Andrew Ward is a freelance writer. His first book, *Barnsley: A Study in Football, 1953 to 1959* (with Ian Alister), was published in 1981. Since then he has completed over thirty books, including *The Birth Father's Tale*, *The Day of the Hillsborough Disaster* (with Rogan Taylor and Tim Newburn), *Football Nation* (with John Williams) and *What Use is a Degree?* (with Alan Jenkins and Lynn Jones). His five books in the *Strangest* series include *Cricket's Strangest Matches* and *Golf's Strangest Rounds*. He has also worked as a statistician, market researcher, careers counsellor and, of course, milkman.

D1138343

NO MILK TODAY

TODAY

ANDREW WARD

ROBINSON

First published in Great Britain in 2016 by Robinson

This paperback edition published in 2017 by Robinson

A CIP catalogue record for this book
is available from the British Library.

ISBN: 978-1-47213-689-3

Typeset in Dante by SX Composing DTP, Rayleigh, Essex

Printed and bound in Great Britain by
CPI Group (UK), Croydon CRO 4YY

Papers used by Robinson are from well-managed forests and
other responsible sources

Robinson
An imprint of
Little, Brown Book Group
Carmelite House
50 Victoria Embankment
London EC4Y 0DZ

An Hachette UK Company
www.hachette.co.uk

www.littlebrown.co.uk

For Ian Alister

Contents

Introduction

Please leave two pints today,
please ring if note blows away.

THIS book is a historical collection of folk tales about milkmen. Traditionally in British society milkmen have been family friends, sex symbols and cheerful chappies. They've been the eyes and ears of the community, and their genetic legacy has supposedly passed into the lineage of housewives. There is some truth in the milkman's Lothario image, as we shall see in chapter seven, but there is also much fantasy. The hero of the milkman's tale is more likely to be a settled family man rather than Jack the Lad, and sometimes the heroine is a milkwoman.

At the job's peak, in the late sixties and early seventies, between 40,000 and 45,000 milkmen delivered to over eighteen million UK homes (about 99 per cent of households). By 2014, however, only 4,000 milkmen and

2.5 million homes remained in the delivery system, and only about 10 per cent of households had a milkman. The doorstep milk market has evaporated and it now feels appropriate to discuss milkmen in the past tense.

During the twentieth century the milkman's working day changed only a little. At the start of World War One, three daily deliveries became two, and then, during World War Two, two daily deliveries became one. Horse-drawn delivery vehicles gave way to electric milk floats and diesel vans, glass bottles replaced measuring cans, security boxes were installed in some milk floats, cartons and plastic bottles took over from glass bottles, the number of products for sale increased, starting times became earlier, and computers replaced mental arithmetic.

The really big impact – the destruction of a much-valued job – was orchestrated by a series of changes elsewhere in British society. The details of the milkman's demise are discussed in the last chapter. In summary, the tale of vanishing milkmen is one of price deregulation, European rulings, improved refrigeration, increased shelf life, supermarket initiatives, competition from other soft-drink companies, the dissolution of the Milk Marketing Board, changing diets, traffic problems affecting the milk float, the increased size of delivery lorries (enabling better delivery to supermarkets) and, eventually, the relative powerlessness of dairy farmers and milkmen. The disappearance of milkmen meant that society lost tens of thousands of gatekeepers.

This book is roughly structured by the milkman's working day. It starts with the milkman's early wake-up call and ends when he returns home in search of sustenance and tender loving care. In between we look at the characters in the job and the many facets of the work.

The milkman's work had some very attractive sides, such as physical fitness, the lack of supervision while out on the round, free time during afternoons, earning the respect of customers, and opportunities to see wildlife. The downsides were long hours, unusual sleep patterns, tiredness, injuries and the loss of independence when returning to the dairy. The job's impact on family life could be positive (e.g. spending more time with the children) or negative (e.g. getting up early and disturbing the household).

A lot of milkmen were transients who stayed only a few months, but some were long-servers. Danny Quigley was seventeen when he started the job in Londonderry in 1945. He intended to stay for a fortnight, but he was still a milkman more than sixty years later. He began his career with a horse and cart in the days when a milkman filled up the jugs that customers left in windows, and he finished in the era of electric milk floats and diesels when a greater range of goods were on offer.

This book celebrates the lives and work of the people who have delivered milk to doorsteps. So come with me into the open air and follow the milkmen from midnight to midnight. Make sure you set your alarm clock or you might not wake up in time.

1

Off to Work

Please leave one dozen eggs. If you don't see me about, kick the hell out the door, put a window through. Must be up early.

IN THE sixties and seventies, most milkmen got up between three and five in the morning and started work between four and six. During the nineties, milkmen in conurbations began to shift their working day so that they started between midnight and two-thirty. This reduced the problems of traffic congestion, parking restrictions and milk floats not being allowed in bus lanes, and it meant that customers were more likely to receive fresh milk before breakfast.

Hughie Duncan was a milkman in Kilmarnock for forty-one years before retiring in 2012. In the last few years, Duncan got up at midnight and did much of his round while it was quieter on the streets. Some milkmen went to bed before their young children.

The Usual Routine

The milkman's day usually started with the sound of an alarm clock. Julian Kearvell, a milkman in Tunbridge Wells, Kent, from 1985 to 2015, set his alarm for 3.45 a.m. and, nine days out of ten, he was awake before it went off. Others had different experiences:

I'd wake at the alarm. In winter I'd switch off the second alarm and dress as much as possible from inside the bedcovers. On a bad morning I'd drop out of bed on to my knees and then try to push up off one foot while hanging on to a bedside table. Then I'd take slow steps across the room and pick up my other clothes. Some mornings I'd spread liniment over the muscles on my stomach, back, shoulders and thighs. I'd finish dressing and then pick up my shoes and wonder how I might get into them. Eventually I'd make my way to the front door and place my key in the lock so I could lock the door silently when I was outside.

I had two or three alarms at five- or ten-minute intervals. I was worried about sleeping through them. I had them on full volume. I was also worried about waking the whole village. I was anxious all the time. I was especially anxious about being late. I was in danger of being late and getting the sack.

With the light evenings, I tried to sleep with the windows blacked out. I found it harder to sleep in the summer. In the mornings I'd wake up and find out what the weather was doing. Some mornings I'd wake up and hear the sound of rain beating and pounding on the house, and I wanted to carry on sleeping. While I was having breakfast I'd listen for the noise of Ray's milk float when he delivered to our street. He always started earlier than me. I'd hear the clink of the milk bottles and the pitter-patter of Ray's feet as he sprinted along our street. I kept thinking that one day I'd lie down on the floor, open the door and grab his hand while it was still on the bottle.

I went to bed reasonably early but still slept through the alarm. I tried two alarms in saucepans, but got used to the sound of the alarm. I tried bigger saucepans one day and then frightened myself to death.

Some milkmen walked their dog before going to work. Others made sure they had a breakfast of cornflakes (and milk, of course). But a lot of milkmen left the house without considering food. Running around without a decent lining on their stomach was an unhealthy start to the day and sometimes it led to headaches and dizziness. Many did part of the round and then stopped somewhere for breakfast, but it could be five hours without food if a milkman was behind with his calls or out on a new round. Sensible milkmen took a flask of coffee. On collecting days they brought sandwiches or stopped at a cafe.

Milkmen's partners might wake up with the alarm clock and then have the second part of the night on their own. Some milkmen's wives worried about the dangers of the road. They might have worried even more after hearing about some horrendous milkman tales (see chapter nine).

By the time they left the house, most milkmen had a clear idea about the weather. They'd have listened to their customers the previous day – 'they say it might snow tomorrow' – and checked the forecast. Milkmen always knew where the weather was coming from.

Off to a Bad Start

Milkmen made two classic mistakes at the beginning of the day. One was to wake up too early; the other was to wake up too late. Here are two cases of arriving for work much too early:

One day I got up in the dark, had a quick breakfast and set off for the dairy. There was a little bit more noise than usual, with some people coming out of restaurants, but I didn't make anything of it. Then I walked past the big clock and it said one o'clock. It turned out I hadn't reset my alarm clock after my lunchtime nap the day before.

My alarm clock was set for 4.15 a.m. and I woke up ten minutes before that. I switched off the alarm and back-up alarm and went through my normal breakfast routine before setting off for the dairy. On the journey to work I noticed that some streets were quieter than normal and other streets had people stumbling around drunkenly as if they were still going home. They've had a good night, I thought, staying out past four o'clock in the morning. Then I arrived at the dairy and found the gates locked. It was eerily quiet. Why is the dairy closed? Have they given us the day off? I eventually realised that I'd read the clock wrong. It wasn't 4.05 when I woke up; it was 1.20 in the morning. I'd got the little hand and big hand mixed up.

A second type of error came when a milkman heard the alarm clock and switched it off without properly waking up:

> My second sense clicked in. It was much too early to get up because there was no traffic noise and no noise from the early starters. The street was very still. It was much too early to get up, so I went back to sleep. I woke up later and it was still very quiet. But the clock said 5.15 a.m. I couldn't believe it. It didn't sound that late. Then I looked out of the window and understood why it was so quiet – there was snow on the ground. I jumped out of bed, dressed quickly and raced out of the house in record time. I was not looking forward to doing the round. I was already behind schedule and I'd lose more time by getting stuck in the snow. That was a very long day.

Another problem arose in the days when milkmen used electric alarm clocks. 'My rival started at 8.30 one morning,' a milkman told me, laughing heartily. 'He'd set his alarm for the normal time but his electricity went off.'

For a period in 1993, one particular alarm on Teesside proved problematic to neighbours. A milkman set his radio alarm on full volume because he'd been oversleeping. Neighbours complained about the early morning blasts so Middlesbrough Council issued a warning. The milkman was later fined £200 for breaking the Environment Protection Act.

Another bad start to the day was a rotten dream. 'Since I mistakenly missed a road out of my round during my first week as a milkman, twenty-six years ago, I've had this recurring dream of it happening again,' said Roy Dyer.

Other milkmen woke up from a bad dream where their milk float crashed silently at the bottom of a hill.

The classic milkman anxiety dream was the one where he delivered the whole round in his sleep. He took two pints to the first house and obeyed the note at the next house ('One extra, please'). Then he drove into the factory and lifted down a churn of milk. After that he dealt with the dog at number twelve, remembered the orange juice at number fourteen and continued with the calls until the alarm went off and he woke up exhausted. Then, to his horror, he realised that he had to do the round all over again.

The most common fear, though, was one of being late for work and getting behind on the round:

> One morning I ran over a cat in the car on the way to work. The cat was still alive, so I tried to find a vet, which wasn't easy at six in the morning. The foreman reported me for being late. He said he would have left it there or run it over to finish it off.

Equipment

Milkmen talked a lot about shoes. They went through a lot of footwear. Some dairies supplied shoes as a perk of the job – 'They weren't bad,' one milkman said, 'with our place I'd expected flip-flops' – but other dairies let their employees buy their own shoes. Some milkmen's shoes lasted nine months, others' only three weeks.

> Did I get through a lot of shoes? Yes. Do you remember back in the days when Tuf shoes were guaranteed for six months? Well, after my third pair they wouldn't replace them any

more. I could wear a pair of shoes out very quickly. You'd walk miles, up and down steps. The shoes very often split along the side there and they'd crack across the sole. I think that was where you were bending your foot on the steps. You were using the ball of your foot a lot.

The right shoe usually went first. Milkmen got in and out of their vehicle up to 250 times a day, so a big hole or a large crack appeared in the right sole, perhaps also caused by pressing the brake and the throttle, stepping down from the van on to the right foot and pushing off for a sprint to the next call. Anyone with two left feet could be served for life by a milkman's perfectly good left shoes after the right ones had been discarded.

The topic of footwear stimulated many discussions. The footwear needed to last but also needed to be light enough so that milkmen could jump from the float and hit the floor running. In summer most milkmen preferred trainers, in winter they wore boots, and in wet weather they sometimes put on galoshes. The wrong footwear could cause nagging tendon trouble, sprained ankles and fall-related injuries. When Jim Hadley retired in 2009, with painful knees after forty-eight years as a milkman, he estimated that he'd got through a hundred pairs of boots in his career.

Winter clothes were essential – gloves, thick jeans, heavy jumpers, jerkins, woolly hats, balaclavas, thick socks, and so on. Some dairies provided an oilskin mackintosh – 'it was great if you were ten foot tall,' said one milkman – and many milkmen wore bobble hats in the cold. Woolly hats changed shape in the rain and grew enough to carry a few pounds of potatoes. In the early days, milkmen touched flat hats as a sign of politeness to a customer.

> I tried all sorts of waterproof gear and in the end I found that the best thing was just an ordinary jacket, come home and get in the shower, because nothing would keep you dry. If you wore all this heavy oilskin type stuff, you sweated like a pig inside and you were just as wet. The biggest problem, you'd find, was that when you got in the van the next morning, the seat was still soaking wet.

Some milkmen didn't wear gloves. 'You were using your hands all the time, picking the bottles up and all that, and trying to do it with gloves on used to slow you down,' said one. But many found gloves essential. One suffered from Raynaud's disease:

> I wore layers of gloves in winter. I had linen inner gloves, woollen gloves, and sometimes rubber gloves on the outside if it was wet. It was well worth keeping the hands dry because I had such bad circulation. If I lost sensation it could take hours to get it back.

Many had problems with swollen fingers. Here is a milkwoman talking:

> My fingers got to look like feet. I used plenty of cream but there were times when I couldn't get my ring off. I think it depended on a person's skin. Some were not affected. My hands were used to being in and out of water, whereas blokes were not used to washing clothes and not used to moving from one extreme to another.

8

Every milkman had an opinion about a torch. Some saw it as essential equipment but others saw it as a nuisance because they had enough goods to carry in their hands anyway. One milkman solved this problem by fitting a miner's lamp on his cap. Other milkmen put their torch in the front compartment of their handcrate. Milkmen also made sure they had their wallets and satchels before setting off for the dairy.

The Journey to Work

Whatever the journey to work – car, motorbike, moped, bicycle or pedestrianism – milkmen greeted other early-morning characters. In the milkman's heyday the other essential workers included bakers, postmen, paperboys, street cleaners, office cleaners, binmen, police officers, taxi-drivers, railway station workers, road sweepers and coalmen. If all those people had ever started a revolution, it would have kicked off between five and six o'clock in the morning. There was camaraderie on the streets at that time, but there was also a hierarchy in the service industries. Dustbinmen took centre-stage with their large vehicles and teams of runners, but they weren't as attractive to female customers as milkmen, who had more opportunities for face-to-face contact.

The start of the day was generally predictable. On most days the journey to work – seven days a week at some dairies – was routine:

> Trying not to disturb my wife, I am up, dressed and eating my breakfast in a quarter of an hour. With a final yawn, I go outside and am soon cycling to the milk depot, still half asleep.

> When I first started, the depot was only half a mile away
> down the road, and I could just nip down on my bike,
> but now [2007], with only one depot left – all the others
> have closed – I have to travel to Leicester, which is half an
> hour journey by car. Now that all the remaining milkmen
> operate from one depot, there's very often a queue when I
> get there.

Hardly any buses were running at three in the morning. Over the years, milkmen lived further away from their dairies and became more reliant on cars for getting to work. Milkmen sometimes phoned the dairy because they couldn't get their car started . . . and who could give you a push start at 3.30 a.m.? Big dairies had someone on stand-by to fetch a milkman whose car had broken down.

Other milkmen were so paranoid about breakdowns that they had a back-up plan. One kept a moped in the back of his car, just in case. Others had a taxi company's phone number handy. Some, such as John Gaunt, cycled six miles to the dairy and carried a puncture repair kit.

Overall, it was hard getting up in the morning and it was even harder getting out of the house. Not everyone was attracted to the early starts, inclement weather and long hours. Being a milkman was also a physical job. Milkmen had to be fit. Like sports stars, they were constantly nursing their injuries, dealing with tiredness and coping with variable energy levels.

2

'Good Morning, Milkman'

No milk today because we have bought a cow.

THE town was asleep, but the dairy was floodlit. It was a surreal scene. A foreman arrived at the dairy before the milkmen. Let's call him Jack. He'd grown up in the nearby streets, started work at the dairy on leaving school and was now close to retirement. Over the years he became virtually irreplaceable and now he unlocked the dairy, switched on the lights and wheeled stacks of milk crates from the fridge ready for the drivers to start loading their floats. Very occasionally Jack took a holiday and chaos descended. Some security-minded person might have padlocked the dairy's doors and no one knew who had a key. A late start made everybody jittery.

Finding the Van
When the milkmen arrived, they walked to the dairy's

garage, found the appropriate van and drove it round to the loading-bay queue. Some milkmen raced each other to get to the queue first. 'It's just like the Le Mans race, everyone struggling to get their vehicles loaded and get away,' said milkwoman Jean Cogar, describing a Co-op dairy in 1984. 'It's every man for himself, it would make a marvellous film.'

The electric vehicles started quickly. Milkmen removed the charge mechanism from the socket, took off the handbrake and away they went. The milk floats roared off with as much noise as their electricity allowed. This simple operation was sometimes made difficult by a practical joke:

> Jeff and I used to arrive about the same time and we'd race to get in the queue first. One time Jeff caught his recharging lead on his bumper and when he reversed at full speed he pulled the plug right off. Another time I ran from my car at full pelt and Jeff raced to his van. Then I walked back round to the queue where I'd already put my van. One of my favourite tricks was when Jeff drove his van to the start of the loading bay and then went off to prepare his load. I'd turn Jeff's van round and reverse it in. Then I'd block him in with mine. He'd have to reverse through the loading bay, loading up on the way.

In the Queue

Milkmen sometimes acted out a comedy routine while they waited in the loading-bay queue. Imagine three milkmen standing talking and a fourth joins them. The conversation starts like this:

'Good morning, milkman.'

'Morning, milkman.'

'Good morning, milkman.'

'Morning, milkman.'

And so on.

The weather was a big conversation topic, and milkmen in the loading-bay queue were ready to tell you what was coming. They might also chat about who'd left the job, potential fiddles, tiredness and new recruits who would 'never make a milkman'.

'Anything happening?'

'Nothing much, just the usual balls-ups.'

'They appointed a new milkman and it turned out he didn't have a driving licence.'

'You've heard that Johno's going to hand in his notice?'

Some dairies had a rest room where milkmen went for a cup of tea, but most milkmen were keen to start their round. While their vans sat in a queue, milkmen collected goods from the stores and searched for the round's book if someone else had done the round the previous day.

On Monday mornings milkmen needed extra crates to collect the weekend's empty bottles. In the late sixties the old metal crates were replaced by plastic crates. 'Wire crates used to be lethal with bits of wire sticking out the side of them,' said one long server. 'The plastic crates were a lot better: a lot lighter, much easier to handle, and it was less weight on the van as well, not so noisy.'

Gradually, the milk floats moved towards the loading bay and the milkmen estimated the amount of milk they needed. One old-time milkman, who did the same round for twenty-nine years from the forties to the seventies, was particularly precise in the days before computers:

There was no messing with Bill. If you wanted extra, he used to leave it the next day. If you cancelled, you'd get that day's milk. And you'd pay for it. Bill used to count his milk exactly.

On the Loading Bay

The physical work began when a milkman's van reached the loading area. Crates of full milk bottles were heavy and they seemed even heavier after a break from the job. The loading bay was big enough for a few vehicles and it was important to drive the vehicle close to the bay so you could slide the crates on to the van. It was easy to lose your footing on a bay that was slippery with spilt milk. It could be very painful if you slipped and a foot went down a gap between the float and the bay.

All sorts of other things went wrong:

I made a typical fool of myself one morning. I was pushing four crates along the bay and swerved them around another milkman. Unfortunately, the bottom crate had no corner notches, so the top three fell off. A few of the lads cheered.

I remember one of the milkmen pushing over a crate of milk one morning. There was a delay while the foreman swept up the broken glass. 'Have you got a hammer?' the foreman asked the culprit. 'I want to see if I can break these bottles up into even smaller pieces.'

'Jack', the loading-bay foreman, counted and checked out the number of pasteurised, sterilised, skimmed, Jersey, creams and goods that were needed for each specific round. Unpasteurised milk (green top) was sold until the eighties, when it failed to satisfy new regulations. Other milk goods, such as evaporated milk, sour cream and UHT cream, were not sold by milkmen because they weren't fresh products. For safety reasons, in the seventies and eighties, cartons were used instead of bottles when delivering to hospitals, shops and other public buildings. In the twenty-first century, cartons and plastic bottles took over from glass bottles.

Sensible milkmen checked each crate to ensure there were no gaps or broken pints of milk. They stacked them on the van in various ways, and on some mornings a milkman argued with the foreman about how many pints were on board. Four people might come up with four different totals. 'When you have a full vanload of milk and churns, you need a degree in building,' said one milkman.

New recruits were often surprised at the amount of hard work involved – loading, lifting crates of full bottles, redistributing crates on the van and lifting churns when delivering to kitchens in factories and colleges.

> The five-gallon churns were fine. The ten-gallon ones were heavy. If you dropped it on your foot you could break it. You would roll it off the bay on to the van. You would be hoping that someone would be in the kitchen where you were delivering.

Most new recruits were surprised by the physical work, but they were soon lifting two crates at a time. (Well, those who stayed in the job.) On the dock, in the morning, the old hands watched how new recruits handled themselves.

It was an important part of the induction course and a step towards acceptance.

Over the years, milkmen have sold lots of goods other than milk. In 1968, they delivered tea, coffee and sugar as well as traditional dairy products. In 1973, a Unigate milkman described himself as a travelling grocery store because he stocked butter, chickens, potatoes, vegetables, canned fruit and biscuits. Bakery products were additional options when the number of bread roundsmen fell dramatically. In 1984, a Co-op milkman stocked bread, eggs, sugar, tea, fruit juice, yoghurts and long-life milk.

An episode of *The Dick Emery Show* in the seventies featured a milkman serving a male customer who had his arm in sling. In the sketch the customer uses his good hand to pile up the goods in the milkman's arms – two pints of milk, a dozen eggs, butter, bags of sugar, a loaf of bread – and then, when the milkman has his hands full of awkward goods, the customer uses his good hand to steal the money out of the milkman's front pocket and runs away.

The job became more complicated:

The milk, I didn't mind. It was all the things that a milkman has to sell with the milk – potatoes, bacon foil, everything else. It's three o'clock in the morning, it's pouring with rain, and I've got two cellophane bags in my hand. One has got a granary loaf in and one has got a brown loaf in. Which one is she having? I've got no idea.

By the twenty-first century, milkmen carried anything that could be sold, including pet food, pot plants, refuse sacks and garden compost. A strange addition to the milk-man's grocery provision was discovered in 2009 when a seventy-two-year-old milkman in Burnley was found to be supplying cannabis to some of his elderly customers. He had amassed seventeen customers for the drug over a three-month period. He was given a thirty-six-week sentence, suspended for a year.

One of the foreman's duties on the loading bay was to check that every milkman was sober. Virtually every dairy has a tale of an early-morning roundsman who was so drunk that he fell off his van when loading up. ('It was a wonder he made it past the first corner,' a foreman said about one such incident.) Here was an ethical dilemma – what could the dairy management do when a milkman came in tanked up from the night before? Should the foreman let him loose on the customers and turn a blind eye? One morning in the early sixties, in the days before the breathalyser, about twenty milkmen went straight from a party to their Midlands dairy and reported for work. The dairy manager took a look at them and said, 'This is a dairy but it smells more like a brewery.'

Drink-driving became even more of a problem when milkmen started their rounds at one in the morning rather than 4.30 a.m. and there were cases of milkmen being arrested. In May 1991, milkman Edward Rolls was three times over the limit when he was tested for drink-driving. He had spent the previous day drinking with friends. The day of the offence was actually down as holiday but a colleague had talked Rolls into turning up for work as they were short of staff. Rolls was banned from driving for eighteen months.

From the Dairy to the Round

In the heyday of milk delivery, in the late sixties and early seventies, one southern dairy had thirty-four milk rounds within a five-mile radius of the dairy. Loaded up for the day, the milkmen roared off towards customers' doorsteps. They were flat out at fifteen miles per hour (for an electric milk float) or over the speed limit (for a diesel van).

Driving away from the dairy was the start of 'Independence Day'. No one was looking over their shoulders and they delivered the round in a way that suited their own pace. First, though, they had to travel to their round. Some had to go a long way:

> When I drove a milk float I had to bring it from out in the country. My first hour and a half was bringing the float along the main roads into Malvern before we even got into town, so that was a nightmare. And then you had to get the milk float back, after it was empty, along the main road. I used to drive almost in the ditch to let lorries through, otherwise nothing could get past me.

On the way to the round, milkmen exchanged more greetings with the early-morning crowd. They'd see cleaners walking through the streets, warehouse night watchmen on mopeds, postmen cycling to the sorting office, and men in builders' vans, hands on the horn, waiting for colleagues to get out of bed. On Saturday and Sunday mornings, anglers sat by roadsides awaiting lifts and cyclists met for their day's ride. But there were still signs of the previous day. Nightclub revellers staggered along the streets and people in evening dress were on their way home from dinner dances.

Sometimes the 'up-all-night' crowd bought a few pints of milk off the milk float. Some milkmen didn't serve them because they were worried about what would happen to the bottles. Others served them and hung around until they had drunk the milk so they could take back the empties.

Everything was wonderful in the outdoors, unless it was 'one of those days'. On some mornings milkmen missed the first alarm and then, behind time, raced to work, loaded the van dozily, and headed for the first call while still wiping sleep from their eyes. Chances were that they were still uncoordinated when they reached the first few calls and that was why they injured themselves on broken bottles protruding from the edge of a crate.

More commonly, however, the milkmen and milkwomen enjoyed the early-morning air. They often demonstrated a temporal arrogance because this was the best time of day. Jean Cogar loved the sunrises, the birds singing, the badgers playing, and other animals frolicking about. At such times it was the best job in the world. And it was a valued role. According to the Milk Marketing Board's training booklet *The Milky Way* (1977), 'you as the milkman are the last vital link in the chain connecting the contented cow with the contented customer'.

3

Different Types of Milkmen

Sorry not to have paid the milk bill before, but my wife has had a baby, and I've been carrying it around in my pocket for weeks.

No two milkmen were the same. Indeed, one of the virtues of the job was that milkmen could mould a round to suit their character. At one extreme were slow, sociable milkmen who provided a social service for customers. At the other extreme came the fast, efficient ones who did the job as quickly as possible. But every milkman had to be fit enough to do the round. A dairy recruitment booklet suggested that the new milkman might drive ten miles and walk four miles a day, but many milkmen covered greater distances.

Slow and sociable milkmen knew their calls for a cup of tea and tender-hearted care. Such sociable types served their customers in all sorts of ways. They posted letters, changed light bulbs, fed cats, mowed lawns, painted houses, cleaned windows and cut hair. One milkman spent most of his waking day on the round:

> They called him The Midnight Milkman. He used to leave at seven in the morning and sometimes not be back by nine at night. He used to do everything on the way round. If you wanted any rabbits skinning or shoes soling, as well as the routine pension fetching. He cultivated cigarette ash the length of his cigarette. Even in a force ten gale he'd still have a cigarette length of ash. One time, when he took a day's holiday, a customer complained to the dairy because the relief milkman hadn't brought the dustbin from the back garden to the front ready for dustbin day.

In contrast to the slow, sociable types, the fast, efficient milkmen galloped up and down paths, carrying bottles by the dozen. They sneaked through hedges, leapt over fences, and trained the customers to line up on starting blocks on pay day. Some runners had little more than a cursory comment for customers, but others seemed to have all the time in the world. The speedy milkmen included an ex-commando who leapt hedges and climbed fences, a round-the-world sailor who bounded down the street with a crate of milk hugged to his chest, various milkmen who trained for London marathons by running their milk rounds, and a collection of wiry cross-country runners who pitter-pattered into the darkness, sometimes stumbling, occasionally falling, but generally emerging with a smile. All these milkmen were athletes of one kind or another.

No Milk Today

When I worked in the kitchen at Minehead Butlins in 1969, our milk was delivered every morning from a dairy in Taunton. The delivery man was bigger, stronger and more tanned than the Incredible Hulk. He used to climb on the back of the truck and pick up the biggest, fullest milk churn with one arm and swing it down for me and Steve Wood to deal with.

In 2010, Gary Qualter walked ten miles a day on his Exeter milk round, so he decided to walk from John O'Groats to Land's End in aid of Macmillan Cancer Support. Qualter wanted to help the charity because he had heard a lot of cancer-related stories from his customers. So, in his forties, he took two months off work to walk the famous route, sometimes taking a detour to meet other milkmen at local Milk&More depots. Qualter walked 1,008 miles in forty-eight days. He lost nearly a stone in weight and had never felt fitter. Then it was back to being a milkman.

Various Backgrounds

Milkmen had various work histories. Some were the third generation of a milkman family, but most had tried other jobs before they signed on with a dairy. I've met a milkman with scars on his hands from working with knives in a slaughterhouse, and I've talked with one who couldn't stand the smell of paint after five years as a decorator. One chef was advised by his doctor to get an outdoor job and lose weight, so he signed up for the milk. Others desiring more exercise included former plumbers, electricians, taxi drivers, lorry drivers, bar stewards and bus drivers. Some milkmen had a professional background – accountant, lawyer, teacher, engineer, etc. – but needed to work on the milk after being made redundant. Others became milkmen after a career in professional sport. Ron Redrup had been a light-heavyweight boxer for over ten years, Jim Sharkey a professional footballer for Celtic, and Tony Fowler a jockey and racehorse trainer.

Jock Kane became a milkman in Hampshire towards the end of his working life. Before that he'd been a GCHQ radio officer in Hong Kong, where he uncovered fraud and security breaches within the government security organisation. Kane's first memoir, *The Negative Asset* (1984), was confiscated by Special Branch and remains unpublished. An injunction was also placed on Kane's follow-up book, *The Hidden Depths of Treachery* (1987). After that experience, dairy politics must have been relatively easy for Kane.

One time, when I was listening to a milkman tell me about his PhD in historical geography, the other milkmen looked at him as though he'd just returned from a milk round on Mars, Jupiter and Pluto. In 1987, an Oxford milkman, Michael Billson, reached the final of BBC's *Mastermind* and missed winning the trophy by only two points. That's two *points*; not two *pints*.

The milkman population included lovable rascals and dislikeable scallywags, but there were also some of the best people you could wish to meet. One milkman summarised his take on the requirements for the job:

> It's not intelligence that makes a good roundsman. I work with one who's as thick as two short planks and can hardly write, but he makes a really good job of the round. Does it matter that he writes *geergorcer* in his round's book rather than *greengrocer*?

Milkman careers varied in length. A high percentage of new milkmen gave up the job within the first year, and one dairy foreman guessed wildly that only 5 per cent stayed for longer than six months. Some experienced milkmen were derogatory to newcomers, resorting to comments such as 'He couldn't handle a pram' or 'He's as much chance of becoming a milkman as I have of being a nun'. New recruits were perhaps unable to cope with the weather, the unusual hours, the physicality of the job or the financial nous needed to balance the books, so they left for a more suitable job. Such transients gave management headaches. They cost a lot to train and the money would be wasted if the recruits left within weeks.

Some milkmen left early because they could see no real career progression. Others stayed a few years before moving on to another job, perhaps one with more sociable hours. Many spent ten to twelve years in the job while they raised children. And other milkmen spent the majority of their working career on the milk, lasting until the physicality of the job brought arthritis, gamey knees, dodgy hips or other chronic problems.

Long-serving Milkmen

Derek Arch was fourteen when he took over his father's milk round in 1943, at a time when his home town, Coventry, had been decimated by German bombs. He started with a bicycle, two buckets and a ladle. Arch was still a Coventry milkman sixty-six years later, when he was interviewed by the *Express* and the BBC. He walked about eight miles a day on his round and reckoned he had delivered over eight million pints in his milkman career. He described himself as 'an old man trying to earn a crust'. By 2014, Derek Arch had taken his long-service record up to seventy-one years and he was still rising at two-thirty in the morning and driving a milk float made in the fifties. The business, D Arch & Sons, had been going since 1873.

Jack Moon worked as a milkman in eight different decades. He started in 1933 and worked until 2004. He never took a holiday. Around Ashwater, Devon, he was known as the Dairy Dynamo. In the thirties, Moon delivered milk, groceries and coal in a horse-drawn cart, and his only break from milkman service was a spell in the tank corps in North Africa during World War Two. When he started, his mother had a small milk concern with a couple of cows, and customers came to collect the milk in jugs, bowls and buckets. He sold up to a bigger dairy in the early eighties, when it became too difficult for him to conform to the new rules and regulations, but he continued to visit doorsteps for another two decades. Moon never considered retiring. Here he is, speaking at the age of ninety, when he was still working:

> I like the exercise and I was getting up early – I'd only lounge about in bed otherwise. I can't remember the last time I had a lie-in, even on a Sunday. I do have a day off then but I hate it – I don't know what to do with myself . . . It's hardly a strain carrying around a bottle of milk. I've just got through the winter and now I have the summer to look forward to. I'm not doing it to keep any traditions alive – just myself.

Stan Robins, MBE, delivered to Wootton Bassett doorsteps for fifty-three years. During World War II, Robins survived Colditz. After the war, at the age of twenty, he ran his milk business with his wife Diana, and his two sons, Adrian and Mark, also became milkmen. Robins dedicated his MBE to his friends and Colditz inmates. He had been secretary of the Colditz Association for ten years.

Ernie Tisdale was a Shropshire milkman who retired from the job in 1995 after forty-odd years delivering milk. Tisdale started his milk-delivery career with a horse and cart but switched to a milk float after his return from National Service. His customers often sang him the Benny Hill song, 'Ernie (The Fastest Milkman in the West)', and they gave him copies of the record. At his funeral, in 2014, 'Ernie' was the last song played.

When it came to milkmen covering large distances, few could rival the career of Alistair Maclean of Borgie, Scotland. Between 1960 and 2010, Maclean spent fifty years delivering to the north coast of Scotland and he travelled over a hundred miles each day. He delivered to Tongue and Melness in the West and Scrabster and Thurso in the East, journeying along many side roads in between. His van carried as many as 2,000 pints on a Saturday. He sometimes delivered coffins to an undertaker in Tongue and he often gave schoolchildren a lift to Berryhill when they'd missed the school bus. He kept the milk money in the same cash box throughout his whole career and handed the box over to his successor. By the end of his working life Alistair Maclean had possibly set a British record – nearly two million miles on the same round.

In the early seventies a survey of customers looked

at the most important assets for a milkman. Courtesy and cheerfulness came top, followed by punctuality, helpfulness, appearance and product knowledge. All new recruits received some training. In the late eighties Unigate training meant two weeks with an experienced milkman, a brief period at training school for milkmen and then three weeks learning a round. The training at some dairies was not so organised and sometimes new recruits were sent out on a round almost immediately.

According to the *Daily Express*, on New Year's Day 1969, a dairy in the Potteries ran a special course for trainee milkmen to teach them about 'the dangers of the amorous housewife' and the importance of 'keeping the relationship on a friendly basis without going too far'. I bet the milkmen enjoyed the role-play in that course. Maybe the course facilitators brought in a couple of actresses . . .

Relief Milkmen

A dairy relied mainly on regular milkmen who delivered the same round every day. When the regulars were ill or on holiday, however, relief milkmen covered a round for a short spell – a day or two, a weekend, a week, or a fortnight.

Regular milkmen thought they did the round far better than relief milkmen and there was some substance for this. A relief man might cut corners as they were less likely to be recognised by customers. Regular milkmen sometimes castigated their reliefs for any number of reasons:

'My relief man is a really messy worker.'

'He never leaves my van looking the same; he demolished a lamppost last week.'

'The customers say he just throws the empty bottles on to the van.'

'He told my customers that I'd won on the Pools and gone to Australia.'

'On one page of the book he collected the money and then forgot to cross them off.'

Relief men had their own complaints. Sometimes they were explorers – more Milko Polo than Marco Polo – and they moaned about the state of the round's paperwork. One relief man looked at the book and saw that the next call was ROYAL INN. He spent five minutes looking for a pub and was about to give up when he noticed the Royal Insurance building.

Regular roundsmen tried to replicate the round day after day, so that customers could say, 'You can set your watch by him.' But it was hard for a relief man to replicate the round exactly. One relief man did an unfamiliar round after being briefed by a foreman; later he learnt that the regular milkman reversed down a one-way street, which saved going all the way round a gridlocked one-way system.

Relief men made mistakes. Here are two examples:

One street had no number thirteen. It was a 'one–two–three street' rather than a 'two–four–six street' and when I got to the end of the street I found I was one house out. And I was up to thirty-something. I had to go back and move all the milk back one house, until I got back to number fourteen.

There was a relief milkman doing my round one week when I was on holiday. The relief delivered to every street except one particular crescent. All these customers in the crescent phoned the dairy and a foreman had to take the milk out to them. It turned out the relief man lived down that crescent and he didn't want anyone to know that he was a milkman. The foreman took him off the round.

On the other hand, some relief milkmen were dismissive of the regular milkman:

> The regular man was so slow. The round took me four hours, and it took him six hours. He spent all his time talking. If he saw a garden gnome he stopped and talked to it. I think he made a social event of it. On a Saturday he was normally half-cut when he got to the end of the round. He delivered to too many pubs.

If relief men were too early with the milk, there would be no empties left out and hardly any notes. They also had to field queries about the regular man, along the lines of 'Is he on holiday again?' or, in university towns, 'Is he on sabbatical this week?'

Relief milkmen who did lots of different rounds got to know towns and cities very well. If people wanted directions they asked a milkman, but the retort could be a wisecrack.

'How do I get to the university, mate?'

'Study hard and get your essays in on time.'

One relief milkman told me how difficult it was to replicate the regular man:

> One of the calls was an old-people's home that didn't open the doors until seven. That meant that I had to go back at the end of the round. It also involved opening and closing

what seemed like twenty doors to get to the delivery point
and find someone who would pay me.

Milkmen on regular rounds thought they had the better
job:

I always felt that relief work was a much harder side of the
business. When you're on a regular round, I could tell you
what all my regular customers had every day. I didn't need
to pick up the book, I knew it off by heart. But when you're
doing relief, you're on Fred's round one week, Johnny's
round the next week.

Sales People

When supermarkets began to gain a bigger share of the
milk market, and the number of customers requiring
delivery decreased, milk rounds covered bigger areas
and customers were more widespread. Milkmen had to
travel greater distances, and they had to become quicker
and more efficient in their daily work. Some changed
from delivery workers to sales people, especially when
they became franchisees. Stroud Creamery was one of
the first dairies to work the franchise system, in the early
seventies, and franchising became more commonplace in
the eighties.

Milkmen distributed leaflets, advertised new goods
and sold produce other than milk. Even in the seventies
some milkmen had their own sidelines. One bought bread
from a bakery on his own initiative and then delivered it
to customers, and another sold paraffin on the side. By
the end of the century, though, milkmen were selling pet

foods and growbags. Sheldon's of Knutsford, Cheshire, delivered 10,000 pints and 2,500 newspapers a day.

At one dairy, the salesmen types started late, around 6.30 a.m., so they could mingle with customers and sell goods as they were doing their rounds. Commission was an incentive for these salesmen. Delivery-only milkmen started very early and just dropped off the milk and goods. Some of them finished early so they could go off and do another job. With new estates, however, the salesmen types were definitely needed because all the new inhabitants needed milk. Ultimately, dairies and franchisees had one key question: 'How is the round profitable?'

Milk rounds were urban or rural in nature but, like census tracts, they were never homogeneous. The type of housing might change from one street to the next. A round with suburban housing could suddenly give way to a few isolated farms. Milkmen on rural rounds drove greater distances than urban milkman, but they benefited from the country air. Milkmen on compact urban rounds might have rows of terraced houses and blocks of flats. Parking the float became trickier in the seventies and eighties, and some milkmen started their rounds much earlier to avoid traffic congestion. One regular milkman was shifted from a round with a rough estate to one of posh houses. 'He won't like that,' said another milkman. 'He won't be able to tell his customers to piss off like he does on the estate.'

Some milkmen lived on their round but others deliberately chose a round some distance from where they lived. I asked one milkman whether it was difficult delivering to his neighbours.

Nah. You just have to say hello a lot. One woman wanted to pay me in the Co-op when I went shopping with my wife on my last week off. I just told her that I was off-duty. I can call in and have my breakfast at home.

The Milkman's Music

In the summer of 2013, Leicester's Kevin Gifford listened to songs on his headphones and whistled along with the tunes, but a handful of customers complained to the dairy about the noise (and others responded with letters of appreciation). Gifford wondered if there would be complaints about the birds, too, because he reckoned they made more noise than him. Gifford's dairy responded by issuing the milkman with a formal written warning, telling him not to sing or whistle until after eight o'clock in the morning, but one letter-writer thought Gifford had near-perfect pitch and saw him as a possible entrant for *The X Factor*, *Britain's Got Talent* or *The Voice*.

Some milkmen were considered 'tuneless whistlers' by their customers and others were nicknamed 'Budgie' by their colleagues. Jonah Moore was billed as 'The Whistling Milkman' when he appeared on television and radio during the fifties, sixties and seventies. Moore started delivering milk with a horse and cart in Camp Hill in the borough of Nuneaton and Bedworth. He played football for Nuneaton, excelled as a darts player and found fame as a whistler.

In his book *The Musical Milkman*, Quentin Falk describes how a milkman called George Bailey murdered his wife in Little Marlow, Buckinghamshire, in 1920. Bailey, a whistling milkman, was using teenage girls to help him develop an unusual musical notation system. He was convicted and hanged. The case was unusual because it was the first time women had sat on a jury.

Paul McCartney certainly appreciated a whistling milkman. McCartney realised that the Beatles had made it big when he was coming home from a nightclub in the early hours and heard his milkman whistling 'From Me to You', the latest Beatles' song. I've arrived, McCartney thought, the milkman's whistling my tune.

In the Scottish borders a sprightly milkman called Bobby Service entertained his customers by singing Robert Burns' songs and reciting poetry. His large repertoire meant he was slow to complete his round. Ian Hardie's tune, 'The Poetic Milkman', was dedicated to Bobby Service, who would sometimes sing duets with customers.

4

Doorstep Delivery

Please do not leave milk at number fourteen as
he is dead until further notice.

THERE is a legendary tale about a milkman who walked up a customer's path on a scorching hot summer's day. The customer had departed for work, but she'd left a bucket of water and a note with instructions to protect the milk from the sun: *Please leave milk in water.* The milkman saw the note and read it. Then he flicked the top off the milk bottle and poured the milk into the bucket.

This story was told at dairies around the country. Maybe it happened, maybe it didn't, but there were days when milkmen felt like emulating the story.

In the heyday of milk delivery, customers loved collecting a freshly delivered pint of milk from the doorstep before pouring the cream on to the morning cereal. Indeed, a 1986 survey found that 80 per cent of housewives preferred to have milk delivered before 8 a.m. But some customers always had to be at the end of the round.

'In an ideal world everybody wants their milk ready for their breakfast,' said one milkman, 'but in reality, even with the 3 a.m. start, I just can't do everybody by seven o'clock.'

'Everybody wants the milkman there at half past seven,' said another milkman. 'Not too early to wake them up, not too late that they've gone to work.'

The milkman's job broadly split into two parts – delivering milk and collecting money – and this chapter is about delivery. However, on collecting days – mainly Thursday, Friday and Saturday – milkmen combined some delivery with collecting. Traditionally milkmen worked on Sundays, like bus drivers, bus conductors and newsagents, but, in later years, from the seventies, Sunday became a rest day in an increasing number of dairies.

Another big change, starting in the seventies, was to deliver parts of the round on every other day. In the 1990s and 2000s, when the distances between calls grew longer, rounds were often split into two separate areas, with delivery on alternate days. A key factor in this change was the increase in the number of customers owning fridges. Only 13 per cent of households had a fridge in 1959, but the figures rose to 56 per cent (in 1970) and 92 per cent (in 1979).

The Milkman's Helpers

Traditionally, milkmen called on young people to help with the milk delivery, but children's work was restricted by various regulations. Kingstanding Dairy, Birmingham, during the forties and fifties, employed young boys of fifteen and sixteen. Known as 'jockeys', they delivered milk but weren't supposed to drive vehicles or handle the money. On collecting days, Fridays and Saturdays, a jockey delivered all the milk and the milkman collected all the money. On the other five days, the jockey delivered the passenger's side of the street and the milkman did the driver's side. By the late sixties, Kingstanding had changed to one-man rounds, but roundsmen still used young children.

Most helpers came out for an hour before school. Someone once told me that he thought about a third of milkmen had helpers, but it is very difficult to estimate. One milkman's son enjoyed being with his father on the round because his dad taught him how to talk to people. Years later, he also thought it was a good psychological experience to have known his dad at work.

Gordon Sumner, the musician better known as Sting, was five years old when his father took over a dairy in the north-east. At the age of seven Sting worked as a helper at weekends and during school holidays. He was shaken awake at five in the morning and bundled into warm clothes, and he learnt to carry six bottles in his hands and two under his arms. When he won the one hundred yards race at the Northumberland County Schools Championship, he put his success down to the running practice he'd had on the milk round.

Some young helpers suffered repetitive strain injury at an age when they were still developing. Rheumatology research in the mid-nineties showed how one milk boy had suffered three months of dull, aching bilateral anterior knee pain. The boy played two games of football a week, but his pain was most obvious when he was weight-bearing, carrying heavy objects (e.g. milk crates), bending or kneeling.

Other helpers went on to become milkmen. Chris Frankland began delivering milk in 1949 when he was ten years old. Working from a bicycle with a carrier, he did thirty calls before school and thirty calls after school. He became a full-time milkman on 1 September 1957, his seventeenth birthday, and he stayed in the job for nearly fifty-seven years (except for a two-year spell of National Service in the late fifties). By the time he retired, at the age of seventy-four in April 2014, Frankland must have delivered over eight million pints. He'd become a franchisee in 1984, adapted to new technology in the nineties (e.g. the electronic round's book) and throughout maintained his jovial catchphrase ('I will do my best, boss'). If he got stuck in the snow, he'd take off his jacket and put it under the offending wheel. In 2007, he was getting up at 1 a.m. and delivering a 900-pint round to 358 customers near his home in Dinas Powys, near Cardiff. When he chalked up fifty years of service, Dairy Crest produced a special milk bottle commemorating his achievement.

Most young helpers, however, were temporary:

I was 'on the milk' for a short period as a teenager. I had vague dreamlike recollections of clinging to the back of a 'speeding' milk float at 4 a.m. as icicles slowly formed on my dripping nose, peeling frosting bottles from my unprotected fingers, and being harangued by irate customers, but other than that it's just a blur. I may have just been imagining it.

It was grim. My hands were so cold and I had to be back in time to go to school. My hands were numb, absolutely numb, and my mother used to start rubbing. Oh, the pain, you wouldn't believe it. The dairy was just across the road. I'd maybe be ten or something like that.

In *On the Milk* Willie Robertson tells the story of milk delivery at Fletcher's Dairy in Dundee in the early sixties. Fletcher's relied on seven milk laddies, all still at school, to deliver the milk. Jim Fletcher drove the lorry while his daughter Avril rode on the back and prepared everything for the milk boys. The laddies swung off the lorry with wire crates of milk bottles, delivered the milk and leapt back on to the lorry. Robertson was only fourteen when he joined the other laddies, in July 1962, and he did the job for fifteen months. His first lesson was all about safety – how to stand on the back of the lorry, one hand on the holding rail at all times and two if you could, and how to get back on the moving lorry by jumping on to the back step. The milk laddies started at 5 a.m. and finished the round before school.

One boy helper, fourteen-year-old Carl Giles, was swept away by a flood on the Fosse Way, Eathorpe, at 3 a.m. on 10 April 1998. The milkman, Vincent Gallagher, drove into five feet of water in the dark and the van was carried away. Gallagher held on to a branch but Giles, a non-swimmer, died. PC Paul Fell won a national police bravery award for harnessing himself on to a lorry and rescuing Gallagher, who had been in the water for about twenty minutes. It was pitch black and there was a torrent of ice-cold water. Another police constable and three members of the public also helped. Gallagher was convicted of careless driving and fined £250.

Using children could be risky if, as was mostly the case, it was against dairy policy and it could invalidate the milkman's insurance. I know of other cases of young people dying when delivering milk. Some were killed by vehicles when running back and forth across roads in the dark or half-light and one was fatally injured by putting his head out of the milk float and hitting his head on a lamppost.

Out on the Round

The first delivery call could be a thirty-minute drive away or it could be just outside the dairy gates. The first street might give the milkman a chance to remove some body stiffness and appraise the day while zigzagging across the road with milk orders. 'First thing in the morning is one of the times I don't like very much,' said one milkman. 'It's that first ten minutes when you think "Why am I doing this?"'

On some days milkmen were tired and uncoordinated. They had to take care not to hit their heads on the van roof or trip over a couple of kerbs. On other days, however, it felt great to be alive. Everyone deserves a period in their life when they feel super-fit, and delivering milk could provide that chance. The tiredness hit milkmen most when they went indoors after a day in the fresh air.

At some point in the morning the milkman started meeting customers, exchanging greetings and discussing the weather.

'What's it going to do, milkman?'
'It'll be lovely weather for ducks.'

'Oh dear, I've just put my washing out.'

The milkman's training manual said that bottles should be put on the hinge side of the door so there was less chance of them being kicked over. Customers asked for milk to be left in all sorts of other places – in cupboards, under bushes, in sheds, on shelves, through cat-flaps, over walls, in boxes, behind car wheels – and the milkman had to remember where it all went. In 1990 a customer could buy a wall-mounted milk-bottle holder for £14.88 (screws supplied) and, apparently, the product saved arthritis sufferers and stroke victims from stooping to collect milk from the doorstep.

One of the milkman's tenets was to get customers to do as much as possible. Rather than climb ten steps to a distant front door, they might ask the customer if they could leave bottles on the bottom step ('I'll need oxygen to get up there'). Some customers asked for the milk to be left at the back of the house because they'd had milk stolen from the front. A few customers kept milkmen to their station by erecting signage (TRADESMAN'S ENTRANCE→). There were calls to make to flats in spooky large old buildings with no staircase lights. And there were celebrity calls ('three pints to the film star at number six'). Milkmen crossed the class divide.

In the sixties and seventies, the increase in high-rise buildings presented challenges for milkmen. The Park Hill estate in Sheffield had a walkway which meant you could drive a milk float around the building and up the floors, but other blocks of flats were particularly demanding. Delivering to a five-storey block of flats was a real problem when the lift wasn't working. Milkmen used a trolley in some places.

One milkman found a set of flats very hard work and time-consuming. He solved the problem by talking the porter into delivering the milk to the flats. He left crates of milk, orange juice and yoghurts, and the porter delivered them. Then the milkman found collecting money time-consuming, so he enlisted the porter for that too. If it was a new porter, he talked him into taking over the job.

Milkmen made special arrangements when serving prisons, old people's homes and sports stadia.

> I deliver to our local football ground. Sometimes it's just one pint for the caretaker. On the day of a big match it may be four or five crates. The caretaker has given me the key to the side gate. Each morning I unlock the gate marked 'private' and go in.

Between 2006 and 2012, Kevin Read thought of himself as 'The Olympic Milkman' because he delivered to building sites before the 2012 Olympic Games. Read was also on duty during the 2011 London riots, but the disruption didn't stop him. 'There were gangs on the streets,' he told *Spitalfields Life*. 'I got lumps of wood thrown at my van, but I just went off to do other parts of my round and came back later to make my deliveries.' Read probably deserved a gold medal himself.

Milkmen made three common mistakes when delivering: (i) they looked at their book, then stopped to talk to a customer and for some reason thought they'd already delivered to that street; (ii) they got the day of the week wrong and delivered Friday's milk rather than Saturday's; or (iii) they thought they'd missed a page of the book, so they turned their vans round, went back to the last street, only to find they had already delivered it and couldn't remember doing so.

A relief milkman had no chance of putting every pint in exactly the right place at precisely the same time as the regular man. Customers were quick to point out where it should have gone, even if they had to chase the milkman along the street in dressing-gown and pyjamas, shouting 'What's been happening to my milk?' Some properties were missed; there was usually someone on duty at the dairy to deal with missed deliveries.

Some calls were jinxed. One regular milkman kept missing one call in particular. He came at the street from one direction and missed the call. Then he tried from the other direction and missed the call. Even the relief man missed the call. Eventually the regular milkman asked the customer to change to another dairy.

Dairy regulations required that milkmen delivered milk using handcrates, but many milkmen found it quicker to grab as many bottles as possible in their hands rather than stop to load up a handcrate. Strictly speaking, a milkman should have carried no more than four bottles without using a handcrate, but a milkman taught me how to carry seven bottles in my hands and two under my arm. I picked up three with the fingers of my right and then used my left hand to push another one between my right thumb and index finger. Then I picked up three between the fingers of my left hand. On some days, when I was feeling confident, I put two under my right arm before picking up three with the left. That meant nine altogether.

'You shouldn't carry them like that because you won't

be covered by the insurance,' a foreman told me one day. 'If you fall downstairs, cut your wrist and lose an arm, you won't have a leg to stand on.'

Collecting Empties, Sorting out Vehicles and Shutting Gates

Traditionally, milkmen collected empty glass bottles – most customers rinsed the bottles but some were slovenly – and they trained customers to leave empties *outside* crates rather than inside them. A milkman could then drop the full bottles into the crate and simultaneously lift the empties with the other hand. It could be difficult to pick up four empty bottles in one hand from a crate. When you did pick them up you had to hope that nobody had peed in them or vomited over them. Other times slugs and snails were stuck to empty bottles or the cream hadn't been properly washed off the inside of the bottle's neck.

Sometimes the milkman found a dozen or more empties left outside because they had been accumulating inside the house for several days. It was difficult for the milkmen to collect that many at once (unless he could see them from a distance and had therefore decided to carry an empty crate to the house).

A few customers hung on to empty milk bottles and made use of them – as a flower vase, an egg cup or a rolling pin for pastry – but the bottles were the property of the dairy. One day a milkman's front door broke off its hinges so he propped it up against the wall in his hall and piled up half a dozen crates of empty bottles in the doorway. Musical milkmen tried to play a tune on the empties by swinging them in the wind with a finger over the top.

At times a milkman had to take empties to the doorstep rather than collect them. In 1978, Sir Timothy Kitson, the MP for Richmond, Yorkshire, gave an example of poverty from his constituency: 'A milkman told me that Catterick Camp is the only place where he has to take with him an empty bottle because on certain occasions he must share two pints among three families.'

At some point on the round milkmen sorted out their floats. They'd been taking the full milk bottles from the nearside crates and putting empty bottles in their place, so they had to rearrange the milk, moving the full pints to the perimeter of the van and the empty bottles into the middle. Some milkmen were considerate about sorting out their float – they'd wait until most people were up or they'd go to a quiet place – but others happily made a noise. One tiny milkman used an industrial estate to sort out his van because it had the highest kerbs on his round. He parked on one side of the street and shifted the crates around on one side of the van. Then he drove to the other kerb and did the same again. One double hernia was enough for him.

Milkmen got a lot of notes from customers and they dealt with them in different ways. Some left them in situ, but others picked up notes and threw them away. Some tossed them into the back of the van. Others saved the best notes for scrapbooks. The saddest note ever read by a milkman was left outside a house in Adelaide, Australia, in 1963: *Milkman please call the police – we are all dead in the house.* The police found five dead bodies.

Gates were a problem. Some you lifted with your foot and others had string over the gatepost. Some swung silently, others grated along the ground. Some clicked into place, others missed their catch when they swung to. Tall milkmen could stride over some gates, treating the round as a steeplechase course, but other milkmen found gates too high for hurdling. There were places on gates where a milkman could rip a finger, tear a uniform, or catch a splinter. And then you had to close the gate quietly on the way out (SHUT THE GATE PLEASE – DOG GETS OUT). Gates were also dangerous for catching your coat, anorak, hand or the bottles you were carrying. On rainy days you could be drenched by the water on a hedge or a gate. Milkmen also walked into cobwebs in the dark.

In the days before cartons milkmen had to look for 'dirty bottles'. Sometimes the dairy machine didn't clean every bottle perfectly on the inside, so milkmen were offered a small reward if they brought back dirty ones. Milkmen got nothing if the dirty mark was on the outside of the bottle.

A foreman told me about a woman who came into the dairy with a snail in the bottom of the bottle. 'It was still crawling around in the bottom of the bottle,' the foreman said. 'I was tempted to tell her that it was a delicacy in some parts of the world.' Early legal cases suggested that dairies were more culpable if they left a *large* object in a bottle (e.g. a snail) rather than a *small* object (e.g. a fly). The small object was harder to spot.

Most milkmen aimed to do the round quickly and get home. As with all seemingly enormous tasks, this could only be achieved by breaking down the targets into smaller chunks. Let's get to the end of this street. Let's see if I can reach the newsagents by six-thirty. Occasionally you heard about milkmen who couldn't handle it. Sometimes they abandoned their vans on the round and walked away from the job.

The Round's Book

What held a round together was the round's book or, in later years, the electronic round's book. The round's book was like a ledger. To save time, milkmen sometimes corrected the book entries while driving, perhaps crossing out '1' for '2' or adding '+1' above the original entry. Other milkmen wrote in the book and then set off. There were little codes, such as UFN (Until Further Notice). Some milkmen kept coded notes in the book to indicate which customers were considered awkward and which ones were too friendly. That gave the relief milkman a heads-up.

Milkmen marked the current delivery page of their book with a bulldog clip or a rubber band. Clip-on pens were another useful asset, but old-timers had pens behind their ear or in the top pocket of their overall. Losing an important item meant a bad start to the day.

Often a relief milkman couldn't understand the shorthand description in the book. If the book had a note saying 'BACK' it didn't explain that you were supposed to walk through a gate that led to the back door and then look in a cupboard at shoulder-height and leave the milk there. A relief milkman might not know whether or not to carry an extra pint (just in case it was needed), and the regular milkman might not have explained that he ducked under a hedge to deliver to the house next door. The relief milkmen didn't always know that the round had exchanges with shopkeepers – a pint of milk for a newspaper, a pint for a pork pie, and so on – because they definitely wouldn't be marked in the book.

From the early nineties, computerised round's books were available, but not every milkman took to them:

> By the time I finished, the big dairies were introducing these hand-held computers. I had a guy ring me up about it and I used to get blurb through the post – did I want to go on so-and-so system? But the set-up cost was quite high. You'd got to buy these hand-held, got to buy the programme, etc. Then you'd got to have someone come in to teach you how to use it. You were looking at about a thousand quid to set it up. And my round's book worked. I knew what I was doing with them, and me and technology don't get along very well anyway.

Routine

Different rounds had different paces. A lot depended on the round's population density, physical terrain and type of housing. If you tried to hurry on terraced streets you might only get ahead of yourself; if you daydreamed on long paths you might be out all day. Each round had a suit-able pace which got you to the right place at the right time and kept you relatively free from traffic jams. Milkmen learnt the best time to tackle a block of flats, a road that had a lot of commuters, an office building or a school expect-ing milk before the morning break. The best method was to set up customer expectancies and conform to them. The greatest compliment paid to a milkman was praise for his regularity and predictability ('You can set your watch by him'). Milkmen could grow irritable if they were behind schedule through no fault of their own.

Consistency in delivering the milk was the most important factor. The milkman needed to know that the milk and other products went on the window ledge, by the wall, at the gate, in the conservatory, behind the kennel, or on the doorstep. Routine was the key thing, but inevitably the routine was disrupted at times. Maybe a milkman arrived at a street one morning and found a change in the road layout or workmen putting in a new gas pipe. Football matches, festivals and Bank Holidays all changed the rhythm of the round. One milkman went out on his normally cushy Sunday round only to find there was a big cycle race that day and he couldn't cross the main road for ten minutes.

Changes in Routine – World War I and World War II
Before World War I, milkmen delivered three rounds a day. The first round was between 5 a.m. and 6 a.m., the second mid-morning and the third at teatime. That was reduced to twice daily when war broke out. Many milkmen in their twenties and thirties went into combat, so dairies employed women, school leavers and men too old for the services.

In the interwar period milkmen continued to deliver twice a day. There were some exceptions, including Mrs Powell of Buck Holt Dairy, Monmouth, who delivered a quarter of a pint four times a day. Her customers were all within a mile of her dairy.

By the thirties, milk delivery was a cut-throat business with competitive roundsmen. Then, at the outbreak of World War II, there was a complete overhaul of the system. Milkmen and milkwomen traded customers so that their rounds became more compact. If customers were registered with a private milkman and moved house, they re-registered with a private milkman; if they were registered with a Co-op milkman, they re-registered with a Co-op milkman.

During World War II, delivery was limited to one delivery a day. In those horse-and-float days a veterinary surgeon might spend nights in stables in case the delivery horses were seriously disturbed or injured by bombing. The roundsmen were supposed to tie up their horses and take cover themselves, but invariably some stayed by their horses and soothed the animals.

The Isle of Wight was one of many places where rounds were rationalised:

In order to save manpower, petrol and tyres, the Ministry of Food decreed that dairymen must either pool their resources or operate in zones. Cowes on the Isle of Wight chose to operate in zones, and a committee was set up to work out a scheme to present to the Ministry of Food before the ministry imposed a plan from above. Shop retailers and three people with very small rounds were excluded from this scheme. A plan was worked out to use twenty-two motor vehicles, seven horse vehicles and three hand carts, using a staff of forty delivery men – a reduction of 30 per cent.

After World War II, Mr R A Claydon summarised the success of zoning:

It was eventually reported that in 575 areas throughout the country where zoning schemes were introduced, the savings effected were 2,450 hand prams, 1,900 horse vans, 2,600 petrol vehicles and 39,100 gallons of petrol a week, which from the viewpoint of helping the war effort, was a most welcome and valuable contribution.

Through the late forties and early fifties, there was talk of nationalising the retail milk business. The zoning continued until about 1954, when food rationing ended. In the mid-fifties, there was a series of letters to *The Times*, starting with a customer who had to switch dairies because he had moved three miles and his old dairy didn't deliver to his new street. Indeed, one street might be United Dairies, another Express Dairies. But voluntary zoning kept the price down by lowering delivery costs. Then competitive practices returned in the mid-fifties.

5

The Milkman's Year

*As we are at the royal garden party on Tuesday we don't need
any milk on Tues or Wed but we will be back by Thursday.*

WINTER, spring, summer or autumn; the milkmen dealt with it all. Wind, snow, rain or sleet; milkmen were on the street.

In winter the weak started leaving and the tough got going, coping with ice, snow, fallen trees, collapsed chimneys, broken bones, cut fingers and road closures. One northern dairy summed up this heroism: 'Acorn Dairy milkmen have been known to tackle hurdles the Milk Tray man would shy away from.'

A milkman's mood changed in spring, the light changed in summer and the colour of leaves changed in the autumn. But there were considerable regional differences in climate. On average, Camborne, Cornwall, had only nine days of air frost a year, but Aberdeen, Scotland, had fifty-three. Skegness averaged 121 days of rainfall a year but Aberystwyth had 158 rainy days. I wouldn't have fancied delivering milk to Seathwaite, Cumbria, in November 2009 when nearly fifty centimetres of rain fell in a four-day period.

The time of the year made a difference to orders. Jewish people required special kosher milk during Passover week, and cultural differences required specific dietary requirements. One London milkman learnt some Bengali to help him communicate with customers.

Winter

Here is a milkwoman talking about the winter months:

> The first thirty minutes in winter were awful, so cold, with ice around the bottles. I used to wonder whether it was worth it. The cold got me down in the end. I wasn't particularly tired. It was just miserable to have rain dripping down your neck. The people were good. There were regular calls for tea, sometimes with rum in the tea. Some milkmen wore pyjamas or long johns.

Harry James spent thirty-five years on the same round in Alsager, Cheshire, but eventually he succumbed to the winter weather. James started delivering milk when he was ten years old because his dad was a milkman. He took over the round for Northern Dairies in 1976 and then, five years later, he bought the round himself and became self-employed. But the winters of 2010 and 2011 were very harsh and at times his milk float was towed back to his Mow Cop base. James was fifty-nine when he retired.

The job had a high drop-out rate in winter and staff shortages could be a problem, but experienced milkmen prepared well for bad weather. They equipped their vehicles with grit, sacks and plenty of salt. Sometimes, when the van was stuck in snow, the milkman unloaded every crate before trying to get out. The milk floats came out more easily in reverse gear. Some milkmen used chains.

When the snow first came, it glistened, virgin and velvet, bright and light, and took away the customary darkness. Some milkmen ran like children in the snow, excited, kicking up the flakes, shaking snow off their hats. It was beautiful at the beginning, but backstreet ice created problems later.

Walking in the snow and ice could be treacherous for milkmen, and customers didn't necessarily clear the snow off their steps or paths. You might slip on a path and put your hand out for the expected fall. Sometimes you corrected yourself, slid around and stabilised. Other times you had to grab a hedge or a gate post. One snowy morning a milkman got his float stuck in a house garden:

I phoned the dairy for help. The garage man arrived in an empty diesel. That's a notoriously unstable vehicle and he was sliding across the ice. I saw him coming but I didn't know where he was going. He was only doing about five miles an hour but he was side-on and I was skating for safety. I asked him what had happened to the breakdown wagon. He said, 'It's broke down.'

In winter, customers rinsed the empty bottles at night and the bottles were frozen to the step by morning. In snow and icy conditions the technique of kicking frozen bottles from the step sometimes resulted in a broken bottle with a jagged edge lurking beneath the snow. Icy ruts in the road caused the van to bounce around and send bottles all over the place. Sometimes a milkman dropped a bottle into the snow and the milk turned to ice cream.

Milkmen tried to remember what the path was like underneath the snow. Was it a dangerous path of slippery tiles? Could it be gravel with good grip for running? Or was it a lawn underneath? Sometimes it was difficult to see the boundary between grass and path.

Milkmen could be very cold in winter. One wedged a brick on his float's accelerator pedal and then ran alongside the empty vehicle to keep warm before jumping into the cab. Some milkmen wore gloves and others didn't. Almost all had headwear. Some wore tights and long socks, and one kept a gas heater in his cab. In some winters the snow cleared and then reappeared a week or two later. The milkmen were not as cheerful about a second fall of snow.

In bad weather it was prudent to leave the van at the bottom of the hill and walk up. But conditions could worsen by the minute. A simple movement could cause the van to be stuck. Maybe the front wheels slid into the kerb and there seemed no way out, forwards or backwards. Sometimes shifting the load over to one side of the van helped.

Before mobile phones it wasn't easy getting help when a van was immobilised. Milkmen had to find a public telephone or use a customer's home phone. But even then there might be a long wait. The dairy's breakdown vehicle could be on another call or, when it arrived, it might not be able to help. Maybe a local resident would come out with a spade and start digging up the ice around the milk float. Then perhaps that same resident repeated the action so that the breakdown truck could move. When one milkman got totally stuck, beyond hope, he asked customers to store the milk in their bathrooms and sheds so he could deliver it the next day.

Over the period 1971 to 2000, the UK had an average of thirty-three days of snow or sleet a year, but most of it fell on high ground, and the snow only settled on sixteen days a year (on average). There were clear regional variations. Cornwall was the least likely place in Britain for snow, and Banffshire, Scotland, the most likely. The really bad winters included 1947 and 1963. Alan Jenkins recalled the latter in *Drinka Pinta*:

> Let us not forget, either, the terrible winter of 1962–3, which seemed endless, with whole areas cut off from normal supplies for days and weeks on end. The dairy industry made spectacular efforts to get the milk through to its customers, and photographs of it doing so were an almost daily feature of newspapers. In its advertisements the NMPC [The National Milk Publicity Council of England and Wales] were quick to echo the theme, and milkmen were shown tramping through snowdrifts, their vans bearing the slogan *Drinka Winta Pinta*.

One milkman described his winters:

> Boy, we had some fun! I remember one day. We started at three in the morning and we finished at half past four in the

afternoon. Delivering a lot of it by sledge. The places we couldn't get to in the car we'd put it on a sledge and drag it. The last three winters we did, we were digging ourselves out. You'd get the van where you could and walk the rest.

When the weather was bad, you'd come up past the police station and you'd wind it up as fast as you could and go straight to the top without stopping because once you'd stopped you'd had it.

A Gloucestershire resident recalled winter scenes from her childhood in the 1930s:

I remember at my first school the milk was put on the range to thaw out before we could drink it. The bottles had cardboard tops and were collectors' items as many different ones were produced during the year. The milk expanded when frozen and I have a mental picture of the cardboard top resting an inch above the neck of the bottle.

Milkmen gave even more thought to their footwear when it was snowy or icy. Was it better to use wellington boots, walking boots, climbing boots or crampons? Like National Hunt jockeys, they knew that another fall might happen sometime and it was a relief if they survived it without a hospital visit.

The snow brought better visibility, although some days were both snowy and misty. When the snow thawed it was a great relief, but milkmen had to be careful where they stood during a thaw. One milkman, reading a note on the front doorstep of a house, was drenched by an avalanche of melting snow from a house roof. On one very dark morning a milkman stood on the doorstep for a minute trying to read a note. Eventually he worked it out: *Beware of Dangerous Guttering Overhead*.

A winter's day without snow offered little light for milkmen. On some days the sun rose around eight o'clock but winter days were often overcast, gloomy and darker than a coalman's delivery. There was always one winter morning when it was the darkest morning ever, when it was blacker than black. Or it seemed like that.

I was petrified driving down some of the farm tracks in the pitch dark. There might be a house every mile and I was aware of every sound. I'd tell myself, 'You're mad, you're crazy, anything could happen, and no one would know for three hours.' I'd look round in every possible direction before getting out of the van. Sometimes I might get out and get back in and decide to go back when it was light. Sometimes I'd sit in the van for two minutes to get the guts to go out in the cold.

It could rain hard in winter. Mud and wet stuck to the bottom of trousers and two pairs of socks slowly dampened until moisture reached the skin. Winter was also a time of darkness, spooky alleys and ice on the float's windscreen. Sometimes the sharp mornings were delightfully bright. When the sun was out and the frost was clearing, conditions were very pleasant, although the milkmen had to keep moving. Those who didn't wear gloves were pleased to see a cat so that they could temporarily warm their hands. They would be even more pleased if a glamorous customer uttered encouraging words – 'The kettle's just boiled'.

Milkmen had to be careful in winter. It always seemed harder to work in the dark, especially around dawn, when slippery black ice lurked under tall trees:

> I had a bad accident coming round a corner down by the railway line. I hit some black ice and was heading for a furniture lorry. I threw myself across the cab, just in time, before the front caved in. My leg was trapped but I was lucky not to get killed.

In the snow visibility was good, but on dark mornings milkmen needed a sense of concealed objects such as rambling plants, washing lines, car aerials, wing mirrors, garden gnomes and kids' trikes. Wet cold was bad for health. Milkmen might be fighting off an early morning cough and a sore throat, or their eyes throbbed from being exposed to blizzards and frosts. Rain coming into electric milk floats sometimes caused ulcers down the exposed leg. Others suffered from chilblains. And one took five or six Anadins a day.

In his milkman memoir *Hey, Milkman!*, John C LaRizzio remembered the really cold winters of his teenage years in the sixties when he delivered milk in Nesquehoning, Pennsylvania, USA:

> These were days birthed barren and brittle, when the cold seemed to penetrate the dark. It pierced the blank curtain of darkness with jagged unseen bristles and shards. It stabbed tears from my eyes and, seemingly, sliced the flesh on my cheeks. Its presence was painful and pointed. It challenged my resolve with a relentless, punitive assault. It hid itself in

brazen breezes that tugged at my hood and contested my every action. Still other days the cold seemed more pervasive, more bland and weighty but every bit the uncontested lord of the out-of-doors. It stole the function from my fingers and the comfort from my toes. It turned my legs to deadened stumps and froze the insides of my nose.

By 2009, Derek Arch had experienced sixty-six winters of delivering milk:

The winters of today are nothing. We've seen the snow waist-high, haven't we? And we've got through. You learn with experience. You don't go up hills. You work your way round to come down them . . . I feel the cold terribly now. I didn't put on half the clothes then as I do now. It's just age, I think. Your blood thins.

During one winter a Gloucestershire milkman called Gary Cowley delivered some of his round by sledge because the milk was freezing in his Transit van. He'd be driving along and he'd hear the ping of milk tops flying off. In the winter months electric floats were freezing cold and the diesels were wonderfully warm. In the spring and summer the floats were beautifully airy and the diesels uncomfortably hot and steamy.

Spring

Compared with winter, spring was a joy. Spring provided optimism. Spring was the reward for milkmen getting through winter. The mornings were lighter and the days were warmer.

There was one drawback with spring. Towards the end of March, a few days after the equinox, the clocks went forward and the milkmen had to wait for more daylight. By the middle of April, however, milkmen were optimistic.

> I really liked May and June. Once you got to the end of April, coming into May, it was beautiful bright mornings. It was lovely. It was really nice to be out early before everybody else. You could hear the birds singing.

One problem was the increased likelihood of flooding in spring. Milder weather meant that snow melted on the hills and the river downstream could overflow. One milkman paid boys in boats to help him deliver to a village after floods had made it difficult to distinguish the river from the land.

In the Windsor floods of March 1947, milkmen and postmen toured the streets by boat, and a baker specialised in throwing loaves of bread through open bedroom windows. Milkmen wore thigh-high waders so they could walk through water while holding on to front walls and property fences. Alternatively they punted along the street in flat-bottomed boats that carried milk crates. The 'Eton Boating Song' was an obvious choice for a sing-along.

One milkwoman entertained herself in all weathers:

> I spoke to animals, such as cats, and looked at gardens. I looked around, watched the seasons change, saw front doors changing colour, what washing was hanging. Sometimes when it was really wet I phoned for dry clothes and changed in the float.

During spring, customers made changes to gardens and buildings. If the changes were radical it might make the milkman hesitate for a moment, wondering if it were the right house. A milkman who identified a house solely by its front door was in real trouble when the blue door became red. In spring, milkmen were cautious about roses, weeds and newly laid seeds. A cobweb could cling to you for the next twenty calls.

By the end of spring the weather was warmer. This was generally positive, but there were some downsides. When milkmen returned to the dairy, there was a terrible stench of stale milk. During the winter, the big dairy lorries created potholes; by the spring the holes had spilt milk sitting in them. The sun warmed the pools of milk, and the effect was a grotesque, putrid pong.

Summer

For many milkmen an early dawn was the best part of the year. They might have seen a panther or a crop circle. When a round red sun bobbed cautiously over the horizon, it felt a privilege to be up in time to see the dawn. The milkmen had the streets to themselves. The birds were singing and so were some milkmen. What more could you want?

> I used to leave home just after three, load up, started about half three. You saw the odd drunks going home, especially Saturday mornings. I did the top of town first; it was amazing the foxes and badgers you used to see around the top of town.

Summer was a time for milkmen in shorts showing off their tanned legs. It was a time for female customers in bikinis enjoying the sun. The light mornings made the round quicker to deliver. Also, customers took their holidays in summer, so there were fewer calls (except at holiday resorts). Compared with wintry conditions, the round was a doddle.

The major problem was getting the milk into a place where it didn't turn sour in the warm weather. Jersey milk, in particular, turned very quickly. Customers needed to protect their milk from the birds and from the sun, and some were remarkably inventive. They provided buckets and pots, and suggested sheltered spots. They asked milkmen to hide the milk in the shade and cover the top of the milk bottle so that the birds didn't start pecking at the silver foil. All sorts of foil protectors were used – yoghurt cartons, plastic cups, pieces of slate, flowerpots, aerosol-can tops, fabric-conditioner bottle tops, Thermos flask tops, plastic glasses, and so on. Of course, the blue tits sometimes attacked the bottle tops on the milk float instead. One milkman outwitted the tits by laying an old fur collar resembling a cat on the top of the crates in the van. In recent years, with homogenised milk, there was no cream on top of a pint of milk and the birds seemed less interested.

During a heatwave some milkmen started earlier in the day to stay cooler, and the company was different during the summer. It might be a big year for greenfly or ladybirds. Bees led milkmen through the flowers, and wasps accompanied milkmen later in the summer. Dragonflies turned up for a brief spell if a customer had the right pond, and the wildlife also included badgers, hares, stags and deer.

People opened more windows during summer. If a milk-man went to bed at 9 p.m. he did not sleep so easily if he could hear the sound of next door's lawnmower or washing machine. On the other hand, tiptoeing up a garden path with a crate of milk was an opportunity to eavesdrop on what was happening behind open windows. You could hear all of human life from doorsteps – arguments, snoring, people making love, residents taking showers and parents trying to get their kids off to school ('John, it's three minutes to eight!'). You might also hear snippets of news from the radio or television.

Some customers left discs and dials to indicate the number of pints they required. During the summer these were much easier to read, but the milkman needed good vision to read a disc from a distance in the dark. A weary milkman might be relieved when a dial was set on zero and there was no need to go up the long drive. Summer was wonderful. The only problem was the crows ransacking discarded chips at dawn.

Autumn

There was a great storm on 16 October 1987. The event was notable for its destruction and damage, but it was also legendary because the BBC's weather forecast under-estimated the likely damage. Twenty-five years later, people logged their 1987 experiences on the BBC website. The contributors included Paul Slade and Mike Bentley. Slade's best memory was seeing a milkman in a crash helmet running from door to door as slates and tiles still fell from buildings; Bentley's, a Thanet Ambulance technician, was off searching for a route through the fallen trees and debris when he came across a whistling milkman.

Autumn also brought fireworks and fog. The fog appeared at any time but the fireworks usually happened around the fifth of November. One milkman asked a customer if she was looking forward to the big bonfire. 'Oh, yes, very much,' the customer replied. 'I'm hoping to plonk a couple of my kids on it.'

The combination of dark and fog meant poor visibility. On some mornings a milkman could see only a few yards. The fog increased a milkman's chances of being run over. A milkman listened for the sound of cars, but sometimes a vehicle appeared suddenly through the mist. An electric milk float was slow enough to see what was happening in the fog, but there was a greater concern about how other vehicles were proceeding, especially given the milk float's vulnerability. Fog was also bad news for the milkman's journey to work.

It was hard delivering a regular round in the fog, but it was even harder delivering a new round. Sometimes it was so foggy that it took some time to find the next house on the round and then the milkman had the problem of finding the van again. 'Mist in town was fog in the country,' one milkman said.

For some, the autumn was particularly beautiful. The comedian Benny Hill once explained to his brother and biographer Lenny Hill about the beauty of an early morning horse-and-cart delivery round:

It was lovely getting up on fresh mornings and galloping for miles out into the country, the Hampshire landscape glistening with early morning dew is one of the prettiest sights you can see. I'd be up on the top of the cart, lord of all I surveyed. Over Station Bridge I'd rumble, cart creaking, bottles rattling. Daisy the mare would pick up speed the other side and we'd bowl along to Bishopstoke.

As autumn progressed, there was more darkness in the mornings. Getting used to the dark was an annual challenge. Milkmen rarely used torches. For most, the skill came in training the eyes to adjust to the little amount of natural light that you could find within darkness. Milkmen tried to avoid looking directly at bright lights because being dazzled made the next few calls harder. One milkman regularly wandered down a dark alley, clinging on to three pints. He knew exactly how to avoid the rambling plant and somehow he got through a high back gate that was locked from the inside. Then he just missed two washing lines in the back garden before he collected some cobwebs on his face. He probably trod on a few snails on the way. The athleticism of snails has been given a bad press. When they crawl up and down empty bottles they seem to move really fast.

Another milkman had a bad experience with a torch:

I once bought a torch at Woolworth's and even bought extra batteries. I got to my milk float one morning, unplugged the float from the battery charger, jumped into the driver's seat and put the torch on the passenger seat. Then I backed the float out of the garage bay and the torch fell out of the van, hit the floor and I swung the van round and bounced the back wheel over the torch. One flattened rubber torch. I never used a torch again.

Running in the dark was difficult. It was too easy to trip over a kerb. A simple object like a car aerial or a wing mirror could do untold damage. Milkmen had to go carefully so they could see planks jutting out from a van roof and the connecting rod on its trailer.

Some milkmen took great delight in listening to owls. Others enjoyed the night sky. Ultimately, though, milkmen were trained to look down rather than up. They studied doorsteps, gate catches, empty milk bottles, crates and customers.

Then, in late October, there came a time adjustment and more daylight. Putting the clocks back was great for the job. Some milkmen thought they should put the clocks back every week.

6

'Merry Christmas, Milkman'

No milk till Saturday cos Santa gave us some.

On the day of the huge Christmas delivery, the milkmen greeted each other at the dairy.

'Merry Christmas, milkman.'

'Merry Christmas, milkman.'

'Merry Christmas, milkman.'

Many dairies traditionally delivered milk and cream on Christmas Day. That could be really dangerous because some milkmen stayed up drinking all night on Christmas Eve and didn't go to bed before starting work. One milkman loaded up his van on Christmas Day, went to a pub on his round and got so drunk that he ended the day standing outside Woolworth's merrily handing the firm's milk to strangers.

The breathalyser was introduced in 1967 and its major purpose was to reduce the number of drink-driving deaths around the Christmas holiday period. On Christmas Day 1967, Sam Ashworth, a sixty-year-old milkman from Southend-on-Sea, was stopped by police at 7 a.m. The officers were suspicious because Ashworth was singing 'The Last Waltz' as if he was on the way home from a night in the pub. Ashworth was asked to take one of the new breath tests. The milkman blew into the bag and was found to be sober. The police wished him 'Merry Christmas' and sent him on his way.

Raymond Briggs, author of *Father Christmas*, had inside knowledge about milkmen because his father was one. Briggs thought that a milkman's job was similar to that of Father Christmas. Both travelled long distances in the cold while other people slept through the night. Santa Claus and the milkman shared the motto that the goods must get through, and both used singular vehicles in the snow – a sleigh and a milk float. In *Father Christmas*, Briggs shows the milkman talking to Santa Claus. He also depicts the milkman's van with the number plate ERB 1900 – the initials of Raymond's father, Ernest, and the year of Ernest's birth. On Christmas mornings young Raymond helped his dad with milk deliveries.

Christmas meant different things to different milkmen. Clive Greenham never forgot Christmas Eve 1970 because he married his sweetheart Patricia on that day. In those days milkmen worked throughout the Christmas period, so Clive and Patricia started their married life by delivering the round together on Christmas morning. Greenham worked for forty-seven years on a Somerset round which covered Kingsdon, Yeovilton and Yeovil Marsh. He retired in 2010.

'Merry Christmas, Milkman'

Stan Wilson, milkman for Claverley, Shropshire, from 1952 to 1988, once recalled a festive Christmas incident:

I remember the shop in the village when Eileen Bryant ran it, especially one Christmas. The shop was very busy and there was mistletoe hanging up, and the lady standing beneath was Elsie Spiller from Danford. She was good for a laugh, so I put my arms around her and gave her a kiss. Everyone was laughing, when suddenly there was a heavy banging on the shop window. We all spun around, startled, to see Elsie's husband outside, banging on the glass . . . and laughing his head off! He would have to have been passing the shop at that time, wouldn't he?

Some dairies delivered on Christmas Day until into the eighties, but it eventually became a dairy holiday and milkmen delivered a double round on Christmas Eve. Christmas required an elaborate plan. Customers were given forms in advance and asked to signify which goods they needed for the holiday period. Because the milk floats weren't big enough to hold the goods for a double round, it meant that milkmen delivered half the round and then returned to the dairy for a second load.

Christmas always seemed special when I was a milkman. Without doubt it was a tiring and difficult time. Extra cream, milk, bread, and even hampers were sold and delivered, and the milk floats used to be stacked high with all the extra goods. Of course you would see all the Christmas festivities in each and every house, and if I had accepted all the alcoholic drinks I was offered I would never have got the milk float back to the dairy. Some of the miserable old milkmen would suddenly cheer up at Christmas and try to be their customers' best friend.

I once had a tree fall across the road when I was out on the big Christmas Eve round. I had a sixth sense and saw it falling, so I braked heavily and I came round with a branch poking through the windscreen and a load of creams tipped across the road. I phoned up the dairy and asked for more creams and was treated inconsiderately.

We used to deliver 365 days a year. One of my earliest memories was getting to the Poltimore Arms at midnight on Christmas Eve. I was only seventeen but the boss came out and took me inside. I got so drunk I had to be picked up and taken home.

Christmas used to be a nightmare. We used to have Christmas order forms printed and the table used to be stacked with these order forms. I'd be sat there forever transferring it all into the book and then counting it all because the dairy always wanted a pre-order for cream and fruit juice and what have you, and 'could you give us an idea how much milk you'll want?' I remember one Christmas we did 120 cases of pop. We used to deliver that separately because you couldn't get it on the van with the milk. Then I'd be out delivering potatoes. It would be nothing to do two ton of potatoes in the couple of weeks before Christmas. We did milk, eggs, potatoes, fruit juice, cream, yoghurt, and then the dairies did tins of chocolate biscuits, chocolate gift packs, and every year they did the dairy diary. That was a brilliant seller. We used to do well over a hundred dairy diaries a year. They used to come in boxes of thirty-six so I always used to order three boxes to start. But latterly, I couldn't even sell one box. The dairy diary was a very good seller, but the dairy cookbook was an even better one. Each year it had new recipes.

Christmas meant all sorts of things to different people. Traditionally it was the time for Christmas carols, office parties, family reunions, special meals, presents, marital break-ups, a holiday from work and so forth. To milkmen it usually meant bad weather and good tips, or, occasionally, good weather and good tips. More milkmen left the job in the period just after Christmas than at any other time of the year. They collected their tips, collected their leaver's forms, collected their cards and no longer collected the empties.

Ernie

Ernie was one of those milkmen who sang Christmas carols in the build up to the holiday period. He had worked in the days of the horse and cart. In his early career he'd had a village round and one day he was soaked. He was invited into the pub by the landlord, who sat him down by the fire and gave him some dry clobber. A young lad came in and said, 'Have you seen your horse, milkman?' Apparently the horse was halfway to the city. But Ernie didn't care.

One Christmas Eve it was cold, frosty and icy. I was next to Ernie in the dairy as we queued up for the first half of the big order. We tended to arrive about the same time and the dairy had worked out a Christmas loading timetable so that the milkmen stuck to their usual schedule. On this occasion Ernie was wearing six or seven layers – tracksuits, wet-suits, pairs of trousers, leather jerkin, his yellow lifeboatman's suit, and a balaclava on his head. The other milkmen called him The Incredible Hulk. Ernie didn't mind what they called him, or what he looked like, as long as he was warm.

On this particular Christmas Eve I finished my double round midway through the afternoon. I walked away from the dairy contemplating the heavy drizzle that had now consolidated. In the first street I watched a battered old milk float swerve dangerously round the corner towards me. The van meandered into another street and stopped in the middle of the road. Ernie toppled off the float and started looking for where he kept the milk. Something didn't look right. I walked towards the van.

'Hello, Ernie,' I said. 'Need a hand?'

Ernie spoke with slurred words. I eventually twigged their meaning.

'I need all the help I can get,' he said.

Then he fell into the pile of crates on his van and I noticed that he had a lot of milk on board.

'I'll give you a hand for twenty minutes,' I said. 'Then I'm going to listen to the carols.'

'I'll shing you all the carols you want,' he said, and then burst into song: 'Good King Wenshlashlush . . .'

Ernie was nearing retirement. His real name wasn't Ernie but everybody except the manager knew him as that. Maybe someone had misheard his name at one time or perhaps it was because Ernie drove the slowest milk float in the East.

It took us twenty minutes to do the next five calls. Ernie had a couple of warming vodkas in the first house, though he called them 'vorming wodkas', and then an assortment of drinks at the next house. While he was drinking, I delivered some milk.

As Ernie became incoherent and wobbly on his pins, I realised that I needed to stick with him. I stayed for two hours. At one point Ernie took out his pen and threw it into the rain. At another house he took my pen and did the same. I started making scratch marks in the round's book.

Ernie picked up two bottles and swung them around like an American cheerleader. One looked certain to hit a lamppost. Then he started juggling with the bottles. He dropped two and I cleared up the glass, leaving the rain to swill away the milk.

'You've been out on the tiddly,' one customer told Ernie when she offered him coffee. I left him in her house and went out delivering, happy that Ernie was safe indoors. I served another street and wished I knew the round.

When Ernie returned to the rain, to offer instructions, I made the mistake of going to a back door and leaving the float out of my sight. When I returned, Ernie was hanging on to the pole at the back, his face beaming drunkenly. Milk was dribbling down one side of the van.

'I'm having a sort out,' he said.

He'd tipped over a crate.

Eventually we'd delivered most of the milk to roughly where it was needed and I drove Ernie back to the dairy. We still had a lot of milk on board, so the man on the loading bay, who dealt with returns, was angry with us. He literally threw the book at Ernie and me in disgust, and the only thing that saved us was mentioning the war. It turned out both Ernie and the loading-bay man had been at Tobruk during World War II.

'I may only be a two-bit milkman now,' Ernie said. 'But I used to be . . .'

I escorted him to his bike but he was too drunk to ride it. He tried a couple of times but fell on top of it. Eventually he realised that it was hopeless.

'If you can't behave, you can go home without me,' he told the bike. He gave the bicycle a push. The bike set off on its own for a few yards and then fell into the middle of the road. Ernie walked past it and staggered away from the dairy, towards the local street where he lived. I picked up the bike and took it back to the shed.

'Merry Christmas, milkman,' I shouted as Ernie disappeared out of sight.

7

The Amorous Milkman

One pint a day, sex on Saturdays.

A N AMERICAN sociologist, Odis Eugene Bigus, once described the interaction between a female customer and her milkman as a cultivated relationship involving courting and wooing. Bigus's research showed that it was good business for the milkmen to nurture friendly relationships with customers. It was even better to leave the customer with the feeling that she was his favourite customer. Naturally, a milkman could have forty or fifty favourites.

Stories about amorous milkmen and uncertain offspring were often based on three assumptions: (i) if a baby's physical characteristics did not match dad's, then someone else could be the father; (ii) in the heyday of doorstep delivery, the milkman was often the most frequent visitor to a house and he was therefore the most likely candidate for an affair and a child born out of wedlock; and (iii) wives were much more likely to be at home in the thirty years after World War II, when milk was delivered to virtually every home in Britain.

In her book *Housework*, based on interviews conducted in 1971, Ann Oakley found that the worst things about being a full-time housewife were constant domestic responsibility, isolation and loneliness. Especially lonely were those women who had moved to new housing estates. 'I could be murdered here and no one would know,' a housewife told Oakley. 'When the milkman comes it's an event.'

In those days women studied milkmen and postmen rather than dating websites and newspaper advertisements. The randy milkman has been the subject of jokes, anecdotes and gossip. Let us start with the jokes.

Have you heard the one about the milkman?

Here are four tall tales to start off the legend of the bored housewife and excitable milkman:

A young girl saw her cat lying on the floor with its eyes closed and legs in the air. Her father explained that the cat was dead and his legs were standing up in the air so that Jesus could come down from heaven, pick up the cat by the legs and take him up to a safe place. This made sense to the child.

Two days later, the father came home from work and found that his daughter was upset. The young child explained that Mummy had nearly died that morning.

'What happened?' asked the shocked father.

'Well,' said the child, 'after you went to work, I saw Mummy lying on the floor with her eyes closed, her legs in the air and she was shouting, "Oh, Jesus, I'm coming." And Mummy would have gone to heaven if the milkman hadn't been holding her down.'

A husband came home and told his wife that he had taken two days off work. The next morning the husband could see that his wife was delighted to have him home because she was jumping up and down and telling the milkman, 'My old man's home, my old man's home.'

A young boy passed his parents' bedroom in the middle of the night in search of a glass of water. Hearing a lot of moaning and thumping, the boy peeked into the bedroom and saw his mum and dad bouncing around on the bed.

'Oh, boy, horsy ride!' shouted the young boy. 'Daddy, can I ride on your back?' The son jumped on his dad's back and the embarrassed father continued what he had been doing. The pace stepped up and Mummy started moaning and groaning. 'Hang on tight, Daddy,' said the young boy. 'This is the part where me and the milkman usually get bucked off.'

A customer's husband came home unexpectedly and caught a milkman with his wife in the hallway. The milkman had his trousers down and his hand somewhere around his groin, so he thought quickly. 'Now listen, lady, I'm telling you,' he said. 'You're gonna pay your milk bill or I'm gonna pee on your porch.'

Sometimes it was risky to tell jokes about 'sex with the milkman'. Take this example from a milkman thread on the American forum Data Lounge:

We had milk delivered in the sixties. As a child I had fire engine red hair. No one else in my immediate family had red hair, not even close. However, I did have an uncle with red hair. Everyone would always ask my mother, 'Where did he get that red hair?' Jokingly, she would reply, 'I don't know, must be the milkman.' The milkman would deliver quite early to an insulated box by the back door and she hadn't even seen him, until one day she did and he had fire engine red hair. She stopped giving that excuse.

The milkman was a central figure in the community. Housewives took him seriously and developed a schedule for paying him. They even ran after him in a dressing-gown at six o'clock in the morning, shouting, 'You've missed me out' or 'What's been happening to my milk?'

Here is a female customer talking:

My milkman always got me out of bed early on a Saturday morning. I used to come down and pay him wearing my nightie. One Saturday, later in the day, I saw him in a nearby street as he was collecting money. There were a lot of people about, waiting at the bus queue and things like that. When I said 'Hello' he didn't answer me at first. I took a few steps past him and then he shouted after me, 'Sorry, love, I didn't recognise you with your clothes on.'

Legendary Lovers

The legend of the amorous milkman contains a little bit of reality and a lot of myth. 'I don't say it never happens,' said one milkman, 'but I am a married man.'

The Amorous Milkman

Milkmen could seem athletic and mysterious to female customers, and they brought an aura of sexual adventure to doorsteps. Milkmen were virile loners, full of mischievous masculinity, possibly as clean and sterilised as their milk. These romeos of the road were secure in their dealings with women; they were full of one-liners, knowledgeable about their round and capable of developing a fan base. Meanwhile, female customers could fantasise about the milkman's potential in the bedroom or in the hallway. A nosey neighbour might notice the milkman disappearing into number fifty-three for half an hour.

Milkmen developed a cheekiness from mixing with women, for it was women who usually paid the bill. Milkmen also had a healthy outdoor look. In modern parlance, they were fit. They walked up the garden path with a worldly independence and knocked on the door advertising vitality and virility. The ultimate professional was the milkman who could go to bed with a customer and still collect her milk money.

Certain roundsmen were known as 'one for the women'. One in particular kept being moved from one round to another because irate husbands would phone the dairy and threaten violence. The dairy manager heard a lot of complaints about him:

'Tell him to leave my wife alone.'
'If he comes round our way again I'll give him a good hiding.'
'He won't be so good-looking if I get hold of him.'

Another milkman took great pride in disrupting female preserves. He'd see an appropriate sign in a house window ('Coffee morning – all welcome') and turn up at gatherings. He was the only man present and no one knew how to handle him. (Well, OK, maybe one or two of the women knew how to handle him and he certainly knew how to handle them.)

In the fifties and sixties, there was usually only one telephone in the house, so a woman who was naked, about to get into the bath, might hurry downstairs to answer the phone. It was even better for the milkman if there was glass in the front door. One milkman was collecting money when a customer came to the door in a see-through baby-doll nightie. Another brazen housewife answered the door in a state of semi-nakedness and said, 'My husband is not here today.' One classic tease was for a woman to ask her milkman to help her move some furniture into her bedroom. Other customers were so hard up that they offered to pay off their milk bill through sex.

I did two rounds at Sherwood to start with and another one around Alfreton Road through to the arboretum and beyond. The latter was remarkable. I remember walking around the machines in textile factories looking for whoever paid me. There were even women who thought they could pay me in kind. Not a chance!

When milkmen met at the dairy, they might talk about the women on their rounds:

I had a bit of luck today. I called on a house expecting an old dear. I've never seen the woman before – she usually leaves her money under a brick – but she'd had a few extra this week so I thought I'd better call. And this bit of stuff comes to the door wearing nothing but a V-neck sweater. 'Just a minute,' she says. 'I'll get my bag.' And she walked back up the hall showing me, like . . . well, you know what I mean.

Sunday mornings would bring some ecstatic noises from the bedrooms and I remember well hearing one of my favourite customers yelling in her bedroom at her husband to get his hands off her tits. Of course I had great delight in informing her about this the next time I saw her.

I have seen a few sights from the doorstep over the years, I can tell you. I got plenty of propositions when I was younger and you have to laugh about some of the tricks we got up to. They were good days and good fun.

Amorous milkmen delivered to the nearby houses before stopping off at the home of a female customer. One milkman made the mistake of regularly engaging in nookie *before* delivering to the rest of the street and the other customers were not amused. They began shaking the milkman's float back and forth until it made such a racket that the milkman came out of the house. That lesson was threefold: (i) look after the customers first and foremost; (ii) park the float somewhere discreet; and (iii) then engage in sexual activity. But maybe the float-shaken milkman was just too excited to deliver the milk first.

An exchange of notes between a milkman and a customer might develop into something racy over a few days:

> *Milkman, you missed me yesterday.*
> *I did miss you. I would have loved to have seen you.*
> *I meant you missed leaving my milk.*
> *I must have been distracted.*
> *Distracted by what?*

Other notes might have set the milkman thinking:

> *Please knock. My TV's broken down and I missed last night's* Coronation Street. *If you saw it, will you tell me what happened over a cup of tea?*

> *When you leave my milk please knock on my bedroom window because I want you to give me a hand to turn the mattress.*

There is a story about a bearded milkman coming back from a terrace house call and getting into his milk float. A stunningly attractive young woman saw him from a distance and drove towards the float. The milkman had his head down, doing some paperwork, so the woman honked her horn, stopped alongside, lifted her T-shirt and exposed her bare breasts. Then she gasped, lowered her shirt quickly and drove away at speed. Oh, dear, wrong milkman, she thought. Hers had a beard just like that, too. She should have looked more closely.

It was a fortunate milkman who had nurses' homes on his round:

> When I reached the nurses' homes I knocked for the money at seven-thirty. They came to the door in negligees and nightdresses, everything hanging out, and they couldn't give a monkey's. I had a good stare.

> I reached the nurses' homes in time to knock on a few doors. One woman came to the door with a hastily wrapped towel and wet hair. I'd obviously arrived at an inconvenient time for her but it was pretty convenient for me.

I was doing the round with a lad called Steve. He was a runner and we worked well together. By the time we got to the nurses' flats we were flying. We did the calls in no time, up and down the stairs, sprinting from block to block. We came out of the last building at speed. I ran round the van, leapt into the driving seat and put my hand on the handbrake expecting Steve to hit the passenger seat. But there was no sign of him. I got out of the van and found him standing in front of the nurses' home looking up to the sky.

'Are you all right?' I asked.

'Yeah,' he said. 'I was thinking. This is the first time I've been able to hold my head up coming out of here at nine o'clock on a Sunday morning. Normally I have to hide.'

Sometimes a proposition was blatant. One woman said, 'My purse is up in my bedroom, follow me.' Then, upstairs, she jumped on her milkman.

The legend suggests that milkmen who do the same round for years can watch their children grow up. Perhaps they pat their kids on the head and give them some extra milk.

'My grandfather was a milkman,' explained one forum user. 'I have a lot of cousins.'

There was also a classic routine told by comics:

> *'I had a milk bath this morning,' says the woman.*
> *'Pasteurised?' asks the milkman.*
> *'No,' says the woman, 'just up to my breasts.'*

'I like to get the round done and then go home at nine,' said one speedy milkman. 'An old boy doing this round used to take until twelve, but that was three cups of tea and leg-over twice.'

Fantasies

In *Monty Python's Flying Circus* there is a sketch where a scantily clad, glamorous woman lures a milkman into her house and up the stairs to the attic. The milkman seems certain he is going to get very lucky. The woman opens the attic door, pushes the milkman inside and then swiftly locks the door and imprisons him with nine other milkmen and two skeletons with milkman caps. The room is full of cobwebs and the milkmen have been there for years.

Did the women of the house have fantasies about their milkmen? What went through the mind of wistful female customers, wearing skimpy night clothes ready for bed, when they rinsed out empty milk bottles before putting them on the doorstep late at night? A few hours later the milkman was the next person to handle those bottles.

Many milkmen had a fantasy customer, but fantasy was as far as it went for most milkmen:

I start collecting money at ten past seven. I like to start the collecting at exactly the same time because there's one who comes to the door in a see-through nightie. One of these days I'll get the sack for putting my hands where I shouldn't.

Just as the sky cleared and the sun came out, a girl with light-red hair smiled at me as she walked past. Until then I had thought of her as 'four pints a day with two Erica Jong books on her front-room bookshelves'. Now it was love. I delivered my milk as she walked the street slowly. I kept running across her path and smiling at her. She smiled back. When we crossed paths for the umpteenth time, I said, 'If we keep on meeting like this, I'll be asking you to deliver some milk for me.' Next day she smiled at me again as she walked one of her three children to school. She was a real dream woman. It was a shame I saw her pushing a pram.

The milkman's fantasy world was about walking into a chemist intending to buy contraceptives in case he got lucky on the round. The real world was more about the milkman walking into the chemist and remembering that he needed to buy lip salve, headache tablets and torch batteries.

Other contributions to the fantasy life of milkmen can be seen in the erotic fiction genre. An example is *The Milkman Cometh*, a fifteen-page short story by Kate Richards. The milkman provides intimate services for the lonely ladies on his milk round and is then pursued by one in particular.

Affairs

Some milkmen became involved in something very real. The musician Sting's mother Audrey had a long-standing affair with a milkman called Alan who worked at the same dairy as her husband Ernie. As a boy Sting heard and saw Audrey and Alan being affectionate through the opaque glass of the porch door. The thirty-year affair became a marriage after Ernie and Audrey divorced.

The mother of artist Grayson Perry took up with a Co-op milkman in the sixties. One night Perry's father discovered the affair and confronted his wife. Grayson Perry's parents split up but got back together a few weeks later. But the affair with the milkman continued. At Easter 1965, Perry's father discovered his wife was pregnant by the milkman. Apparently the milkman had three women pregnant at the same time – his own wife, Perry's mother and a teacher. The milkman left his wife and moved in with Perry's mother. They lost the first baby but had a child two years later. Grayson Perry lost touch with his mother.

Angie Smith was a divorcée with two young sons when she had a brief affair with a milkman and became pregnant. Smith was twenty-three in November 1968 when she gave birth to a daughter in her dad's garden shed. Her parents were unaware of the pregnancy so Angie Smith smuggled the baby out of the house in a laundry bag and left her in the lobby of nearby flats. A resident of the flats thought the bag contained rubbish so she put it by the dustbins. The baby was found twenty-four hours later by a tenant who'd heard her cries. The media called the lost baby 'Dustbin Baby' but her adoptive parents named her Michelle. Birth mother and baby were reunited forty-six years later.

And here is a story told on a Birmingham Co-op Dairy forum:

> The affair I remember was between a Birmingham Co-op milkman and one of his female customers, and it was a scandal at the time as all the neighbours were talking about it and saying how disgusted they were about it. I can remember the family moving in. He was a long-distance lorry driver . . . and his wife was a really good-looking woman and they had four or five children, the eldest being

about six. I'm not sure but I think this couple stayed together but left the area. The milkman either got the sack or was moved to another round as I am sure he was reported to the Co-op about it.

The Real World

It was early July when the milkman's wife went into labour. This particular milkman hadn't had a day off since Boxing Day, but now he left his round to visit his wife in hospital. His appearance in the maternity unit, wearing his milkman's uniform, provoked typical comments. 'Oh,' said one nurse, 'it's the milkman's, is it?'

Another milkman gave the eulogy at his father's funeral. His first words were, 'Yes, I am the milkman's son.' And he really was. His father had had a long career as a milkman.

At one house a relief milkman saw a note outside the house – *If I buy ten pints and a dozen eggs will you snog me?* The milkman was unsure how to react. He tried to remember who lived in the house but he was new to the round. If he rang the doorbell a bloke might come to the door with a grin on his face and say, 'Got you there.'

In the real world the milkman often had evidence of other people's sexual adventures. For example, at 3.15 a.m. one day, a milkman came across two suspicious characters sitting in a car in a quiet place. He phoned the police, but his call sparked trouble. The pair were courting but they were both married to other people.

Here are more stories from milkmen:

A woman on my round told me about a man who ran across the playing-fields at the back of her house. The man stood in full view of a row of houses while he was tossing himself off. 'Did you call the police?' I asked her. 'Yes, I did,' she said. 'But I waited until he'd finished before I called them.'

One morning, doing a new round, I found an intriguing note: *Hello, handsome, hope you can read this in the dark. I forgot to tell you yesterday that we need three today. I've been making too much coffee. Have a nice day.*

One snowy winter's day I'd delivered a pint to this one house. I was back at my van when a young woman in a nightie opened the door and shouted for an extra pint. 'Here it is, love,' I shouted back. 'At the van.' I took it over eventually.

It was dark and quiet one morning at about five-thirty. I took two pints to this one house and a nearby front door opened. The girl who came out was new to me. She couldn't stop smiling.

'Good morning,' I said.

'Good morning,' she said. She was really grinning. 'Say, is Mill Road at the top or at the bottom?'

I pointed towards Mill Road. She grinned again. Then she ran off, following my directions. I could hear her clogs as she entered the early morning mist. She looked as though she'd had a good night in a stranger's house.

I thought I was in with a good chance one day. I was having a coffee with a young teacher who had taken a day off sick. Her husband was away and we were getting on like a house on fire. Then the postman delivered a letter and it fell into one of the wellington boots I'd left at the door. We thought this was funny, but the letter turned out to be a really big gas bill which upset my customer. It sort of spoilt the mood.

Some milk rounds were much coveted because they had film stars living on them. One milkman delivered milk to a star and knew exactly when to be there in order to catch a sight of her. One day he saw her in a dressing-gown preening herself in the kitchen mirror.

Milkmen lived for such moments. They never knew who they'd bump into. One relief milkman knocked at a house and a naked woman, just out of the bath, came to the door. Calmly, unembarrassed, the customer counted out the money and settled the bill.

Some milkmen used strategies to catch a customer naked, such as ringing the doorbell when she was about to get in the bath or suggesting that hoovering in the nude was the latest fitness craze. A canny milkman waited until the shower stopped and then rang the doorbell so the customer had to come to the door with a towel wrapped around her.

'I know I'm getting old,' Alf Milton told the local newspaper when he retired after forty-seven years as a milkman in the West Midlands. 'If I see someone with nothing on I just turn away.'

Misunderstandings

Some stories can be elaborated in the telling. Here are two examples:

One day a woman was sitting on a bus with her four-year-old grandson. She was telling her friend that a noisy milkman was waking her up at 5 a.m. every day. Then the friend got off the bus and another friend got on and asked the woman how she was.

'I'm fine,' said the woman.

'No, she's not,' said the four-year-old grandson. 'She's very tired and it's the milkman's fault.'

A woman was painting the lounge walls with a pair of old knickers on her head to stop paint splashing her hair. Then the doorbell rang. Her young son answered the door and saw the milkman. 'Mum,' the boy shouted. 'Take your knickers off – the milkman needs paying.'

Paternal Discrepancy

In recent years DNA tests have opened up a more precise awareness of genetic inheritance. Sometimes this is critically important. If, for instance, a young child has a serious congenital kidney defect, other family members can be DNA-tested to see who has the best fit for a kidney transplant. But what happens if tests show that none of Dad's genetic material matches the child's? This is known as paternal discrepancy or, in some quarters, 'the milkman scenario'. The child has been biologically fathered by someone other than the man who believes he is the father.

A literature review by Professor Mark Bellis and colleagues found big differences in seventeen studies on paternal discrepancy. The authors' best estimate was that about 3.7 per cent of men who believe they are the real father are actually not the real father. Doctors may feel it is not their job to explain this to members of the family. The mystery of milkmen and paternity continues.

8

Never Work with Animals

*Could you please leave us one pint a day because
my dog is getting fat.*

'WHILE I have yet to meet many of my customers,
I must know every dog, cat, child and parrot that
lives in the streets on my round,' wrote John Huins, in his
book about being a milkman.

Sometimes a gate had a sign warning the milkman
about an animal:

> SHUT THE GATE
> DOG GETS OUT
> BEWARE OF THE DOG

Other signs might be needed, such as THIS VEHICLE IS
BEING DRIVEN BY A DOG. On 23 January 2004, a pensioner
was treated in hospital after he was hit by a milk float with

a dog at the wheel. A milkman at Morton's Dairies regularly took his dog Monty with him when delivering a round in the Wirral, Cheshire. Monty, a black Labrador, stayed in the float while the milkman collected the money. The customers loved the dog and often brought out titbits. On this occasion a seventy-five-year-old man went out to join the dog while the milkman was away from his van. The dog came across the cab to greet the pensioner and accidently trod on the float's accelerator. The vehicle lurched off, hit the man on the knee and then crashed against a lamppost. The man was taken to hospital and the dog was taken to a vet. Monty had a damaged paw.

Never work with animals, eh?

Dog Bites

In 1997, milkman Jack Roberts suffered a severe hand injury when attacked by a Rottweiler in Farnworth, Lancashire. His injured hand needed microsurgery. Magistrates ordered the dog to be destroyed, but the Crown Court reversed the decision. Interestingly, Roberts and his wife agreed with the decision to spare the dog because they were both animal lovers and they saw the problem as the dog's owner rather than the dog. The owner was banned from keeping a dog for twenty years.

Ian Cooper, who delivered to the Cheshire villages of Chelford and Birtles, was once bitten on the ankles by a feisty Jack Russell. After that bad experience he made sure he carried dog biscuits. Similarly, Thames Ditton milkman Roy Burton's number-one tip was 'make sure you bring some dog biscuits'. It was better for the dog to bite the biscuit than munch the milkman.

Never Work with Animals

In the community of milkmen there were dog-lovers, dog-haters and people who were somewhere in between. Dogs on a milk round could test a milkman's patience. 'I needed butterfly stitches after a dog bit my arse,' one milkman told me.

Here are a few more doggy tales:

I was once showing a relief man my round. I warned him about this dog that was prowling around the garden. 'Whatever you do, mate, don't go in this garden,' I said. I pointed out the BEWARE OF THE DOG sign and said, 'Leave the milk outside the front gate.' Well, he saw that the dog was over the other side of the garden and he thought he could get to the doorstep and get out before the dog ran across. 'Don't even try it,' I said. Well, he did it. He opened the gate, raced up the drive, plonked down the milk, raced out, shut the gate behind him and stood there laughing. 'I bet you thought it couldn't be done,' he told me. Then the dog came through the hedge and bit him. I knew it would.

I've got a Jack Russell in one street. It lets you in all right, and lets you play with it, but just you try to get out. I won't go in there now. I leave the milk outside and throw an empty bottle at the dog. I carry a bottle to all calls with dogs. Just in case.

I was bitten by a little black and white mutt. It leapt up and bit my right bicep. The customer said, 'He's never done that before – what were you doing?' I told him I just went to ring his doorbell. 'Oh, that's it,' the bloke said. 'He doesn't like hands.' I thought, I'll ring your bell with my foot next time. Back in the dairy, I unloaded the van and then went to pay in. A foreman was sitting in the cashier's office as I walked in. A few milkmen were counting their money at the edge of the room. 'What do we do about dog bites?' I asked the foreman. Another milkman turned round, grinned at me and said, 'Have you bitten a dog?' I never did get an answer to my question.

There's this huge St Bernard dog on my round. I've got three bottles in my right hand and three bottles in my left hand, and the dog's owner says, 'He's all right if you stroke him.'

On one delivery there was a Labrador that used to sit serenely in the garden and watch me as I delivered the milk. The customer warned me that it had been in a car accident and was a little crazy and that I should watch it as I came up the garden path. No problem. I did this every single day until one day I was so busy looking at a sexy housewife in her underwear that could just be seen through the window that I forgot about the dog. It didn't bark but crept behind me, bit the back of my leg and then ran. It didn't break the skin but it still hurt and I only had myself to blame.

Dogs raised complex legal issues. The sign BEWARE OF THE DOG was a warning to milkmen but it could also count against the owner because it implied that the dog's owner knew that the dog was dangerous. Sometimes police asked the local milkman if a particular dog had a history of biting people. In many cases dogs were allowed one free bite. After that dog owners definitely knew their dog could be dangerous. Legislation in the early nineties tightened up issues of dog bites and dangerous dogs.

Other Dog Stories

Some milkmen were very confident with dogs. One milkman tamed barking dogs by getting down on all fours and barking back, but that technique generally came with a health warning.

Sometimes a dog led the milkman through the round:

I was doing relief work one day and I was joined by a black-and-brown dog. The dog was lame, running in an odd way, but it knew the round far better than me. I found it disconcerting to study the round's book only to look up and see the dog already outside the next call, pissing on the gatepost, waiting for me to catch up. The dog's lameness had obviously arisen from an accident. He'd probably been run over by a milk float driven by a relief man who didn't know the round.

There was a dog at Cossington that used to wait for me and then jump in the cab and get taken round the round. It was a cairn called Dicken. This drove the relief men ratty because the dog jumped into the cab when *they* were doing the round. There were also two Irish wolfhounds at one house, which meant you couldn't go into their garden unless they were inside. I didn't push my luck with them.

There was a classic interchange between a dog's owner and a milkman. 'It's all right, he won't go for you,' says the dog's owner. Then the milkman replies, 'He just did.'

Another big doggy problem was dog fouling. Milkmen were in and out of their vehicles and had to be careful where they trod:

One day I leapt into my van without realising that I'd just picked up a giant dog turd on my foot. My heel skidded across the cab floor and I banged my knee on the steering wheel. I wiped my foot on the grass and cleaned the van floor with paper. I had to clean my shoes as best I could.

One female customer used to give her regular milkman a couple of apples a day. The milkman ate one and then gave the other one to a spaniel.

Wild Life

Milkmen were on guard for creatures other than dogs. At one house, as the milkman approached the front door, a cat regularly dived at the lounge window as if trying to attack the milkman. Milkmen might see a dead cat or a dead hedgehog in the road early in the morning or a live household rabbit loose on the streets. Dedicated milkmen would catch the rabbit and take it to the right house.

Milk delivery could be a scary business in the dark:

I nearly trod on a hedgehog one morning. It frit the life out of me. On another morning a huge cat, or a rat, flew across the chip-shop alley. If it wasn't a cat it was a rat as big as a cat. I left the milk at the front after that.

I have come across geese guarding their property and you have to move fast with them. They have long necks and can suddenly give you quite a peck, but my worst experience was with two Siamese cats. I can do a good cat meow (as well as Donald Duck and chicken noises) and when I came across these two cats in the garden I meowed at them. Big mistake. They went bonkers, started hissing and jumping up at my chest, trying to scratch my face, and this big brave milkman ended up running as fast as he could to escape the attack.

I was late one day because I had a bit of a spill with the van. I swept round a right-angled corner and all the cream fell off. You should have seen the cats. They came from all over the neighbourhood. Spoilt rotten. All my cream orders in the middle of the road and all these cats.

One time a relief milkman knocked on the door of a house and a woman came to greet him.

'Yoo-hoo,' someone called from the back of the house.

'No, it's not the regular man,' the woman shouted behind her. She turned to the milkman and said, 'He's upset. The regular man usually says, "Where's the milk money?"'

The voice in the back squawked and gurgled.

Then the milkman realised what was happening.

'Where's the milk money?' the milkman said in a squeaky voice.

'Where's the milk money?' said the parrot.

Hedgehogs were predatory when it came to milk – they might knock over a pint of milk and then drink it – and snails and slugs could be inconvenient for milkmen. One morning a milkman had to knock on the front door of a house. The customer had left out a cheque but a snail had eaten across the cheque during the night and it was now useless.

Sometimes the wildlife wasn't really wildlife but it seemed like it was. One day in the mid-fifties, a regular milkman visited a familiar house and jumped a foot in the air when he saw he was about to be attacked by a scary giant in the garden. But the giant turned out to be a new scarecrow. It had been built by householders who were trying everything to keep birds off the garden produce. This scarecrow was a blonde-haired maiden with an expressive face, raincoat sleeves waving in the wind, and eyes not missing a trick. The scarecrow was so realistic that neighbours said 'hello' to her, gentlemen doffed their caps and the milkman contemplated seducing her. Well, it was dark.

Another scary moment occurred in Biggin Hill, Kent, in 1965. A 2ft 6in monkey called Mickey attacked a milkman and a few other people. Police were called, but Mickey the Monkey eluded all attempts to capture him. It took three hours to catch and subdue the animal.

On another occasion a milkman was in a quiet lane on a pitch-black morning. The high hedges made the setting spooky. Then the milkman heard a low, heavy cough right by his ear. The milkman thought he was about to be mugged. Then he made out the shape of a cow behind the hedge.

Overall, though, the milkman saw wildlife at the best time of the morning. Derrick Weaver, a West Midlands milkman, loved the winter frost, the autumn sun lighting up the leaves on trees and the early morning smell of flowers after a rain shower. In the hours around dawn a milkman might settle down with a flask of tea and study the birds and animals in a rural setting. The early hours packaged peace and tranquillity. This was the day at its best. As one milkman told me, on one such day, 'It was so quiet this morning that two dogs copulating in the middle of the road were undisturbed by my electric float.'

9

Injuries, Crashes and Emergencies

Hey, man, don't tread on the flowers, it hassles me.

MILKMEN have been injured in all sorts of ways. They've walked into washing lines, fallen on broken glass, stabbed themselves with car aerials and got podgy fingers stuck in doorbells. They've kicked loose paving-stones, trodden on garden rakes, slipped down potholes and stepped on children's toys. They've banged their head on roof-racks, trapped fingers between milk crates, skidded across wet tiles and toppled into outdoor swimming pools. They've been tripped up by caravan tow-bars, smacked in the face by planks on a van's roof and sprained ankles when slipping off kerbs. They've been the victims of bad weather – ice, snow, rain, wind – or been involved in a collision. They've come into a warm house from the cold outdoors, set off to visit the upstairs toilet and suddenly found themselves at the foot of the stairs.

No Milk Today

Here's an accident story to get us started:

One day I fell head first into a bin. It was a call where I had
to lean over the fence and put the milk into a bin. Being not
so tall I had to jump, but I jumped too far and fell over the
fence. After that I walked all the way round.

One milkman bent down to read a note and then banged
his head on a hanging basket as he stood up. The basket
was swinging and creaking at five o'clock in the morning
and the milkman was shaking soil out of his hair for the
rest of the day. Another milkman, known as 'Mad Harry',
always stood up as he applied the brake, so he hit his head
several times a day. Sometimes, by the end of the round,
blood would be streaming down his face. Here is an
example of a milkman who was blown into trouble by a
freak gale:

One morning there was a whirlwind that blew down a
signal box and parts of some houses. I was blown over a
fence. I thought someone else had got hold of me by the
throat and thrown me over. I had bruises but no serious
injury from that.

One milkman escaped relatively unharmed when a tree
fell on his van, but another one died when he fell on broken
glass and severed an artery. Milkmen have been killed by
passing cars when stepping out from behind their float.
A boy helper had his leg broken when a milkman drove
too close to the kerb and the lad's dangling leg was trapped
between the kerb and the van.

The milkman's body took a long-term battering. Some long-serving milkmen developed arthritis or a nagging pain in the right leg from jumping off the float and landing on that leg. Others needed a brace to support their back, and most long servers had a scar from a broken bottle. Clive Greenham needed two knee-replacement operations towards the end of a career lasting nearly fifty years, Walter Pettitt had a hip operation after thirty-eight years in the job, and a persistent knee injury caused George Bell's retirement when he was sixty.

Broken Bottles

The most common injury involved a fall and a broken bottle. Here are four hand-injury tales:

I was carrying twelve pints of milk in a large crate when I tripped over a kerb. I fell with my hand over the crate, breaking the bottles. This was about 11 a.m. on a collecting day. It was so cold I couldn't tell what damage I'd done. I drove back to the dairy with my left arm in the air because it was fairly bloody. They gave me a sherry at the dairy and took me to the hospital. There was glass in my finger which trapped the tendons. I had it stitched but two weeks later the fingers were trapped shut. Three hospital visits later, a X-ray showed there was still some glass in my hand so I went in for a general anaesthetic. They took the glass out. I was off work for about ten weeks.

On the loading bay I found a broken bottle in a crate I was pulling over. I took out most of the broken bottle and then I felt the familiar pinch of glass on skin. I looked immediately at the wound and it didn't seem a problem. But then the smallest movement of the finger opened up a deep narrow cut. Blobs of blood came out. I licked the cut and continued loading. I forgot about the finger for a while. When the round started I realised that I wasn't licking blood away, I was drinking it. I put a plaster on but the blood was soon seeping through it. Since then I've always carried spare plasters with me.

I've only had one bad cut in fifteen years. It was on the thumb. A woman left out a bottle with a broken top. She couldn't understand why I shouted at her. Another woman told me she never left broken bottles but one day there was one outside. Her young son had kicked it over, broken it, and stood it up again.

I cut my wrist badly and there was blood pouring out. I knocked on a customer's door and she came to the door.

'Can you help me, I need bandaging?' I said.

The next-door neighbour opened her door at the same time.

'Can I pay you now?' she said.

'Not today, love,' I said. 'I'm bleeding to death.'

'Let me get you something, milkman,' said the first woman. 'Try not to drip on the carpet.'

A foreman offered advice for avoiding hand injuries:

We get a lot of cut hands in the winter. If you feel yourself falling, throw the bloody bottles. We can always buy more bottles, but we can't buy any bloody hands. I was delivering to this block of flats one day and I felt myself slipping on the stairs. I was on the fourth floor, and I did what I always do – I threw the bottle of milk I was carrying so I didn't fall on it. The milk went down the chute between the stairs. All the way down. It was like a bomb going off.

The combination of bottles and winter weather caused all sorts of bother. One milkman was confident about seeing in the dark but one morning he tripped over a rose stump in a garden in half-light. He was carrying an empty milk bottle, which he tried to throw but didn't throw far enough away. His hand came down on the broken milk bottle and gravel. He cut the middle finger and the palm of his hand. He was still suffering from frostbite two months later.

Ernie, the milkman who enjoyed Christmas, once went to hospital with cracked ribs on an icy day. A nurse in casualty saw him come through the door and said, 'Oh, no, not another milkman, we've had three in already today.'

A milkman might go weeks without breaking a bottle and then he'd go home one day, put the kettle on and accidentally knock a full pint off the kitchen table. My own technique was to catch a falling bottle on my foot and ease it to the ground as gently as possible. Sometimes, though, the top came off anyway and milk poured out.

Crashes

Delivering milk could be dangerous. Lionel Jones had an example from the mid-1920s:

Even after the car came into use my brother Fred would still help out delivering milk using the old bicycle and sidecar. This ended, one evening, in near disaster when he caught the sidecar wheel on a raised stone kerb at the roadside, which tipped the bike over into the path of a car coming from the rear. The car then proceeded to push him and the bike towards an oncoming bus. Fortunately for Fred, he got away with just torn trousers and cuts and bruises. The milk, of course, was wasted and the old tricycle written off as scrap.

It cost a lot to insure a fleet of milk floats and the premium was justified because milk float skirmishes were plentiful. In most large dairies a milkman had been killed or seriously maimed while on duty. The story was a warning to others. One milkman died while driving a Commer diesel. The front tyre punctured and the vehicle somersaulted at speed.

A milkman told me a story about driving a diesel along a country route. He looked out of the window and saw a tyre rolling past his vehicle. He turned to his young helper, about to say, 'Some poor bloke's lost his wheel' but everything went 'BANG', the van lurched to one side and the milkman realised that he was the 'poor bloke' who'd lost his wheel. Suddenly his vehicle was out of control.

Another milkman lived on the round where he delivered. This was really good because he could drop in at home for cups of tea and meals. But one day he was arriving home for his breakfast when the brakes on his milk float completely failed, just as he was reversing into a parking space. Consequently he backed into a neighbour's car. That was very embarrassing.

Some crashes were caused by a loss of concentration:

One winter's morning I was out on a second round with another milkman and his boy. None of us knew the round. We started clumsily with the three of us running into each other as we left the van for the first calls. Then, back in the van, while making the first turn, all three of us were trying to read the round's book. Suddenly two of us yelled, 'Look out!' and the third, the driver, slammed on the brakes. The van came to an emergency stop on the pavement about two inches from a lamppost.

I was late starting on a round because I'd refused to take out a museum float and they wouldn't give me anything else. Then I couldn't find anybody to hand my notice to. Well, Paul was back early before I'd even started, and the foreman said that Paul knew the round, which was good because I didn't know it. Paul said it would be quicker with his electric float so we loaded it up and set off, and Paul asked, 'Where does the round start?' I said, 'I thought you knew.' 'No,' he said, 'I've never done it before.' I swivelled round and sat on the foam passenger seat and tried to read the book. By this time Paul was craning over and then we looked up together: 'Shhhhhit!' A yard from the windscreen was the six foot six-inch car park barrier. Paul ducked instinctively. Even at milk-float speed the effect was devastating. The front half of the fibre-glass roof was lifted on to the floor. The next half and the supports at the back were bent back ninety degrees, parallel with the floor. The front and side windows dropped out, leaving me with the side-window rubber round my head. There was glass everywhere – in our pockets, on the floor, across the car park. But there were only three broken bottles. Paul must have been thinking he was going through the car park on his way home after doing his round. Had Paul not ducked and had I not sat down, both of us might have lost our heads.

One classic milkman accident was taking a corner too quickly and losing the outside crates. It took a while to sweep up the glass fragments, and it seemed like hours when rush-hour drivers were laughing at you. If you were lucky, someone from a nearby house would come out with a dustpan and brush. One milkman got an endorsement on his driving licence after losing his load:

> I was going back from the round on a Monday. I was bringing back a lot of crates on one side of the van. That was just the way the round was organised. I was going round past the bus station and a stack of four crates fell off. All over the road. It was a white and yellow job. My predecessor had done the same but he'd done a runner and driven off leaving the crates. A policeman arrived and brought a broom from his Rover. I thanked him and he asked me what had happened. I told him it was the damned crates; the clips had worn away. The policeman told me how to stack crates with three sideways and one lengthways. The dairy hadn't told me. The policeman said doing it that way meant a more stable load. He said my way was dangerous. What if there'd been a motorcyclist behind? I thought that might have been the last of it, but the policeman reported it and I got a summons: *Having unstable load*. I told the foreman about it and he told me that it was my responsibility. I had to sort it out. I got a fine.

It was easy to forget to engage the milk float's handbrake. One very experienced milkman lost a float once when he left the handbrake off and failed to turn the front wheels into the kerb on a steep hill. The float set off on its own, knocked down a lamppost, wiped out a rosebush and hit two cars.

In a similar incident, in August 1984, a driverless milk float rolled down a steep slope in Botley, near Oxford. The van picked up pace until it was travelling at over twenty miles per hour, making a tremendous noise, bottles bouncing and clattering around. It ploughed through a garden fence and demolished a kitchen wall. A policeman arrived at the scene, turned to the milkman and said, 'Had trouble parking, did you?'

Another milkman described the problem with one particular hill:

> I took the float up to the top of the hill, ever so slow, because it's very steep, and then rolled it into a driveway, did the milk, pulled the float out and rolled on to the next one. There was no way you could leave the float on the hill, even with the brake on. I used to come down hills with both feet on the brake. In ice, or any sort of bad weather, you'd know to walk all the milk up. You'd never get the float up there. It was so slippery and so bad.

'Look Behind You'

A milk float had blind spots at the rear. Drivers had to rely on side-mirrors when crates were stacked up high. In one incident a six-year-old boy jumped on to a milk float without the milkman seeing him. When the milk float set off down the road, the boy fell off and died of a fractured skull.

Reversing into a low object was a common cause of crashes. 'There was an invalid car on my round and I hit that twice,' said one milkman. 'I reversed out and didn't see it because it's too low to spot.'

Here are two more tales:

Nobody parks behind a milk float, especially where it has to reverse out. Well, a car parked behind me. I should have looked, but I pushed the car from one end of the car park to the other.

I was showing a new starter my round so that he could take it over. I was chatting away to him at seven o'clock and I reversed out of a parking space on a quiet estate only to find a trailer in the way. I hit it with a real bang. There wasn't a scratch on the side I'd hit. That was lucky, I thought. Then people came out of their houses with looks of horror. I walked round the other side of the trailer and saw that it had caved in completely. The nearside wheel was lying flat on the floor, broken through ninety degrees, while my milk float was unharmed.

In 1999, a seventeen-year-old had two cars written off by the same milk float within two months. Two different milkmen caused the collisions. Both milkmen were trying to reverse out of the cul-de-sac where the seventeen-year-old lived. The first car, a C-registration Fiesta, was parked outside a house in Stoke Gifford, South Gloucestershire. The float hit the offside wing, the car was written off and £550 compensation was paid. The second car, a D-registration Vauxhall Nova, was parked in the same place. It had only been there for three days when it was written off with a smashed driver's door.

But the roles could be reversed. Some residents routinely reversed out of a parking space into what they thought was open space and didn't notice a vehicle as large as a milk float. 'This old boy came out one morning and reversed right into me,' a milkman told me. 'I was stationary, working on my book and he said "Where did you spring from?"'

Fatalities (Part 1): Victims of Crime

Some milkmen have paid the greatest sacrifice in their line of duty. In 1973, Frank Kidwell, twenty-seven, was killed during a £160,000 robbery at a Unigate depot in Surrey. The culprit was later sentenced to seventeen years in prison for manslaughter and an unsuccessful campaign to bring back capital punishment was launched. The following year, in 1974, Leonard Munson, a fifty-one-year-old milkman, was beaten to death and robbed of £100 on a staircase in a block of flats in Hornsey, London.

In December 2003, Ronnie Kettridge, a milkman from Barnsley, South Yorkshire, was stabbed to death on his way to work in Sheffield. Two teenagers, Adele Silkstone and Jamie Lee Osbourne, were later convicted of the crime. Silkstone stopped Kettridge's car at a zebra crossing and then she and Osbourne tried to steal the car. But the boy's mask slipped and he killed Kettridge to conceal his identity. Osbourne received a life sentence and Silkstone eight years.

In Northern Ireland, during the troubles, a number of milkmen died prematurely. Thomas Cahill was a victim in Belfast in 1971, Trevor Close was killed by gunfire in north Belfast in 1983, and Paddy Brady was shot dead in Belfast in 1984. In the last case a young helper was found hysterical beside Brady's body.

Milkmen in Northern Ireland feared for their lives at that time:

> A car pulled up alongside me, wound down the window, and I thought, Oh, God, I'm away here. But it was a woman running out of petrol. She just wanted to know where the nearest petrol station was.

Fatalities (Part 2): Victims of Road Collisions

Milkmen were particularly vulnerable when they were rearranging their load on a busy road. Geoff Reynolds was critically injured in 1987 when a van hit his milk float and he never recovered his faculties before he died in 2006 at the age of fifty-five. Dairy Crest milkman Allan Knight died in July 2007 when he was struck by a lorry while sorting out his milk float in Alresford, Hampshire. Knight was hit by a 7.5 tonne vehicle driven by a fellow Dairy Crest worker, who was found to have amphetamine and cocaine in his system.

At 4.30 a.m. one day in March 2007, a milkman was killed by a hit-and-run driver as he stepped from his float. The victim, Christopher John Losper, suffered a fractured skull and multiple rib injuries on his sixtieth birthday. The car driver, Tony Revell, was returning from a night out but he lost concentration in Ferndown, Dorset, because he was exchanging text messages with a girl he'd met that evening. He was sentenced to four years in a young offenders' institution and banned from driving for five years.

Another classic accident is the one where a milkman runs across the road from behind his milk float only to be killed by a passing car. Nicholas Sutton, twenty-three, was hit by a car as he stepped out from behind his milk float in Cleve Road, Goring, Oxfordshire, at about 8.35 a.m. on 17 April 1991. His life-support machine was switched off the following day.

A variety of other incidents have caused fatalities. In 1912, a milkman on a bicycle was killed by an omnibus while delivering his round. Milkmen driving diesel vehicles have been involved in high-speed crashes, and children have been killed when playing at the rear of milk floats or sneaking under the vehicle to hide from their mates. In November 2004, a milkman died after being hit by a police car on an emergency call in south-west London.

'Call the Police'

'Every milkman I know has been able to call the police out at some time or another because he has seen something suspicious or someone suspicious,' said one long-serving milkman.

One day in 1957, a milkman in Greenford, Middlesex, saw yesterday's milk on an old lady's doorstep, so he walked round the house to see if everything was all right. Through the back window he saw the woman's body. She had been murdered during a robbery.

On 2 May 1972, a gang of armed robbers hijacked a lorry as it was bound for Harwich. The lorry had £400,000 worth of silver bullion on board. But the gang hadn't planned for a milkman called Owen Whymark, who saw the hijack and spotted the lorry coming up behind him. Whymark settled his milk float in the centre of the road at ten miles per hour, causing a different kind of hold-up to that achieved by the robbers. When Whymark drove into the car park of the nearest police station, the robbers abandoned the lorry and took off separately with only 15 per cent of their haul.

Brian Hockley, MBE, had a fifty-year career as a milkman:

> One time I witnessed a robbery taking place and ended up being taken down to London to look at these men on an identity parade. Another time I spotted two people stealing a couple of milk bottles from my cart. I noticed they were driving down a dead-end so I followed them and made them pay up.

Milkmen and postmen needed police escorts on Southwark estates in the eighties. A lot of people were out of work at that time and the inner-city problems included rioting. This led to intimidation of milkmen, robberies, milk theft and unreliable milk deliveries. At the same time, competition from supermarkets and convenience shops was growing.

By the nineties, milkmen faced all sorts of problems. In the winter of 1992–3, two milkmen were the victims of Super Glue attacks: a Cheltenham milkman had his eyes glued at 3.45 a.m., and another, in Tooting, had his hands Super Glued to his float's steering wheel. The following year a milkman in Bicester, Oxfordshire, was held up by a masked knifeman at 3 a.m.

Milkman Roy Dyer has wryly described the milkman's vulnerability: 'If some drunks or druggies, on their way home from a club, shout out, "There's a milkman, let's get him," there's a good chance of escape if they're over ten seconds away and the float reaches fourteen miles per hour heading downhill.'

At six-thirty one morning in March 1991, milkman Bert Boyce was delivering his Hemel Hempstead round when he heard a woman screaming and shouting. Boyce called the police. The woman had spent six days in captivity. John Warrington was later sentenced to fifteen years' imprisonment for kidnapping and falsely imprisoning his victim.

In August 1998, an eighteen-year-old burglar was caught with a £6,000 haul and sentenced to eighteen months in a young offenders' institution. He was chased and captured by two men. One was the burglar's victim, who had run from the house naked. The other was the milkman.

In 2000, one of the key pieces of evidence against the murderer David Munley was a note he'd left for the milkman. Munley's victim, eighty-seven-year-old Jean Barnes, was a Cambridge graduate and retired civil servant. Munley had crept around her house several times in order to steal antiques before selling them to dealers. Then, on one visit, he was confronted by Miss Barnes, so he killed her. Munley then pretended that the woman was still alive. Eventually he wrote a note to the milkman to stop the milk, saying that Jean Barnes was in hospital and would be going into a nursing home when she was discharged. This note to the milkman was shown on the TV programme *Crimewatch* and a viewer recognised Munley's handwriting. In December 2000, David Munley was found guilty of murder and sentenced to life imprisonment.

Just after Christmas 2000, Andy Bates was delivering milk to a quiet road in Bricket Wood, Hertfordshire, when he saw a man dragging a woman into the nearby woods. It was 3 a.m. and he could hear the woman's screams. Bates parked his milk float so it blocked the assailant's car to prevent a getaway. Then he phoned 999.

Not all milkmen are angels, of course. A teenage milkman in County Durham, a member of a group called Aryan Strike Force, was found guilty on three terrorist charges. And a Finchley milkman once attacked a customer after a long-running feud over a milk bill. The customer thought the milkman had swindled him out of thousands, an accusation later disproved, and the police had been called out on two previous occasions. This time the milkman punched the customer and hit him with the milk bottle he happened to have in his hand.

In 2002, a Merseyside milkman was kidnapped and taken on a fifteen-minute terror ride by a gang of thugs, an incident which led to a Float Watch scheme whereby every milkman on Merseyside was issued with a mobile phone. In 2007, a milkman in Normanton, West Yorkshire, suffered broken fingers and a neck injury when a man jumped into the milkman's Ford Transit cab and drove away. In 2009, a milkman in Arnold, Nottingham, had a gun pointed at him. In 2013, at Church Warsop, near Mansfield, a milk float was hijacked when a man wearing a goblin mask kicked a milkman in the face before driving the float away. And a teenage gang terrorised milkmen in Bradford-on-Avon, Wiltshire, over a six-year period. All sorts of major incidents occurred, but most milkmen got through long careers without any such problems.

In 2005, the Rhondda Dairymen Association entered an arrangement with the police so that a special code word put them straight through to Bridgend police control room. Here are two Rhondda milkmen speaking about 999 incidents:

> It was very early, about 3.15 a.m., and me and my partner in the van saw a man obviously acting suspiciously at the rear of some houses. We know who's about at that time but he was carrying a torch and it just didn't seem right. A little while later he reappeared, carrying a garden strimmer, and we knew he was up to no good. The police came really quickly and arrested him a little way down the street.

> You have to look out for your community. Sometimes we are the only people old people see. You give them the news, have a cup of tea, or change a light bulb. I've done milk rounds in this area since I was a teenager in the sixties and we've always reported crimes to the police. But as community bobbies retired, we've lost contact with the police. Now we can get through to an officer straight away rather than be passed to different stations. You often see people acting suspiciously, damaging a car or breaking into a house.

When urban milkmen brought forward their starting times, it meant that milkmen mingled even more with the nightlife. In 2011, a Cardiff milkman was banned from driving for eighteen months after failing a breath test in the early hours of the morning. Apparently he'd drunk a bottle of wine with his dinner before reporting for work at 10.30 p.m. Then he committed a number of traffic offences before his float was pulled over by the police at 1 a.m. The police took the milk float away on a transporter.

In 2015, a milkman in Crieff, Perthshire, failed a roadside breath test after the police were summoned at 4.30 a.m. The milkman, nearly three times over the limit, was banned from driving for twenty-four months and fined £360.

'Call the Fire Brigade'

Occasionally a local newspaper would report a classic incident: 'An electric milk float caught fire and was slightly damaged while being recharged.'

Milkmen have called the emergency services for lots of other blazes. A Merseyside milkman called Danny Brown earned the nickname 'The Lemonade Fireman' when he put out a caravan blaze with four bottles of lemonade he had on his float. Brown shook up each bottle in turn, sprayed the contents over the blaze and dragged gas canisters out of danger.

In 1972, a milkman got his name in the local newspaper when a hotel on his Cambridge round burnt down. The alarm was sounded at 5.45 a.m. Two people died in the fire, and one woman was injured when jumping from a first-floor bedroom window. The milkman rescued two young women – one Swedish, the other American – and led them to a nearby safe place. The next day it took him hours longer than normal to do his round. Everybody was saying, 'I've been reading about you in the newspaper.'

In 2014, Phil Taylor was delivering to Tregarth, near Bangor, Wales, when an electrical fault started a fire in his milk float. Aware that his van was parked next to cars, he jumped in the burning float and drove it twenty yards to a position where it couldn't set fire to other vehicles. He poured some bottled water on the blaze and customers brought him buckets of water. Taylor went back to his depot, got another van and finished his round.

Other milkmen have been heroic in the face of fire. In 1923, a milkman helped to rescue a child from a burning building in Lambeth. In July 1983, a milkman from Ely, Cambridgeshire, received a bravery award for rescuing two children from a burning house and the following year Allan Frame helped to save a family of four when their house in Wishaw, North Lanarkshire, was ablaze. In 2003, David Knipe of Levens, Cumbria, rescued an eighty-eight-year-old woman from a house fire.

10

Community Workers

Please ring – I have a letter I need posting.

MILKMEN were the dawn patrol. They were often the first detectives on the scene. They were also good support when a local resident needed to investigate an ambiguous situation. One particular lane, at the edge of a large village, was a magnet for incidents. Here is a resident recalling one event from many:

> I woke up one night and the lights were on at the house next door. I thought that was funny because there was no house next door. There's just the field. It turned out there was a car overturned in the field. The headlights were on all night.

The lane's residents also told tales of abandoned cars and suicide victims. One night kids set a car on fire in the field. Another night someone dumped stolen crates of whisky there. It was a dark lane, with a history of trouble, so it wasn't surprising that local residents waited for the milkman before venturing forth. A milkman recalled one such time:

> It was six one morning, at the end of the lane, and a man suddenly appeared in front of me. The man was dressed in pyjamas, a long overcoat and wellingtons, and he carried a walking stick. He wanted me to go with him while he investigated a car that had been parked all night because there was someone inside the car. I went with him and the local resident tapped on the window with his stick. It turned out the driver was a relative who had arrived too late to disturb the residents so he'd decided to sleep in his car until it was daylight. That one ended happily.

It was not uncommon for a policeman to seek the counsel of a milkman. 'Have you noticed that car before?' a policeman might enquire. 'It looks suspicious with the windows open and the wing dented.'

One situation that was more common than you'd think was to turn up at a customer's doorstep to find the house keys still in the front door. Most milkmen took the keys out of the lock and pushed them through the letterbox, as one milkman explained:

> I've lost count of the number of keys I've pushed back through the door first thing in the morning. They leave them in the door when they come back from the pub. Mind you, I pushed a set through the letterbox at six o'clock one

morning and the bloke was in the garden. He hadn't been able to sleep so he'd got up to do a bit of weeding. I had to climb in through a window to let him back into his house.

Another scenario arose when the previous day's milk was still on the step. The milkman's mind went into overdrive. Have the residents gone on holiday and forgotten to cancel the milk? Have they been called away unexpectedly? Are they ill? Have they left the milk there because it is cold outside and they haven't got a fridge? Could this be an emergency? Should I check with the neighbours to see if they have gone away?

Most regular milkmen then did a quick tour of the house, looking through windows to see if anything was amiss.

Community Workers

In the early 1900s, milkmen didn't only deliver milk. They also delivered messages, carried laundry around the village and took a basket of pigeons from a fancier's loft to release them in the countryside. Milkmen posted letters and collected shopping. One customer sent her milkman out to buy a bottle of sherry every day.

In the modern era, one considerate milkman shut garage doors left open by mistake to prevent the passing public from seeing expensive mountain bikes inside the garage, and another, Paul Radford, fitted a customer's false leg every day. But the most common request revolved around height: 'Oh, you're tall, milkman, can you change me a light bulb?'

'I'm not just a milkman, you know,' Liverpool's Ian Clark once told the *Mirror* newspaper. 'I'm a social worker, a policeman and your very own Neighbourhood Watch all rolled into one.'

Once upon a time, British society had many gatekeepers – milkmen, bus conductors, park-keepers, petrol-station attendants, etc. – but most of those functions have either disappeared or been much reduced. In 1961, in the House of Lords, Lord Taylor spoke of how suicidal people could be very lonely and it was often a landlady or a milkman who made the discovery after milk bottles were uncollected. In the late seventies, a group of American suicidologists had the idea that gatekeepers such as milkmen could be educated to spot suicidal signals.

People who worked outside normal hours could do things that nine-to-five workers couldn't do. But the decline in the number of milkmen – from 40,000 in the early seventies to 4,000 forty years later – has taken away some informal community support. It had taken years to build up a cadre of milkmen into a community service. Some were so trusted that customers gave them burglar alarm codes and keys. And in census years milkmen were a source of help for enumerators who were trying to find out who lived in particular houses.

Nigel Crocker was honoured with an MBE in 2004 after thirty-eight years as a milkman. The sixty-one-year-old grandfather lived and delivered in Broad Town, Wiltshire, where he'd been born (on his mother's kitchen table). On his milk round he delivered groceries to the old and frail. He gave lifts to people who were walking home after a late night in the local pub, and he checked on those who'd been ill. He cut people's lawns and hedges, did odd jobs around their houses and kept an eye on properties while people were away. He saw his customers as friends and he tried to look after the local people while delivering the milk. Crocker was not only a milkman but also a parish councillor and chairman of the village hall committee. It could be argued that people from milkmen families were especially well suited for political office because they knew their community well and understood its constituents. Milkman Cliff Trotter became Mayor of Harrogate in 2007. Kevin Hollinrake, a member of parliament, was a milkman's son. And another member of parliament, Greg Clark, had a father and a grandfather who both worked as milkmen.

Trevor Jones was one of a third generation of milkmen in his family. He delivered milk around Tredegar, Wales, for fifty-three years and was awarded an MBE for community service in 1998. Jones decided not to collect his award in person because his priority was delivering his milk round on that day. Many years later he talked to the *South Wales Argus*:

> That [the MBE] was for things like the customers of mine who were blind. I would read their mail for them. I always tried to help the people on my round. One time a man called Bryn Gardener came and said his wife was stuck in the bathtub. Because I knew my customers, I knew there were two nurses who lived on the street. They brought some towels and looped one under her arms and hoisted her up and 'pop!' she came out! I have heard that my father saved a girl's life while on his round. A customer said his daughter had swallowed a marble, so he held her upside down by her feet, slapped her back and the marble fell out.

Essex milkman Kevin Stoneman delivered on the same round for thirty years. He changed light bulbs, put the rubbish out, and once helped the police to catch a burglar. When someone hijacked Stoneman's float and drove it away, the milkman took great pleasure in flagging down a taxi and telling the driver, 'Follow that float.' Stoneman grew so close to customers that he went to their weddings and funerals.

'I need one of them automatic waving hands, mate,' a milkman called Bert told me. Bert was another multitalented milkman. He was a driver and deliverer, birdwatcher and bookkeeper, garden adviser and house protector, money collector and converser, social worker and nurse. His round had plenty of 'old dears'. Some were getting over hospital sorties and others were recovering from nervous breakdowns.

'I've got a customer on my round,' said another milk-man. 'When she goes away on holiday she asks me to carry on delivering a pint a day and pour half in the cat's bowl.'

In February 2013, ninety-one-year-old Peggy Thomas stepped out of her stair lift at the bottom of her stairs and her legs gave way. She fell on the floor and couldn't get up. She was on the floor for nearly twenty-four hours, until her milkman, Pete Edmondson, knocked on her window at 7.45 a.m. Edmondson found a way into her house and lifted her from the floor. Knowing that Peggy Thomas was a diabetic, Edmondson made her a drink, gave her some bread and butter, and then brought her medication to her. He called Homeline and stayed with the elderly lady until more help arrived. 'You just do what you have to do,' Edmondson told the *Swindon Advertiser*. He had been a milkman for twenty-four years.

Some elderly customers, living in upstairs flats and having difficulty with stairs, lowered a bucket with a note so that the milkman could deliver the goods vertically. Some of Kevin Pierce's elderly customers couldn't open the lids of beetroot, pickle or medicine bottles, so they left the bottles outside for Pierce to unscrew. A customer on Mark Haynes' round slept with a whistle around her neck so she could blow for help from her milkman. In John Millington's career he delivered millions of pints of milk and donated a hundred pints of blood. Another community service, especially after the 1960 Betting and Gaming Act, was for a milkman to place bets with bookmakers on behalf of customers. Elderly people confined to the house could watch horseracing on television and track their wins and losses.

John O'Malley worked as a franchisee in Stockport, Greater Manchester. In 1995, he rose at 12.30 a.m. and arrived at the dairy half an hour later. He ran eight miles in seven hours to serve 680 customers before 8 a.m. 'My customers are not just getting a fresh product delivered to their homes every morning no matter the weather,' O'Malley told the *Guardian*. 'They are getting a Neighbourhood Watch scheme and community worker too.' He had twice disturbed burglars on his round and once interrupted car thieves as they were wheeling a Ford Orion off a driveway.

Here is another edgy tale:

I came back to my van one day and found a woman teacher in my cab. 'Drive me to the spaceship,' she said. I thought I'd humour her. Then she said, 'They'll never take me on the spaceship when they find out what I've done with the children.' I drove her home, not knowing what I'd find. It could have been bodies in the tower, that sort of thing. It turned out to be a broken marriage, and her husband had gone off with the children. The woman went to a psychiatric hospital the next day.

Derrick Weaver started as a milkman's helper in July 1966 when he was fifteen. One of Weaver's first Saturdays was the occasion of the 1966 World Cup Final, when England beat West Germany 4–2 after extra time. A lot of milkmen were late back to the depot that day because they'd waited to see the outcome of the match. When Weaver was interviewed by the *Guardian* in 2009, he had chalked up forty-three years in the job. His community roles in Harborne, Birmingham, included unscrewing the tops off water bottles for a lady with arthritis and checking houses where yesterday's milk was still on the step. On two occasions he'd entered a house only to find that the householder had died.

South African golfer Bobby Locke won the 1952 British Open Golf Championship at St Lytham St Annes thanks to a helpful milkman. Locke's car was kept overnight in a locked garage but the garage owner with the key was some distance away. The milkman drove Locke to and from the garage owner's house to collect the key and unlock the garage. Locke then drove his car to the golf course and arrived just before his tee-off time.

By 1996, Dennis and Jean Knight had lived thirty-five years in the same house so they decided to mark the occasion. Their milkman, Peter Simpson, had served them for all those years, so they included him in the celebrations. They left Simpson a full bottle on their doorstep, and it contained something stronger than milk. The Knights calculated that Simpson had delivered over 19,000 pints to their door during those three and a half decades.

When Eroline O'Keeffe's son Trevor was murdered in France in 1987, her milkman Mick Fitzpatrick immediately lent her money so she could go to France to identify the body and make funeral arrangements. O'Keeffe spent many years battling the French authorities until the serial murderer Pierre Chanal was finally proved culpable for the death of her son.

A Listening Ear and a Watchful Eye

David Watson, the 2011 Milkman of the Year, saw his customers as friends. Watson used an expression common to milkmen – 'we are the eyes and ears of the community'.

At some homes, the milkman was the only person to visit all week and he had a lot of listening to do when customers unloaded their concerns:

'I can't get about so well these days.'

'I've just come out of hospital.'

'It's awful when you get old.'

'I'm glad someone else is about at five o'clock in the morning, only I've lost my husband, and I can't sleep, and I have to keep making myself cups of tea.'

One woman had the front door open ready to collect the milk at 5.30 a.m. She needed to confide in her milkman:

We buried my niece yesterday. She was knocked over on the bridge. Only fourteen. Such a nice girl, not like my two.

No one came forward about the accident. But there was a good turn-out at the funeral. The whole class came. She was in a coma for twelve days.

Peter Fry retired in 2014 after fifty years in the milk business. His depot manager spoke highly of Fry's expertise with customers: 'Peter became someone they could talk to in confidence; they told him about their worries and he was always happy to provide a listening ear, even if it meant his round took longer than it should.'

Occasionally the role of the caring milkman has been more formalised. The Care Code was introduced in 1975 and there was a plan in place to alert neighbours, the dairy and emergency services if necessary. It was successful in places where the milkman had a direct link to essential workers if a customer was in trouble.

'I found one of my customers in the river,' said one milkman. 'Her feet were stuck in the bottom, but they reckon she died instantly – probably from the cold and the shock, like.'

'I once found an elderly lady who had collapsed on her kitchen floor and had been lying there for days,' said another milkman. 'If I hadn't called round I don't know what would have happened to her.'

Jonah Moore, 'The Whistling Milkman', was credited with saving three people's lives. On one occasion he could smell gas in a couple's house so he broke down the door and rescued them, and another time he drove a woman to hospital after finding her slumped on the lawn suffering from hypothermia.

Some milkmen took a first-aid course with the St John Ambulance. Ian Smith, from Moira in Leicestershire, was trained in CPR and used his skills while doing the job. Smith started delivering milk on his dad's Coalville milk round when he was eleven and then, as an adult, he had his own round.

Here are some more stories of the milkman's community role:

I used to help a guy out with a milk round when I was a student. One particular winter we had some snow and we found an old guy had fallen down outside his home in the snow. God knows how long he had been there. We managed to help him back on to his feet and get him into his house and called an ambulance. If we hadn't been delivering milk, the poor old guy might have died from hyperthermia.

Very often I was the only person they saw: 'Can you change my light bulb?' 'Can you put new batteries in the doorbell?' One old lady had a wall clock. Her husband had put that clock up on the wall in nineteen-thirty-something. It had a massive key and she couldn't reach to wind it up, so I used to wind the clock up.

One time I went to an old boy's house and he'd got himself in a bit of a state. What's happening is that he's been fitted with a catheter and he's waiting for a nurse to change the catheter but she's running late and he's quite desperate. This catheter is overflowing so I've got to get him into the toilet and empty his catheter for him.

The oddest one I ever had was an old lady who came out at about five o'clock one morning. She said, 'Can you help. My sister's stuck under the bed.' Two old ladies lived together. I get up into the bedroom and they've got one of these old-fashioned beds that were quite high. She'd gone to get out of bed and obviously fallen and she was wedged under the side of the bed and couldn't get up. I sort of gently helped her out and got her up and sat her on the bed. She was all right. The other lady said, 'Thank you ever so much, she's been there for two hours.' Twenty minutes later, you're on to the next customer.

The milkman was a lifeline for the elderly, the housebound and the vulnerable. Old people trusted the milkman and they were generally right to do so. Through the fifties, Richard Greenhalgh called for several years at the home of an elderly lady, brewed her tea, lit her fire and made her bed before continuing with his round. Another customer, nearly blind, asked the milkman to look for her purse or under the bed where there was a boxful of money.

Martin Williams once chaperoned a woman who was being stalked and, in recent years, some milkmen have texted infirm customers to check they were all right. When a drunken man set fire to his mate's leg on a park bench in Truro, Cornwall, the local milkman poured milk over the fire.

Dave Sargeant walked at least five miles a day while delivering to over 500 households in Hutton and Shenfield, Essex. One of his customers was so blind that she put her rubbish just outside the door so Sergeant could take it to the bin at the end of her drive. One day, as he was returning to the dairy after completing his round, he noticed that the milk was still outside one particular house. It turned out that the woman had fallen over and couldn't get up. 'It's the people that make the job,' Sergeant told the *Brentwood Gazette*. 'Everyone is concerned about you if you are off.'

Bolton Evening News reporter Frank Wood got to know a few milkmen in his time. Here Wood talks about one in particular:

> Ronnie Brundrett has seen enough 'life' in forty-five years to write a book. He's lost count of the people he's found drunk in the front garden and had to help them to bed. And he once took two lads home after he found them wandering around the streets stark naked after a stag night. He's helped people who were ill, pregnant, fed up with living and scared of dying.

The milkman had to be a good listener:

> I stood and listened as a widow with arthritis told me how she'd been conned. A man had called at her house and had seemed trustworthy. He left his van, with its ladders, at the front of her house, and explained how he'd spotted a crack in her chimney. He offered her an expert appraisal, and she asked him to do the job. After he had 'done the job', he kindly offered to drive her to the bank. She withdrew £300 and paid him. He had done nothing to earn the money . . . The same woman told me another story. A man was weeding her garden during the summer and he asked to use her toilet. He came into the house, burst into the lounge, knocked the door into her back and snatched £75.

Milkmen needed practical skills. Here is Dennis Nock, speaking in 2008:

I've changed light bulbs, unblocked sinks and opened jars. It's not in your job description but people ask you to help and when you do, they think you're a saviour. I remember turning up to collect the money one evening some years ago, and this chap was packing up ready to move into a retirement flat. The van hadn't turned up and he looked at his pile of furniture and said, 'You wouldn't mind, would you, Dennis?' What could I say? The customers expect it of you.

The 1969 *News of the World* Personality Milkman competition was won by Tom Spurr of Sheffield. One customer summarised Spurr's qualities as 'invariably punctual, nothing is too much trouble for him, VIP of the world's best delivery service, always cheerful, makes light of the weather, clean and tidy, and will always help in an emergency'.

An Award-winning Milkman

Tony Fowler was a jockey and racehorse trainer before he turned milkman in the early nineties. He delivered milk and other products to over twenty villages around Melton Mowbray, Leicestershire. His achievements included helping the police to put over fifty people in prison, and his honours included a MBE, Pride of Britain Award, Milkman of the Year, Conscientious Tradesman Award, Rural Hero Award, Openreach Extra Milk Award, Co-operative Local Champion, a place on the *Independent on Sunday* Happy List and a special award from the chief constable of Leicestershire. Speaking in 2013, Fowler told *Weekender*, 'I've been shot at, mugged, you name it, on my round, but it has been all worth it, to turn in the likes of car stealers and drug dealers.'

He described one of his incidents to the *Leicester Mercury*:

Me and crime just seem to bump into each other, but while I'm out and about I'm bound to see things. I'd spotted a flash-looking car driving a bit fast a little earlier in the day in Thrussington. Then, later, I was going down Church Lane and I saw it again, outside the school. As I came up, I could hear the engine running and it all seemed a bit strange, so I called the police. Then I thought, I can't do anything more, and went on with my round. Apparently the police arrived soon after and got them.

Tony Fowler worked fifteen-hour shifts and drove about 100 miles a day in his van. He slept for about four hours from 8 p.m. to midnight. Then he started work again, finished at 3 p.m. and rarely took a holiday. Fowler's dedication to his customers included dropping off prescriptions to the elderly and helping out with odd jobs. He replaced light bulbs, changed fuses and unscrewed tops off jam jars, bleach bottles and lemonade bottles, and he checked customers' houses when they were away. One pensioner described why Fowler was so special:

He put a lock on the shed door saying I needed increased security and he changed the spotlights in my kitchen when they went. Once, when he came round, he saw I had a flat tyre. I was just going to call the rescue people but he said there wasn't any point and did it himself. I also know of an occasion when he waded through flood water to rescue an elderly lady's kitten, which was stuck up a tree.

Fowler had images of Batman and Robin on the side of his van. His crime-fighting exploits included chasing burglars and blocking off a getaway car to help police make a drugs bust. On another occasion he put out a customer's frying-pan fire by soaking his jumper in water and dowsing the flames. 'He's like another arm of the Neighbourhood Watch,' said one customer.

When Fowler got an invitation to receive his MBE, he wanted to wear the cow suit he used on his milk round, but he was put under pressure to conform. He posed for photographs in his white cow leggings but switched to dark suit trousers for ceremony. But he wore his normal work top, which had a distinctive black-and-white pattern common to a cow.

11

Collecting the Money

I'm not home. Go into the house and help yourself to the money.

O N COLLECTING days milkmen combined milk delivery with money collection. A 1984 recruitment brochure estimated that a milkman collected 15 per cent of the money on Thursdays, 30 per cent on Fridays and the rest on Saturdays. This meant a 1 p.m. finish on a Thursday, 3 p.m. on a Friday and 5 p.m. on a Saturday. This tradition began when most customers were paid towards the end of the week.

It might take four or five hours to do the round in the early part of the week, but milkmen could be out for ten or twelve hours on Friday and Saturday, and maybe six or seven on Thursday. They paid their receipts into the dairy office and then had the further task of listing each address with its arrears and calculating the amounts still owed. A few days later, the milkmen learnt whether or not they had balanced the books. From the early nineties, computers made the bookkeeping easier but milkmen still had to be methodical. These financial responsibilities separated milkmen from postmen, dustbinmen, road sweepers and other workers. The paperwork and money management involved shouldn't be underestimated.

On collecting days milkmen drove a float and carried a float. Most had a 'magic' wallet and a leather satchel, but some carried change in their pockets. The wallet might go in the top pocket or in the satchel, which was strapped over the head to reduce chances of theft. In 1971, when Post Office giro payments were introduced, milkmen in Eccles, Lancashire, paid giro cheques into post offices as they did their round. On Saturday afternoons, when banks were closed, issues of safety and security arose.

The job had a strange paradox. Milkmen were loners for most of the week, working off-peak hours, hidden from customers, enjoying the peace and quiet. Then, on collecting days, the same milkmen had to be sociable. Some ran fast to deliver the milk but collected the money slowly, enjoying the chat and the gossip, getting to know families. Others were always in a hurry. And some shy milkmen posted bills through letterboxes and collected cheques without meeting the customers.

Training the Customers

Milkmen presented themselves to customers with both a hard side and a soft side. It was important to choose the right approach for the customer and the situation.

'Collecting the money is not a challenge,' a brawny milkman told me. 'If they don't pay me, they don't get any milk.'

Well, that's the hard side. Underneath the friendliness and pleasantries, milkmen could be ruthless. They knocked loudly on doors, thinking, 'If I'm up, the customer should be.' If the house was divided into several flats, they'd ring all the bells. It didn't matter who paid as long as somebody did.

Other milkmen preferred to charm the customers into doing what suited the milkmen on collecting days. They liked to have customers leave money in a safe place so it could be easily collected, and customers were often keen to oblige. In the fifties it was common for customers to leave doors unlocked so the milkman could enter an empty house and collect the money. Sometimes, in those days, there were several piles of cash on the kitchen table. Here is Quentin Thompson of the famous Beverley firm Thompson Dairies:

> In Everingham people would be out to work on the fields. Doors weren't locked and you would go into the kitchen and the money would be on top of the fridge. There would be money for the butcher, the fishmonger and the milkman, all in separate heaps. You would look in the fridge and see how much milk there was.

One long-standing milkman liked to have his customers on starting blocks on collecting days. He sometimes signified his arrival by being noisy. He might slam on the brakes to make the crates shake, and then jump out with a few pints in one hand, rattling the bottles with a noise to make a town crier proud. This type of milkman had gradually brought his collecting forward over the years, a minute here, a minute there, without his customers complaining too much. Eventually he started collecting money about seven o'clock. He slowly increased the number of houses where he delivered the milk *and* collected the money. The milkmen's classic rule for collecting days was to ensure they didn't walk up too many paths twice in the same day.

One milkman explained why he never wrote down too much information in his round's book:

> I've got a lot of people who leave their money out for me when they're out. I try to teach the relief men where it is if they come with me, but I don't write it in the book in case I lose the book and someone learns where to look for it. Mind you, sometimes I scratch my head when I walk up a path because I can't remember what we agreed on.

That same milkman organised his round so that he could do almost all his money collection on a Friday. In one street, for instance, he collected the money at number two and then drove to number twenty and picked up the money for all the other customers in the street from an elderly couple. He explained his secret for collecting money:

> You have to have a ready answer. If they're not in, they can leave it outside. If they are worried about leaving the money outside, they can leave it with a neighbour.

Some customers were a mystery to the milkman. One round's book had an unusual instruction at the house of a recluse – *push the milk through the cat flap, then reach through on Saturday and there'll be a cheque left there.*

The round's book had to be kept in proper order. It was important to note cancellations, alterations and payments as soon as possible. The electronic round's book totted up accounts for the milkman and printed out bills. Machines also catered for debit- and credit-card payments. Before computers, it took milkmen one afternoon per week to add up the bills for every customer. But not everyone adapted quickly to new technology. Derek Arch's wife Betty helped her husband by doing the accounts. In 2009, she was still using a comptometer from the forties.

Knocking on Doors

One day a milkman in Cardiff knocked on a customer's door to collect the money. The Swiss au pair answered the door.

'Milkman,' said the milkman.

'No,' said the young girl, speaking slowly. 'I am Josie.'

American police officers use the acronym GOYAKOD – *Get off your ass and knock on doors*. Once upon a time that was how milkmen collected most of the money.

At one sheltered housing complex, a milkman knocked on the door of every house before collecting any money. He didn't want to waste precious minutes waiting for old ladies to shuffle up and down the hallways.

Long collecting days raised the issue of sustenance. Proper meals were unlikely. Milkmen might survive on chocolate or something from the corner shop. Some went to the pub, where they grabbed a sandwich and a pint. Others became drinking partners with customers. Local legend has it that when actor Oliver Reed lived at Okewood Hill, Surrey, he once took his milkman off on a two-day drinking binge in London. The milkman lost his job but Reed hired him as a gardener.

Only well-organised milkmen took a packed lunch on collecting days. Some survived for five or six hours on a bowl of cornflakes, and others bought something in a shop. 'There was never time to eat,' one milkman said. 'It never occurred to me to take food on the round.' Indeed, there was a tradition of milkmen not eating much. Back in 1947, when food was rationed, milkman Fred Stevens was interviewed for a Pathé News film:

> I think the rations today are plenty for everybody. All I have is about five cups of tea during the day and one dinner at night, six o'clock. I walk about ten miles a day and climb two thousand stairs. I seem to be fit enough, I don't see why other people shouldn't be.

Some milkmen resorted to consuming the goods on their float. Maybe they drank a pint or two of milk and ate yoghurts while on the round.

Access to toilets was important on long days. On a country route the woods were your toilet. In towns, milkmen got to know the pubs, cafes and public toilets, or there might be a customer with an accessible outside toilet. Here are two milkmen talking about toilets:

> Twice I got caught with my little acorn out. One delivery was up a track where I used to drop off a couple of pints into a crate at the end of a long drive. No house about, just nice Kent countryside so the ideal opportunity to have a pee. One day I did and was startled by someone whistling and

then calling out, 'Morning, Milky.' It was embarrassing but she did not seem to mind as she had a big smile on her face and had come up to collect her milk and pay the bill.

In some posh homes you could ask to use the toilet and they would say, 'It's not working.' Some were funny like that. They might shut the door and leave you out in the rain while they fetched their money. At one posh house a woman invited me in for tea. 'Shall I take me shoes off?' I said. 'No, it doesn't matter,' she said.

When customers opened doors, milkmen had to listen to comments from the occupants:

'I thought it was the nurse.'

'I can't get about so well these days.'

'I've just come out of hospital.'

'It's awful when you get old.'

'You'll have to shout – I'm a bit deaf.'

'Are your cows kept in a pasture because I want to be sure I'm getting pasteurised milk?'

Most customers were happy to wait for the milkman's knock or the bell's ring, but others took advantage of every sighting of the milkman, as one milkman explained:

They used to pay me while they were waiting for the bus. I'd set off for a few calls and the whole bus queue would pay me. I'd go back to the van and have to work out who they were. Sometimes I'd cross twenty off.

In Dundee, in the mid-sixties, Avril Fletcher told milk laddie Willie Robertson that there were three parts to collecting the money on Saturdays and Sundays. First you got the money from the ones who could pay you. Then you got the money from the ones who couldn't pay you and had some excuse or moan. And finally you had to get yourself as much in tips as possible. One trick was to hand out the change in such a way that the customer would let the laddie keep the last coin. Fletcher's milk boys were paid £1 a week in the early sixties, plus all the tips they could get.

The best time of the year for tips was Christmas, but milkmen in rural areas did well for seasonal fruit and vegetables. One milkman came away with fifteen pounds of carrots after a productive day collecting. Some milkmen took payments in kind.

Co-op customers could pay with tokens. A token from the local Co-operative Society was one of the hundred objects in the BBC's 'History of the World' radio series. People bought tokens from their local Co-op and then left them out to pay their Co-op milkman. It was considered safer than leaving out money. The colour of the tokens changed whenever there was a price rise, but people could go on paying with the old tokens if they left the additional sum in real cash. The token system continued until the late seventies.

On rainy collecting days it was difficult to keep the paperwork dry. The rain came into an electric float if the vehicle had no doors. You could shut the door on a diesel but there were times when you took the round's book out of the van, stood on the customer's step and tried to read the book while the ink started to run.

Inevitably there were bad payers. A milkman might ring the front doorbell and catch sight of a customer hastily going out the back. When one milkman knocked on the door of a long-term debtor and listened carefully, he could hear a woman saying, 'Shush' to her kids. Another milkman had difficulty at one particular house:

> A wee girl comes to the door and when I say, 'Milk money' she says, 'Just a minute.' She goes off and when she comes back she says, 'Mummy says she's not in.' 'I'll call back later,' I say, and as I'm walking away I hear the kid shout, 'He'll call back later, Mummy.'

The voices inside the house could be so loud that a milkman couldn't get the customer's attention. The classic case was a milkman ringing the doorbell several times while the couple indoors argued loudly about whose turn it was to pay the milk bill. Sometimes the milkman put his foot in the door, either because there was a danger of a debtor shutting the door in the milkman's face or because it was a windy day and the front door would slam if the back door was open. Occasionally a milkman took pity on a hard-up customer and, in true Robin Hood fashion, shifted the debt to a rich customer elsewhere on the round.

A milkman never knew what the customer's reaction would be.

> I went for the money at one house and the woman was lying in the sun in her bikini. I asked her for two weeks' money. 'Oh, I can't be bothered getting up,' she said, even though the door was only a few yards away. So I said, 'Oh, I can't be bothered leaving any milk.' I picked up the two pints and took them back to the van. The dairy manager backed me up.

Some rounds were more frustrating than others, especially those with high arrears. Collecting could happen on any day of the week and sometimes a customer left an appropriate note: *Please make us pay today*. Other times a milkman would put a bill through the letterbox and tell the customer when he was calling for the money.

Collecting the money was also an opportunity to be a salesman, and some regular men developed a doorstep patter ('Extra milk for the school holidays, cream for Sunday?'). Even in the heyday of milk delivery, in the early seventies, about 10 per cent of people moved house each year, so the milkman had to be continually looking for new trade. In some areas, such as student ghettos, there was an even greater turnover. Ways of recruiting new customers included posting a WELCOME card to new residents and leaving a free pint on their moving-in day. Sometimes it was the customer who took the initiative:

It was always the first thing we sorted out when we moved. Find a milkman (who came daily and before 9 a.m. in those days), then organise the daily newspaper delivery. But I haven't done either for at least twenty years when we moved away from London.

A milkman called at a house in Margate in the early sixties. The house had two self-contained flats. One flat had a pint of sterilised a day and the other a pint of jersey milk. The milkman knocked on both doors and the women were soon at the doors ready to pay. The milkman checked his book and calculated the two bills. Then he turned to one woman and said, 'Let me see, you're the sterilised lady, aren't you?'

Relief milkmen were more likely to be out of synch with the regular man's timing and that made it harder to collect money. Sometimes the regular man collected at an unusual time, such as between 4 p.m. and 6 p.m. (although that raised the question of whether milkmen working peculiar hours were covered by insurance). Also, in the winter, when it was dark at 5 p.m. or 6 p.m., customers didn't like opening their doors to strangers. There was some fear of mugging, but, more likely, people didn't want to answer the door to a pedlar, carol singer or potential burglar. Also, customers were correctly suspicious when an unfamiliar milkman came to collect the money without his van.

Milkmen had to keep the money safe. Some roundsmen split it up by keeping some in their satchel and the rest in between crates and under the seat. Sometimes they forgot where it was hidden.

I always had a cash bag across from one shoulder to the other hip. My wife and I used to walk round the top of town in the dark on a Friday night. I used to say to my wife, 'If you see anybody suspicious or anybody following you, go straight to a customer's house and stay there.' Because I'd been round the top of the town for so many years, I knew most of the rogues, shall we say. We never had any trouble but we look back now and think, on a Friday night I'd be walking round with £300 or £400, by the time I finished. I'm not sure I would do it now.

From the mid-seventies the arrival of safes and security boxes offered milkmen more protection against the increasing number of muggings. On some rounds an experienced milkman discussed bad payers with other local tradesmen – tobacconists, newsagents, etc. – and then decided whether or not to stop a customer's milk.

Price increases changed the mathematics of collecting days. In 1978, when the price of a pint of milk went up from 12½p to 13½p, a lot of customers couldn't afford to pay the bills and some milkmen couldn't calculate them. They felt much more comfortable when the price increased to 15p, in 1979, but customers were angry at the 20 per cent increase in a year. 'The only thing that comes down these days is the bloody rain,' moaned one customer. Milkmen were frustrated because price increases reduced consumption and that made it harder to earn commission. Besides, some customers didn't believe the increases and thought the milkmen were trying it on.

Collecting days were improved by computer technology. In olden days milkmen relied on mental arithmetic to calculate bills for weekly and monthly accounts, and milkmen had to write out addresses and regular orders when they switched to a new round's book every two or three months. The introduction of computers meant changes to orders could be quickly tapped in, bills calculated and printed out, and the addresses and orders no longer needed to be laboriously carried forward into the new round's book.

12

The Hardest Round

Please do not leave me any milk tomorrow,
or in your case TODAY as I wrote this yesterday.

MOST milkmen had some specific criterion which made their round sound like the most difficult one in the dairy:

> *I take out over 900 pints.*
> *My round has the longest driveways in town.*
> *I carry more goods than any other round.*
> *I've got nearly 700 calls.*
> *My round gets up to 900 calls in the summer.*
> *I have to drive thirty-one miles in an electric.*
> *I cover 100 miles a day in my diesel.*
> *I reckon I run about ten miles on my round.*
> *I have to deliver to a twenty-storey block of flats.*

The best way to gauge the hardest round is the reaction of other milkmen. When I worked as a relief milkman there was one round which stood out – Jeff's round.

One week, when I covered for Jeff, I tried to estimate the round's extent. While delivering milk I paced out some calls with my running steps and then converted to yardage. I ran about 280 yards in total, there and back, for three driveways in one avenue. Twenty calls in three other roads added another 870 yards. Then there were other incidental walking steps – getting to work, loading the van, delivering to the nurses' homes, and sorting out the crates. By the end of the week I'd calculated that Jeff covered about thirteen miles a day on foot (mostly running) and he drove eighteen miles. What particularly shocked me, though, was that he cycled six miles to and from work during the summer months.

The reactions of other milkmen convinced me that Jeff's round had no rival.

'Oh, no, not Jeff's round,' said one milkman who had done most of the dairy's rounds.

'I hope you're fit,' said another, while pulling a face.

'Good luck,' said a third.

'It never ceases to amaze me what streets Jeff turns up on,' said one customer. 'Yet if you stop and talk to him, he's got all the time in the world.'

'He was the dark milkman who was like lightning,' a customer on Jeff's previous round told me. 'If you see him, tell him we'd like him back.'

Jeff

Jeff was a tall slim man with a fast, loping stride. He was an athlete, 6ft 2½in tall, weighing thirteen stones, and he was almost too fast to watch. His hand actions were quick and his thinking even quicker. He had the hardest round in the dairy but he still had time for part-time jobs such as landscape gardening and delivering coal. He also played pool, snooker, darts and bar billiards.

On a number of mornings, when my milk float was behind his in the queue, I studied him from the moment he started to prepare for his round. He was so quick, so athletic that it was difficult to spot all he was doing. When he loaded the van I started to worry whether there would be enough produce left for other rounds. He took out so much milk that he had to show me the only way to stack it on his van. He took cartons of milk for the hospital, over 250 small bottles for a school and a ten-gallon churn for a college. I remember waking up at one o'clock in the morning before I did Jeff's round for the first time, thinking, 'How does Jeff take that churn off the float when he gets to the college?' I spent the rest of the night trying to work out how much ten gallons of milk weighed. When I got to the college, lifting the churn was easier than I'd expected.

Jeff did his round in four to four and a half hours. It took me an hour longer. Some of the driveways felt like bus routes that stretched into Never-never Land, but I found their doors eventually. It was much harder to deliver to the hospital flats. I wrote down Jeff's briefing to me about those flats:

When you're collecting you have to get to the nurses' homes by a quarter to eight. Otherwise you might as well give up because their shift starts at nine. I get two crates of milk and set off for the fifteen-storey building first. I've held the lifts for four years, but I had a complaint a few weeks ago and I'm not supposed to do it now. If anyone asks you, you don't know anything about it. It was a maintenance man who complained. Anyway, I got in the lift last week and this maintenance man was in the lift, and he'd just pressed fourteen. I said, 'Don't you want to stop at this one and this one and this one and this one?' and all the time I was pressing the other numbers.

Jeff told me more about his technique of taking the lift to the top floor and then working his way down:

I block the door with one crate, keep the other crate swinging, and grab the cartons two at a time. If you're really quick – really, really quick – you can dash out and back before the lift doors shut. I got my finger trapped once and it didn't half hurt. I was just a bit too slow. I wouldn't advise you to do that though. If you're not quick enough, your milk will be going up and down in the lift all morning.

Jeff had very low arrears on his round, but a lot depended on getting to the nurses' flats on time. 'You can be there at eight or even eight-fifteen if you're very fast,' he said. 'I do two flats, look across the other side, see what they want, then I come back and work out what to charge all four while they're answering.'

He was a good role model for me because he had been a relief milkman himself, a veteran of forty-four different rounds. He had unlimited stamina and an excellent vocabulary. He used words like proficient (to describe one milkman) and truculent (to describe another milkman's reaction to a customer). He had rejected the position of foreman in favour of 'a less dogsbody job', as he called it. On collecting days Jeff had his customers on starting blocks.

'The worst thing about this job is going back to the dairy,' he told me.

The Fastest Milkman

While delivering Jeff's round I had a conversation with a milkman from a rival dairy.

'How does Jeff do the round?' I asked. 'Does he jog? Does he trot?'

'No, he runs, like you do. He gallops round. He likes to be in the pub by eleven-thirty on a Thursday morning. When the bad weather was here, he still ran round. He took a few bad tumbles but he was only twenty minutes behind his normal time.'

I spent about fifty-five hours a week on the round. It was planned so that I had a week off whenever I completed a week's stint on round nineteen. Jeff didn't seem to need the same amount of rest as me and he had a good time away from work. He gave his wife his wages and then took the money from his bag (commission and perks) for his lunchtimes and evenings.

I wrote down some of my frustrations in my diary:

Nearly everybody is in residence at the moment. There are no listings in the round's book saying UFN [until further notice], and Jeff is so energetic, so brilliant, that he's forever adding calls to the round. This round has more back-door calls than any other I've done, not to mention all the goods that go out. When you see a note in the far distance, at a front door, you don't know whether it's for extra milk, grapefruit juice, lemonade, cream, yoghurts, or what, and you can't carry one of each just in case.

One morning Jeff was wheeling out his cartons while I was waiting for the foreman to check out my milk. I asked Jeff why he came off relief work. His reply:

Well, they messed me about. For example, one Saturday I started a round and they took me off it at seven to start another round. Then at ten they took me off that to start a round that hadn't been collected for four weeks.

On another occasion, during the snow and ice of a bad winter, Jeff's van was just in front of me on the loading bay. I climbed on to the bay and Jeff paced towards me. He suddenly collapsed to the floor in a crumpled heap and said, in a croaking voice, 'The van's loaded.' That nightmare – doing the hardest round in the snow and ice – lasted only a moment. Then I realised that Jeff had seen me and it was all a good act.

The loading bay had room for three vans. Sometimes a few of us would watch Jeff as he stuffed the goods on to his float. He had hardly put his van on the bay when he had almost finished loading. He dragged the churn along, tossed on his skimmed milk and sterilised milk, and he was ready to go while two other milkmen on the bay were still sorting themselves out.

'Did you see Jeff?' one milkman asked a group of us.

'He just grabs crates two at a time. And have you seen him out on the round? He's like a kangaroo.'

Another milkman told me a story about Jeff's days as a relief milkman:

Jeff did Fred's round once. Now, Fred's as slow as they come. He'd put four pints into a handcrate in slow motion and then he'd take them to the doorstep ever so slowly. Fred never got back before twelve. His round was designed to go past his house six times. Well, Jeff got to Fred's house about eight o'clock and Fred says, 'You've got off to a good start,' and Jeff had finished the round.

One morning, I asked Jeff if he'd had many accidents.

'Only one,' he said. 'One day I turned into a manor house and skidded into a gatepost.'

On another occasion Jeff came in a little earlier than usual. 'I have to get back early today, I've got to build a brick wall,' he told us, as we stood around in the loading bay queue. I suddenly felt very tired.

I learned that he set his alarm-clock for 3.45 a.m. and came straight out of the house without anything to eat. He combed his hair in the van.

Eventually, one day, I discovered the man's weakness. I bumped into him after he had just picked up his wage packet. He was tearing at the paper to get at the money.

'How long have I worked here?' he asked me. 'And I still can't open these wage packets.'

The man was fallible.

13

Milkwomen and Milkmen

Just had a baby, please leave another one.

DURING World War II, when many men joined the armed forces, the milkman's job was continued by youths, milkwomen and men too old to serve. The door was opened further for women with the 1976 Sex Discrimination Act, but it took some time for women to establish themselves in the male-dominated milk-delivery business.

By the end of the twentieth century, however, milkwomen were reaching the final shortlist for the national Milkman of the Year competition, which rewarded special service provision for customers. The first female national winner, in 2001, was Annette Hicks, who came from Kelly Bray, near Callington, Cornwall. Hicks was very popular with customers for her cheerful disposition. She was also a long-distance runner who visited the gym a lot.

Signing up for 'the milk' was the gateway to an unusual

lifestyle. This chapter illustrates the nature of the job in the seventies and eighties by focusing on two women and two men.

Jan

Jan worked as a milkwoman in the East Midlands for two and a half years, until a really bad winter. The job was hard work. It meant seven days on, one day off, then a four-day weekend break (Friday to Monday inclusive) every fifth week. She had previously worked in a hosiery factory . . . until it burnt down.

Her interview with personnel was a general chit-chat. They asked why she wanted the job and gave her a simple arithmetic test. The dairy was a family business and they knew what they were looking for. The interview lasted thirty minutes and Jan got the job. It probably helped that she'd spent eight years as a bus conductress.

She had a short walk to the dairy. After a week's training a round came up that the dairy thought would suit her. A supervisor showed her the round for a week and then she took it over, although the supervisor drove out daily during the first fortnight to check she was all right.

Jan arrived at the dairy at 4.45 a.m. and spent about fifteen minutes queuing for the loading bay and putting all the goods on the van. Her dairy relied solely on custom-designed electric vehicles and had no diesels (except the tankers). The loading bay was big enough for two vans and the dairy had about fifty rounds. Her round covered a lot of miles and visited a number of villages. Sometimes the batteries of her float ran out and she was either towed back or another van brought out to her.

She wore jeans and Doc Martens on the job. She had woollen hats (knitted for her by customers), mittens with no fingers and sometimes proper gloves while driving out to the round. The first thirty minutes in winter were awful. It was so cold that ice formed on the bottles and she used to wonder if it was worth it. The cold got her down in the end. She wasn't particularly tired. It was just miserable to have rain dripping down her neck and never really warming up.

The people were good to her and she had regular calls for tea (sometimes with rum). She usually skipped breakfast but two elderly men befriended her on the round. She had tea with one in the mornings and sometimes bacon and eggs. One customer brewed beer and bottled fruit. Some customers called her 'Milkie' but a lot got to know her by name.

The dairy's overalls were old brown cotton, much warmer than nylon, and the dairy laundered them daily. Her shoes lasted about two months. In the mornings she always took a coat with her, just in case, and was never without a flask of coffee. In summer she wore boots, unless it was unusually dry. Even in summer she dressed for winter. On collecting days she took sandwiches.

On normal delivery days she returned to the dairy about noon, sometimes earlier. Her major collecting days were Friday, Saturday and Sunday. On Fridays she finished around 2 p.m., on Saturdays between 2 p.m. and 3 p.m. She wasn't worried about handling money – she had often worked with cash – and she never thought about being mugged. She worked on Christmas Day and got £250 in tips one Christmas. Jan thought most milkmen stayed up on Christmas Eve and turned up pissed on Christmas Day.

She bought a Teasmade thinking that a cup of tea in the morning would get her up. She rose at 3.45 a.m. and took the dog for a thirty-minute walk. Her last winter was a bad one so she slept in more often. It was really cold in bed. She'd just be getting warm when it was time to get up. In her thirty months in the job she had the flu once but was generally fit and healthy.

Her dairy's milk floats were like little tankers, but they skidded around on snow and ice. They had solid wheels with no inner tubes, so the grip could be poor. She carried a big block of salt and old sacks to put under the milk float's wheels. One time she reversed into slush and snow and couldn't get the van out. People from the dairy came out to help but they had to unload every crate. Her breakdowns were mainly electrical faults. The steering went once and the contacts failed on another occasion.

She liked the smell of milk but recognised that it offended some people. She thought the dairy had a sour smell. She enjoyed the job but working early mornings on seven successive days was arduous. She got tired but thought that sleeping in the afternoons was a waste of the day. She worked an allotment by the canal.

When she finished work her first requirement was food. Sometimes she called in to the pub near the dairy and had two pints and a cob with some milkmen. Other times she cooked something at home.

The snow got her down in the end. One day she set off from home with no sign of bad weather. She loaded up the float and it started snowing while she was on the round. The streets were soon thick with snow and she was not properly prepared. The float couldn't go down some streets, which meant that she had to carry two crates of milk a long way while wearing the wrong clothes for the job. It was a ten-hour day.

She occasionally regretted leaving. 'It's the sort of job you can make something out of,' she said.

Peter

Peter lived near the dairy so a foreman came round to knock on his door when he overslept. In his time as a milkman he saw most of human life, and yet he was a shy milkman. He disliked collecting money from customers. He preferred to post a bill and ask them to leave a cheque for him to collect. Occasionally he debated with customers about the rights and wrongs of a bill from weeks or months before.

At the dairy he collected his diesel van and set out to deliver a country round. He got into a few scrapes with the van and his driving cost him several fines. One Sunday morning he drove through a village at forty-six miles per hour and was caught in a radar trap. He had a few minor collisions, including one time when he backed an electric float into a brick wall and another time when he misjudged his parking on an icy road.

One day he was driving into a pub car park when he noticed that the brick wall next to the entrance had been knocked down. He took a closer look at the damage on exiting and demolished another wall. In a separate accident, he left a set of traffic lights hanging by the wires after hitting the pole. On another occasion he nicked a big truck in the dairy. He never had a puncture but he suffered countless breakdowns. One time the engine virtually blew up and another time the exhaust rattled its way off his vehicle. After being repaired, the exhaust fell off periodically.

He would have been all right if he'd had a full quota of sleep but he never did. Sometimes, out on the round, the tiredness affected his brain and he felt he was John Coltrane 'Going Insane'. The whole world seemed to be a collection of psychedelic artwork, and the different pedals on his diesel van didn't mean much to him anymore.

The work brought some advantages. He loved the luxury of an extended lunch when he came in from the round, desperate to eat, and sometimes he went to bed for two or three hours in the afternoon, either sleeping or listening to the afternoon radio play. He'd get up and do some cooking for an evening meal. Having a social life was difficult. Friday night was the worst time for milkmen to go out as Saturday was always a very long day.

Peter fared better with his shoes than most milkmen but he probably didn't walk as far as some did. His ordinary black shoes lasted about nine months. They rubbed his feet and gave him blisters, but he put pieces of card inside the shoes to prevent the rubbing. He was a cross-country runner and he used all his athleticism on his round. He never stopped running, even though he had several falls and one very bad cut on his hand.

He had some run-ins with dogs. He used one of his 'lasting nine months' shoes to kick one yappy dog and it didn't bother him again. Another dog had a vicious growl and Peter was lining up his other 'lasting nine months' shoe when the owner came out and said, 'Don't worry about the dog, he won't harm a soul, but he doesn't half growl.'

He never took packed lunches. Most collecting days he survived from 5 a.m. to 2 p.m. or 3 p.m. on his breakfast of cornflakes. Throughout the day, winter or summer, he drank milk. On the round he was often stopped by the police, but he became less tense when he realised they were after free pints.

He arranged his round so that it finished with a guaranteed cup of tea. At that final call he relaxed a little and discovered everything anyone needed to know about village life.

Linda

Linda had done driving jobs before becoming a milk-woman. She was used to rising early because she'd worked at stables and on a dairy farm. She got up about 4.30 a.m. to work on the milk. She did the job for nearly a year.

On normal days she arrived at the dairy between 5.30 and six. One time, on her eight-mile drive to work, she ran out of petrol. It was a Friday morning and she had pounds of change with her so she left that in the car. She needed a lift to work but she was also worried about getting a lift. As it happened, another milkman picked her up. When she got to the dairy she told them that she wanted to get the money out of the car before she started the round.

Linda wore as much as possible – oilskins, jeans, boots, long socks, T-shirt, polo-necked jumper and woolly hat – to cope with soaking wet days, and she ducked her chin under her scarf. She found that leather palm gloves were better than other gloves when wet. Her gloves were generally warm and had a good grip on the milk bottles. But sometimes her hands got so cold that greasy bottles slipped through. When she was very cold she wore two pairs of gloves.

Her fingers were smaller than men's. She could carry only four full bottles in her hands rather than six. Her jeans were always dirty from resting crates against them. Because she was only half an inch over five foot, Linda had to rest the crates on her chest or shoulder when lifting them down from stacks of six. The coats came in two sizes – large and extra-large. She turned her coat up six inches, and she washed her overalls every two days. The dairy provided oilskins.

Linda bought an expensive pair of Nature Trek shoes but they lasted only three weeks. After that she bought cheaper shoes and wore them for three or four months until they split across the sole of her right shoe. She reckoned the right shoe was damaged by the accelerator pedal, which was sharp on the edge. Sometimes she wore her ring and sometimes not. She noticed that her fingers widened and she used barrier cream to treat the calloused skin. Her hands were sore and chapped in winter.

One dark morning, at 5.50 a.m., she had a shock when she nearly bumped into a tramp outside the vicarage. After that she dreaded getting to the vicarage at 5.50, so she drove the milk float to the door, regardless of the noise on the gravel, and she put on every light. Sometimes she'd miss out the vicarage and go back later. Another eerie moment came when the lights went out while she was in a lift at a block of flats.

Sometimes, when it was really wet, she phoned the dairy for dry clothes and changed in the float. Two or three customers offered cups of tea. One woman was quite trusting;

she was nearly blind and would ask Linda to look for her purse. Under the bed was a box full of twenty-pound notes.

She suffered one dog bite during her year in the job. More friendly was a collie she spoke to through the letterbox. The collie jumped on the float and she'd take it for a ride down the road. Another dog sat and waited at a house with two old people. The old people hardly had two pennies to rub together, but they'd be waiting for their milkwoman with tea on a tray.

Her diesel floats sometimes broke down, usually when she'd started early and wanted to finish early. Some vans would be dead in the dairy. Others failed on rounds. The noise of a big van caused her headaches.

Linda ate no breakfast and nothing while on the round. On collecting days she might buy a bag of chips or two sausage rolls. She would ask to use the toilet at some customers' homes and they might say, 'Not working,' but she found an outside toilet that a customer let her use.

One morning she was stopped by the police when out on the round. They couldn't believe a woman was doing the job so they asked her lots of questions: 'Where did the milk float come from? Name? How long have you been working there? What time did you start? Where are you going? What time will you be back? Who is your foreman? What's the number of your vehicle?'

Another time she stopped her car to wait for a lad who was learning her round. A police officer watched her and then drove his car alongside, perhaps thinking that she was a look-out: 'Name? Where are you going? Work? Delivering milk? Where did you buy the car? How long have you had it?'

She was concerned about safety on collecting days and thought about taking one of her dogs on the round. Sitting in the open float the imagination flowed and there could be paranoia on collecting days. She kept some money in her bag and hid the rest in various places. Sometimes she forgot where she'd hidden it. She worried first thing in the morning when it was dark, and worried when she left the float at the end of a road and delivered on foot. Anyone could nick the float. On collecting days she stayed out until 3.30 p.m. or 4 p.m.

Some houses had notes outside nearly every day. One house had blue wood for one order and orange wood for another, and seeing the colours from a distance helped her to deliver correctly at the end of a long driveway. She rarely used her torch but made use of her float's inside light. Without a torch it was easier to carry four or five pints. Handcrates were gold dust. She took her handcrate home in the car.

Some milkmen were misogynist. Some sat in their floats while she was struggling with the loading. Some stood with their hands in their pockets. She got the odd sarcastic comment when lifting crates, and there were some knowing male looks if she made a mistake. She'd see a few men elbowing each other. They never offered to help.

Customers were surprised to see a woman but they took her to their hearts: 'Are you getting on all right? You're really brave!' Others looked at her as if she were a wizard and thought it was a great thing. The older ones, in particular, said, 'Good for you, it's fantastic that you're doing the job.'

At Christmas she got presents – boxes of chocolates, talcum powder, fruit and vegetables. Notes were written to 'Dear Milklady' or 'Miss' or, for those who got to know her, 'Dear Linda'. It got to the stage that if she missed a day they would ask if she was all right. She carried people's shopping bags and posted their letters.

When she got in from the round she made a cup of coffee, tended to the dogs and then had a bath. Others could smell her when she was at home. The smell of milk was continually in her nostrils, her gloves and her overall.

On Boxing Day Linda injured her left ankle when getting out of the float. Earlier she had hurt the same ankle when doing the splits across the cab after slipping on the wet floor. She was off work for six weeks and that was the beginning of the end.

Robert

Robert was trawling through advertisements when he saw one for milkmen. He needed something to support his growing family. He went for an interview at the dairy and the job was portrayed as 'get up early, get home early'. They gave him some reading about a day in the life of the milkman and tested him on basic mathematics. Later, working in the job, he learnt more about the unsociable hours and the repetitive nature of the work.

Robert was a naturally fit man, lean and wiry, and he played squash regularly. He lived about twelve miles from the dairy so he cycled to work at first. Then he switched to a moped. He was up and out early after a cup of tea and he ate chocolate to keep him going.

He never carried a torch so he walked into things in

the dark, and he could never wear enough clothing to keep dry in the rain. He got through a right shoe every six weeks, pivoting on the ball of his foot to get in and out of the float. He tried to even up the wear and tear on the shoes by exiting the float on its nearside, landing on his left foot, but he soon subconsciously pivoted on his right foot again, so there was no advantage. Landing and pivoting caused the occasional twisted ankle.

Milkmen could never stay dry on rainy days, and sometimes their paperwork got wet. Rain seemed to fall horizontally into the cab of a travelling electric float. It gave a new meaning to 'driving rain'. Robert never ran unless there were prevailing conditions, such as the wind at his back, and he found running on his own tiring and demoralising. He didn't like the idea of doing the same round every day so he worked on different rounds and found that the vehicles all seemed slightly different. He would have plenty of headroom in one and then he'd bang his head on another.

Robert was athletic, but he was really astonished at the fatigue caused by the job. In the first weeks it was a long haul to the end of the round and the loading and sorting was hard physical work. It was more arduous than he'd assumed, but he got super-fit very quickly and was quite capable of coping with the demanding work. He was careful about how he lifted crates, using the strength of his legs rather than bending his back too much. When it was time to relax it was like all the strings went. He got to the point where he enjoyed doing nothing and his energy for doing jobs around the house was suddenly zero. His prime ambition was to finish the round and get home. Invariably a round took longer than he'd been led to believe and longer than he'd hoped. He found the milkman's life a tough one. He gave up playing squash.

One time his van was stuck on the edge of a grassy meadow and it took some time to organise tractors to pull it out. Another time his electric float ran out of juice and he couldn't make it over a humpback bridge. On one occasion, driving a Commer diesel, he turned a corner quickly and a dozen crates toppled over the side in the middle of rush hour. Another time he was involved in a milk-float collision.

He sometimes took a spare bottle of milk up the garden path, either because a customer might want one extra or because a dog looked threatening. Lots of houses had BEWARE OF THE DOG signs but no sign of a dog.

At times he came close to abandoning a round, leaving the van and going home. Sometimes he sensed he was getting nowhere. He found that the way to succeed was by setting much smaller targets and taking the round one stage at a time. Let's get through the next fifteen minutes. Let's deliver another forty pints of milk. Let's get to the end of this street.

In the end he concluded that there was too little training for what he was asked to do. The senior staff were so familiar with the requirements of the job that they no longer pointed out the basic issues. Robert reckoned that half the people who packed it in would have eventually made satisfactory roundsmen.

14

The Milkman's Vehicles

*Sorry about yesterday's note. I didn't mean one egg and
a dozen pints, but the other way round.*

THE history of milk transportation includes foot-
slogging with a yoke and pail, pushing prams and
handcarts, the horse and cart, bicycles, motorcycles, motor
cars, electric barrows, electric milk floats and diesel vans.
A surprising number of milkmen claim to have delivered
by sled or sleigh in snowy conditions, and some used skis
and tractors in the winter of 1963.

The story of the milkmen's vehicles includes several
overlapping periods. Changes to transportation happened
at different times in different regions of the country. For
example, the horse and cart started to disappear from
urban areas in the early fifties – one big dairy in London's
West End withdrew its last horse and float in 1953 – but it
continued until the eighties in some rural places.

The Yoke and Pail

By the 1880s, milk was purchased in one of two ways: (i) those in rural districts went to the nearest farm once or twice a day and bought loose milk from the farmer; and (ii) in towns and cities milkmen bought a few gallons of milk and then hawked it around the streets on a yoke, a solid piece of wood which rested on the shoulders.

> I was about nine when I helped deliver milk with the local farmer at Brimscombe, Mr Wilkins (Wilky). I would go to his farm each morning in the school holidays and watch the cows being milked by hand, the milk being cooled and put into churns. Then Wilky would hook two churns on to the yoke across his shoulders. I would take a couple of one- or two-pint cans and we would go to the local houses. Wilky ladled the milk into the cans and I took them to the housewives, who poured the milk into their jugs.

> As a very young boy in Dursley of the late 1920s, I can just remember seeing two strong young ladies carrying milk from door to door in buckets suspended from a wooden yoke across their shoulders. However, most of the milk was delivered in horse-drawn 'floats', specially designed carts with a low floor base for ease of lifting churns and buckets in and out.

In the late forties, the streets of Clovelly, Devon, were too narrow for vehicles, so milkman Leslie May used the yoke and pail until 1951, when new regulations meant that milk had to be supplied in bottles.

Handcarts, Prams and Bicycles

From the mid-nineteenth century, the yoke and pail was slowly replaced by small handcarts and three-wheeled vehicles which resembled prams. With a large churn on board, the milkman set off on foot, wheeling the handcart or pushing the pram. One dairy assigned a pedometer to a pram and discovered that the milkman pushed it about fifteen miles a day.

Churns of milk were left standing in a stream to keep the milk cool and milkmen with handcarts visited customers two or three times a day. Some milkmen delivered by bicycle with a three-gallon container hanging from the handlebars and measuring jugs hanging from the container.

Here is a story about prams. Mr Kimmins worked for four years at Tom Mitchell's Dairy, Worthing, starting in August 1915 when he was nine years old.

I used to get to the dairy at 5 a.m. Often Tom and his wife were still asleep, so I would climb over the back gate in the dark and get in the dairy, which was in a small building at the bottom of the garden, and wait for one of them to get up and unlock the gate. Though I was only a young lad I used to do a round by myself. In those days we used an iron-shod three-wheel milk pram.

To get out of the dairy and start the round I had to push the pram down a passageway which was only just wide enough. Often the cans around the side of the pram would scrape the walls. Those prams were a real devil in ice and snow; the ice would pack around the wheels. Even in good weather, with a full churn of milk they could be difficult to bump up and down a steep kerb. Often I delivered the milk with lumps of ice floating on it. The round took me out to East Worthing. When I finished the round, at about 7.30, I went on to Skinner's, the newsagent, and did a paper round before going to school at 9 a.m.

At some time I must have helped Tom with the second round. I suppose it was in the school holidays because I can remember that on the second round we poured the milk from the hand can into the customers' jug and collected the cans to take back to the dairy and wash up in a galvanised trough. At some point, I can't remember when, we changed to a half carrier bike with a four- or five-gallon churn and the hand can on the side, and the cans hooked on all around the carrier with two more rows inside each other so that they were three deep. Many a time I lost my balance and went base over apex.

The Horse and Cart

Horses were used more extensively in the first half of the twentieth century. Lord Rayleigh's Dairies switched from handcarts to circus ponies just before World War One. During the period from 1900 to 1939, the horse and cart (aka 'horse and float') gradually replaced the handcart.

Welsh cobs were particularly popular. They could be broken in to traffic, taught not to kick, bite or bolt, and they had delivery careers of around ten to twelve years. In 1935, United Dairies had a stable of thirty-three ponies in Milner Street, Chelsea. Bought as four-year-olds, the ponies went out at 6 a.m. and came back about 4 p.m., and some lasted longer in the job than their milkmen. When horses defecated in the streets housewives raced with shovels to collect manure for their vegetable patches.

Here are some memories of the horse and float, beginning with Emily Filmer in 1916:

Well, the first [horse] I had was all right, but when it went lame I had to borrow one from a local farmer. Going down one of the hills it tripped and its hind quarters came over the shafts. This was just outside the Co-op, in which the upstairs hall was full of wounded soldiers. Of course it was a big laugh but, eventually, when we got it up, it was OK.

In the 1920s, milk was delivered to the door in Charlton Kings by a horse-drawn float with large churns on board. The milkman stood on a step at the back with his reins in his hand, but the horse knew exactly where to go and would walk along the road stopping at the appropriate customers' houses. The milkman came to the door carrying a metal milk bucket with metal measuring containers, or dippers, hanging on it. He then ladled milk out in pints or half pints, into your large china jugs. In some places they were not too particular about clean hands and a dirty thumb sometimes came into contact with the milk being poured into your jug.

Horses understand words of command much better than some of the human beings who are attempting to ride them. One had only to watch the milkman's horse on his round. We can send to the Ministry of Labour for a new assistant and put the new assistant in charge of the milk cart, and as sure as light follows dark that horse will see that the milkman calls at every one of the customers. The horse knows the round. One can sometimes see horses moving through traffic with the wagoner fast asleep.

Our horse was called Goblin and she was a placid and gentle horse and let anyone stroke or pet her. She knew every inch of the round, and when I had to go down one entry to serve the back houses and had to come out at another entry thirty yards further down the road, she would be there waiting for me. How she got round the odd car parked at the side of the road without hitting them I don't know.

In the forties, a blind white horse called Queenie learnt her way to customers' houses on a milk round in St Helens, Lancashire. Queenie responded to the command 'Walk on' and dutifully went to the next house on the round. At the corner shop the horse poked her head inside and the proprietor gave her a piece of bread or an apple. But one day Queenie was indisposed and an inexperienced horse deputised. This replacement horse was an untested, bad-tempered beast. A woman came out of one house and fed the horse a few titbits. The horse enjoyed them so much that he followed the woman up the garden path with the float in tow. The horse smashed two fences and made a mess of two gardens. The milkman had to pay compensation.

In 1950, two brothers, both milkmen, became famous for having their photograph taken on a horse and cart. The Jones brothers were sitting on the cart in Park Place, Tredegar, South Wales, when *Time Life* photographer Eugene Smith asked permission to take the photo, which was later seen around the world. 'The picture makes me very proud,' Trevor Jones told the *South Wales Argus* many years later, 'proud of the work me and my brother used to do, working on our horse and cart in our town.'

Simon Jenkins wrote in *The Times* that in the fifties he and his childhood friends visited the stables, cleaned the brasses and recited, 'He's cheaper to run than a lorry.' Kids loved a milkman's horse and some people believed that horses had more sense than humans. The only real drawback was the noise horseshoes made in the streets. There were experiments with rubber horseshoes, but they could make the horses lame.

On returning to the dairy the horse was unharnessed, rubbed down, combed, fed, watered and bedded. The float was cleaned and the churns washed and polished with Brasso. Emily Filmer found that milk delivery in the twenties was a 6 a.m. to 6 p.m. job, seven days a week, with one hour for lunch. She qualified for a week's holiday after two years.

A lot of young boys loved being with horses. A good example was Tam Connery, who grew up in Edinburgh in the thirties and forties. As a nine-year-old, Connery was up at six in the morning to deliver milk for Kennedy's Dairy. He left school at thirteen, during World War Two, and got a job at St Cuthbert's Dairy. He progressed from barrow boy to dairy transport worker and became a junior horseman. He borrowed his mum's dusters to rub down his Highland garron pony Tich:

> I bought her rosettes and chains, which looped down
> from each ear, along with a martingale or bracelet, which

hung down her front. I added 'birlers', roundels which birled or twirled in the wind, or when she trotted. I was so proud of Tich that I entered her in the annual horse and cart competition for the best-dressed horse and she won a Highly Commended.

The slow speed of the horse and cart allowed Tam Connery plenty of time to appreciate the elegant buildings of Edinburgh. Later, better known as the actor Sean Connery, he rode horses in several movies (e.g. *Shalako*) and was knighted in 2000. Connery, like former prime minister Tony Blair, went to the prestigious Edinburgh school Fettes College. In Connery's case, however, it was to deliver milk rather than receive an education.

Other film stars can be linked to milk delivery. In the thirties, Robert Redford's father worked as a milkman in Edinburgh before emigrating to the United States in 1936, and a young Roger Moore was a milkman's helper in Stockwell, South London. Presumably, given Connery and Moore's acting careers, working as a milkman was essential training for depicting James Bond – super-fit, quick-thinking, attractive to women and capable of dealing with emergencies.

During World War II it was again left to women, children and older men to keep doorstep deliveries going. Alfred Hawthorne Hill was sixteen when he started work at Hann's Dairy in Eastleigh, Hampshire. Hill's old mare, Daisy, would do anything for her master except sit up and beg. Hill was soon promoted to milkman and he did the job before joining the army in 1942. On his round Hill fantasised that he was driving a stage coach into Dodge

City, 'hoofs drumming, bottles rattling and every living thing flying out of our way!' Later, as Benny Hill, he wrote the song 'Ernie: the Fastest Milkman in the West', a 1971 number-one hit record. In July 1999, seven years after Hill's death, a commemorative plaque was unveiled in his honour near Hann's Dorset Dairies in Eastleigh. At one point in his early working career Hill rose at 5.30 to do a milk round; later in life he got up at 5.30 to write television scripts.

Every good horse knew its way home and people in a hurry were described as 'like a milk horse heading home'. But horses could be ill, lame or unpredictable. They might get cold and want to move on, or they had to be pushed up hills. Sometimes it needed two horses to get a float up a steep hill in winter. On other occasions a horse took fright and bolted, and that occasionally led to a serious accident. In May 1961 a horse drawing a milk float bolted into a crowd of people during a carnival procession at Watford, Hertfordshire. The driver and five people were injured.

The horse-and-cart era provided an old tale about a racehorse which had finished last in his first twenty races. Before the horse's next race, the trainer told the jockey, 'Give it all you've got – if the horse finishes last again I'm going to give him to the dairy to do a milk round.' Well, the horse trailed right from the start of the race. The jockey slapped and whipped the horse, but the horse got slower and slower. Suddenly the horse came to a complete stop and turned its head to look at the jockey. 'Go easy with that whip,' the horse said. 'I've got to be up at four in the morning to deliver milk.'

Richard Greenhalgh used a horse-drawn vehicle from 1906, when he helped his father as a lad, to 1962, when he retired from the job. Greenhalgh spent those fifty-six years delivering to the Stand Lane and Outwood areas of Radcliffe, Lancashire. When he retired there was still one other horse-drawn vehicle being used in the district. Greenhalgh didn't go far in his retirement. 'I wouldn't leave Radcliffe for a gold clock,' he told the *Radcliffe Times*.

In 1918, Express Dairies relied solely on their 1,000 horse-and-float vehicles. By 1964 the remaining four show horses were dominated by 2,729 electric vehicles and 971 motor lorries. Some redundant horses were sent to the knacker's yard, but others were stabled at the dairy and used for other purposes. As road traffic increased, it became more and more dangerous to continue with horses. At Hygienic Dairies in New Milton, Hampshire, the last two working horses, Trixie and Queenie, were pensioned off in 1955. Jimmy, a five-year-old bay gelding in London, was made redundant in 1959 and hired by the Wimbledon Common ranger. Edgar's Dairies, Hampshire, retired their last three horses – Patch, Alice and Darkie – in February 1964, but a few horse-drawn floats continued. A horse called Molly was used by Malcolm Jackson in Church, Lancashire, until the mid-nineties.

Motorcycles and Motorcars

Lionel Jones explained the progression to motorised transport in Dursley, Gloucestershire:

Not long after we arrived at Mill Farm, Uley Road in 1926, my father, Alfred William Jones, started his milk round. He delivered his produce with a bicycle and sidecar in which he could put two pails of milk. Milk delivery from the farm took a giant technical leap forward in 1928 when Dad had an old 1922 Albert open-tourer type car modified by Mr Paul Greenaway, the local builder with his workshop by the Broadwell, so that the rear portion was removed and replaced by a wooden box structure with a hinged tailboard section. After a few years the old Albert car was replaced by an adapted canvas top Austin Seven and later still by a new Austin Seven van.

In 1934, William Bailey bought a one-round dairy business, Yeatton Dairy, in Horden, near New Milton, Hampshire. The business came complete with one roundsman, Les Haines, and a motorcycle and sidecar. Initial deliveries were made with a large churn mounted in the sidecar. The business amounted to eight gallons a day.

By the outbreak of World War Two, in 1939, Yeatton Dairy was known as Hygienic Dairy, and there was a total change in vehicles. The dairy's output was now a hundred gallons a day, so four horse-drawn floats and a Singer van were used. Old Farm Dairy in Nottinghamshire used motorbikes and sidecars.

Trevor Jones' round in Tredegar, near the Brecon Beacons, was motorised after World War Two:

We got our first van in 1952. It was an Austin 10 and I can still remember the registration – FDD 540. The van was easier. You didn't have to start work at seven o'clock in the morning to muck it out and feed it. With a van, you pressed a button and it all worked, much better until the bills came in! It was more expensive to run than a horse.

Electric Barrows

Hand-pushed barrows, prams and the horse and cart also gave way to electric barrows. These battery-propelled handcarts appeared around 1938 and stayed until the seventies.

In the late forties, milkmen who used electric barrows without a driving licence had to display an L-plate at the front and rear of their vehicle, even though the barrow's maximum speed was only three miles per hour.

In July 1962, James Hay, speaking in parliament, was concerned about the new legal clause for mowing machines and vehicles controlled by pedestrians. He cited the strange case of David Crane, an experienced milkman, whose career was under threat because he could read a number plate at twenty-one yards but not at twenty-five yards. His electric barrow never did more than two or three miles per hour, and it stopped instantly when he let go of the handle. Some exemptions were eventually allowed.

Electric barrows continued in some terraced house areas, usually until a long-serving roundsman retired. It would have been cruel to make a roundsman redundant because he had no driving licence.

Our milkman in Ledbury Road, when I was very young, was Mr Len Oliver, quite an old guy with a horse and cart. And the stories are true. This horse knew to the blade of grass where to stop for him. They delivered milk on Christmas Day and Mr Oliver had a whisky in every house, so the horse took him back at the end of the day. Absolutely Brahms and Liszt, he was. Towards the end of the time I was living there, before I moved away, they called in the horse and cart, and gave him one of these electric barrows. It was like a box on wheels. It had a handle coming out the front, and you turned the handle and that was the power, so as you went along you pulled it and it came along behind you. I remember talking to Mr Oliver and I said, 'It's not the same as having the horse there,' because we took carrots and apples out for the horse. And he said, 'No, he jerks, stops, jerks, stops, and wherever I leave it, I have to go and get it.'

Electric Milk Floats

Electric milk floats have been described as macho Dinky toys with batteries supplied, but they are also one of the most environmentally friendly inventions in history. Built to carry something like two tons of milk bottles, they were relatively quiet vehicles, spewing no fumes into the environment, and, unlike motor vehicles, they used no energy when stopped in traffic. The purchase price of a milk float was perhaps 70 per cent more than a petrol equivalent but the running costs were much lower.

In the early thirties, Express Dairies experimented with electric trucks for doorstep deliveries. They were so impressed with the ones made by T H Lewis of Camden Town that they took over the firm. Kirby & West in Leicester also manufactured their own electric floats.

Milk floats were flimsy at the front (especially the three-wheelers) but very strong at the back. They were uncomplicated vehicles. Nothing much could go wrong and, when it did go wrong, the vehicles were relatively easy to repair. Milk floats were fairly easy to steal but useless as a getaway vehicle.

In 1956, thirty-eight-year-old Jim Banks was asked to test a prototype for his manager at Kirby & West Dairies. Banks couldn't find much fault with the electric float. It carried a good load, was reliable, quiet, and easy to get in and out of. But Banks advised slowing down the vehicles because the batteries wouldn't last if they went too fast. Fifty-six years later, in 2012, the *Nottingham Post* reported that some of the fifties' Kirby & West electric milk floats were still being used, even though they were older than their drivers. One float had clocked up 485,000 miles, making a mockery of its life expectancy of fifteen to twenty years.

Milkmen had to be careful if they took their float near water because electric vehicles didn't fare well when wet. On the other hand, the float's roof was useful if a milkman climbed up there to scrump apples. A milk float in Scunthorpe was once decommissioned for five weeks because a dove with two eggs was nesting on the float's roof.

Most electric floats had no doors. That made it much easier to get in and out of the vehicles, but there was nothing to protect the milkman. Wind whistled through the cab when a car passed a milk float at speed and on snowy mornings milkmen would be white on one side of their clothes. But some electric milk floats came with doors – sliding doors, jack-knife doors or inner-glide doors. The Oxcart, made by Oxford Electrics, had a walkway through the centre of the deck and a half cab for the driver.

In 1967 Britain had 55,000 battery-operated vehicles in total on the road, more than could be found in all the rest of the world. The early electric milk floats were designed solely for milk delivery. Then vehicles were adapted so that other products could be transported in freezers, racks and trailers.

Electric milk floats resembled dodgems. They had only two gears – forward and reverse – and a setting for overnight charge. They worked on electrical contacts rather than a gearbox. You put your foot on the pedal and made the first contact. When you put your foot to the floor you made the other contacts. You'd hear the clicks and sometimes saw sparks as the vehicle accelerated. Finally, you pressed the booster button with panache. To slow down, you had to take your foot off the throttle and let it hover over the brake. Most milk floats didn't have seat belts, but, after 2005, seat belts, if fitted, had to used on journeys of more than fifty metres between stops.

Milk floats were generally unthreatening but they frustrated car drivers because they went at half the speed of a saloon car (and that could lead to risky driving by other road users). The suspension on the float was not wonderful, so milkmen approached bumps and ramps carefully. Otherwise they could be sweeping up glass from the road.

> One of the college areas I did was almost like an estate. You drove in and their sleeping policemen felt like they were six feet in the air. Everything banged and rattled when you went over them. You almost had to stop and pull the van over. Bonk, bonk, bonk . . .

Milkmen looked in their mirror a lot because cars were going at twice their speed and came up quickly from behind. A milkman's pulse rate quickened when he signalled and pulled out to pass a row of parked cars while traffic kept overtaking him. One day a relief milkman took a wrong turn on an unfamiliar round and found himself on the M1 motorway. He tooled along at ten miles per hour as traffic raced past at seventy or more. Fortunately his batteries held out for eight miles until he reached the next exit.

Electric vehicles worked well in flat areas but not so well on steep hills. On a long round the batteries sometimes ran out of juice and the float had to be towed home. Electric vehicles were sometimes decommissioned by half-shaft problems, handbrake failure or being wheel-clamped after a parking offence.

> I once got through five vans in one day. They kept bringing out them that had been out all day already. I'd get a hundred yards and the battery would go. I had one van so bad that I had to unload it when I went over a bridge. Otherwise I wouldn't make it. They brought a coal lorry out to me in the end.

> My float broke down at five o'clock on a Saturday morning. I phoned the dairy and I got the number wrong. Got some poor bloke out of bed.

Sometimes a milk float caught fire in the loading-bay queue and there were stories of flames a foot high and a milkman scarpering from the scene. Other times a wire came loose and the milk float was suddenly out of action. Milkmen had their own version of Sod's Law – the milk float that broke down on days when you needed to finish early.

The optimum speed for an electric milk float was between twelve and fifteen miles per hour, and there was usually a metal sign in the cab: *Downhill speed not to exceed 25 mph*. Of course, such signs were very tempting to milkmen:

> I remember delivering one round where there was a great chance to test the speed of the float. The load was still heavy – it was still early in the morning – and the slope was gentle and long. I had the speedometer indicator hovering around twenty-two or twenty-three miles per hour but an island loomed and I couldn't break the barrier.

Others did break the speed limit:

> One day I was chugging up the final hill to the dairy, doing all of four miles an hour, when this lorry crept up behind me, dropped down a gear and with a loud roar of the engine shunted me up the hill at a good thirty miles an hour. I thought Old Nick himself had got me as I had been dreaming and not looking in my rear-view mirror.

British sprinter Linford Christie once raced a milk float in a staged advert for milk-sponsored school athletics (MILK: IT'S FULL OF NATURAL GOODNESS). At one time top-class athletes could beat a battery-operated electric milk float from a standing start. But modern souped-up milk floats have been clocked at over eighty miles per hour.

One day a milkman made a mistake with his milk float when he was delivering to a cul-de-sac on a downhill gradient. The milkman parked the float and inadvertently left off the handbrake. He delivered to the street's eight houses, all on the same side of the street, walking across the frontages without looking at his van, and then, looking back, he saw that his van had crept silently down the road until it came to rest on a piece of level ground at the end of the cul-de-sac, right next to the last house. The milkman was quite fascinated by this.

In future he decided to leave the handbrake off in this quiet cul-de-sac. He let the van roll down the hill while he delivered to his eight calls and then met the float at the bottom to continue the round. It was a throwback to the days when a milkman whistled and the horse came.

There were other risky milk-float techniques. A milkman told me that if you were turning right into a busy main road you could press your foot down on the accelerator pedal while keeping the handbrake on. Then you let off the handbrake and the van leapt into the traffic like a long jumper. Personally I think that is a shaggy dog story . . . starring a lurcher.

The electric milk float's heyday was the late sixties. Various manufacturers benefited from the electric vehicle boom, including Morrison's Electrics, Morris Cowley, Smith's Delivery Vehicles and Brush. When I worked as a milkman I had an image of somebody driving a new milk float from Gateshead to Brighton, stopping at several dairies along the way to recharge the batteries. Then someone told me it probably arrived on a lorry.

Injured people were sometimes taken to hospital on a milkman's vehicle, and milkmen have used their vans for other purposes. Milkman Geoff Dean once drove a twelve-foot man-eating plant from Bromley Cross to Deane

School, Bolton, Lancashire, in preparation for a school production of *Little Shop of Horrors*. Another milkman kindly lent some props to a schoolgirl for use in the school play – a milk carrier, a woolly hat and an apron – only to find out later that the girl had brought the house down by impersonating the local milkman in a series of sketches.

Diesel Milk Floats

Diesel milk floats were much faster than electric ones and they were invaluable when customers became more scattered. Traditionally, diesels were used for country rounds some distance from the depot or in hilly regions. In recent years, when more customers were lost, rounds grew bigger and diesels became essential if a milkman was going to complete the round on the same day. Diesel vans made more noise than electric milk floats. They were the big bruisers of the dairy, as recalled by a contributor to the Gransnet forum: 'When I lived in a quiet Test valley many years ago, the quiet electric milk cart was replaced by a noisy diesel one and in summer with all the windows open it woke everyone up at silly o'clock in the morning.'

15

Petty Crime

No milk thank you. We're away for the weekend, which is why
I'm hiding this note under the doormat so nobody finds it. . .

MILKMEN have been the perpetrators and victims of small-time crime. In the past some milkmen served short measures and more recently some have fiddled dairies or customers. But they have also been the victims of crimes (e.g. milk stolen from doorsteps).

Let's start with a fiddle by milkmen in the days of measuring cans.

Short Measures

In the early days, before sealed glass bottles, milkmen were often caught for selling short measures or watered-down milk. In 1918, William Eaton was imprisoned for a month for diluting twenty-two quarts of milk delivered to a restaurant. That same year Henry William Smith was sentenced to twenty-one days in prison for wilfully damaging milk. Some milk was adulterated so much that it was nearly 80 per cent water. A Camberwell milkman was jailed for three months for selling watered-down milk. If milkmen spotted the authorities closing in they might tip over their cart so that the milk content couldn't be tested.

Lionel Jones recalled the 1920s and 1930s:

A major concern was that unscrupulous suppliers would add water to their milk. To guard against this practice the police would make random tests throughout the year, taking a pint sample at the roadside which they divided into three officially sealed one-third pint bottles. This they took for analysis and one was left for the milkman to have analysed himself should he wish.

Some old-time milkmen took their horse to the water trough and hid behind the animal while watering down the milk. Others topped up the milk with water from a nearby pond. Short measures could also be produced by denting the can or leaving the top off the can when it was raining. Old-timers joked that you could tell a milkman by his white thumb because he'd put his thumb inside the measuring can in order to raise the level of the milk. Other customers sometimes looked carefully at the midday milk and said, 'I'll wait for the evening round, thank you.'

In the American film *Great Guy* (1936) James Cagney played a food inspector who was trying to clean up the city. His problems included adulterated milk, crooked weighing scales and incorrect delivery notes. Cagney's tough-guy character combated organised crime. Some dairy foremen and managers had similar roles.

Stolen Milk

Milkmen were the victims when milk was stolen from door-steps and vehicles. Most milkmen learnt crime-prevention techniques. They were alert to proven neighbourhood milk thieves, and they safeguarded their milk by deliver-ing bottles to the back of some houses or inside cupboards. The theft of full milk bottles from a doorstep was both trivial (in terms of the value of the product) and important (as it really annoyed the customer and the milkman).

In 2007, Rowner Infant School, Gosport, Hampshire, faced a chronic milk-theft problem. The milkman put the delivery inside the school grounds behind a locked gate but occasionally someone took a crate of cartons. The problem continued for over a year.

In 2013, a South Wales milkman started collecting keys to customers' houses so that the milk could be left inside rather than outside, where it was being stolen from doorsteps. Hundreds of pints of milk were stolen in the Cynon Valley. Look-outs were stationed but there was not much the police could do.

A milkman in Crewe was another victim:

Yesterday fifty-five pints were stolen from doorsteps and that's a lot of homes. Whoever is doing this is not stealing it because they want it, they're throwing it away. My customers have told me broken glass bottles have been found. This is getting serious now and I'm beginning to wonder if I'm being followed when I do the round. Yesterday one of my customers rang me at about 5.45 a.m. to say her milk had been stolen so I went back with some more and I noticed the rest of the milk had gone from the other doorsteps as well. I replaced them all and then the second lot was stolen again a bit later. I can't leave people without milk and I can't charge for what they've not had. When I've run out, I've even had to go to a supermarket.

The theft of milk could be painful for victims. 'One old man saw a kid stealing his pint of milk,' a milkman told me, 'so he chased him, fell down, and broke his hip.' After that incident the milkman knocked on the door, called 'Milkman here', and took the milk indoors.

Some milkmen kept a weapon (e.g. a rounders' bat) in the float to deter people from stealing milk off their van.

A newsagent told me a story from the eighties:

I unlocked the door of my shop one morning and a policeman walked in with a man. The policeman asked me if I'd sold any milk that morning? I said, 'No, we're not open yet.' The policeman said, 'Well, this fellow says he bought two pints off you.' The thief was later fined £60.

At 2 a.m. one Friday in 1999, a milkman in Rayne, Essex, was fifteen minutes into his round when a car sped up alongside him. The occupants took the milkman's keys from the float's ignition and stole about twenty-pounds' worth of eggs, orange juice and bread. The dairy manager had to get out of bed to bring a spare ignition key. He wasn't pleased.

Milkmen Fiddles

Some milkmen took advantage of the firm on an assumed principle – 'If you rob me, I'll rob you'. One dairy manager reckoned that if he blocked one hole the milkmen would find another one. Milkmen could build up exploitable trust with customers and with the dairy.

Milkman fiddles could be elaborate or simple, well-planned or impulsive. Sneaking a few extra goods out of the dairy was a crude fiddle, but some milkmen were conjurors on the loading bay. Maybe a pot of cream slipped up their sleeves or into their pockets. Perhaps a few extra pints of milk eluded the foreman's count. Dave Sutton has summarised why milkmen felt this was acceptable:

> It is a simple fact of a milkman's life; you have to fiddle a little to make your books come straight at the end of the week. It is easy to forget to book a half a pound of butter or have something nicked from your float and it has to be made up somehow. Some milkmen would try overcharging the customer but that would be a road to disaster because the customer would soon find out and then you'd have an embarrassing situation trying to explain why. One way to make a little money was to under-order on some of the goods and then buy them elsewhere at a cheaper price and resell them.

In his book *Cheats at Work*, Gerry Mars explained how milk roundsmen and other delivery workers were expected to make up shortfalls:

> And it is among these occupations that there is a particularly high turnover during the first six months. After six months

the situation stabilises and workers tend to stay on, often for several years. This suggests that the first six months is a necessary period for adjustment to the mechanics of fiddling in these occupations and, more important, of the *need* to fiddle and of the self-acceptance of the role of fiddler. Those workers who cannot adjust, leave; those who can adjust find that the working environment satisfies them and they stay on.

In the seventies, after the ending of school milk for children over seven, there were still deliveries of small bottles (a third of a pint) for children under seven and children in special schools. One milkman's round included a school delivery of several crates. The milkman picked up the empties the following day. He began to notice that some of the bottles still contained milk, so he went to a quiet place and then poured the unfinished milk into a pint bottle. When he had nearly a full pint he'd slap a silver top on the pint bottle and call it a return when he got back to the dairy. Another milkman told me that he'd drink half a pint of milk and then include it among his returns as a spilt pint.

Sneaking a few pints out of the dairy could escalate into a major scam where hundreds of pints were being stolen. At one dairy a foreman and a milkman were involved in a long-term scheme and they were eventually charged with stealing nearly 600 pints. Another court case arose when a milkman in Wales charged double the standard price for twenty years when delivering to a family business.

Petty crime could escalate into something very serious. Some milkmen looked at how they could use the dairy's money for investment purposes. In one case, a milkman collected three weeks' money over one weekend before leaving his milk float in an isolated spot and taking off for Australia with the cash in his pocket.

A few milkmen used the firm's money to finance their betting habits. One milkman's round went past a bookmaker's shop five times a day because customers used to give him money to place on bets. Another used the firm's money to back favourites with substantial sums. During a bad spell he tried to conceal the losses by adding sums to his round's arrears but the dairy office staff discovered the anomaly. A former colleague remembered him:

> He started with me. He used to vault fences like he was Red Rum. But he was gambling from the outset. His got his first wage packet and said, 'My missus'll want more than that,' so he bet it all on a horse. It came up at seven to two.

Another milkman burnt his wallet, his book and his bag; he claimed to have been robbed but the police got a confession out of him. Another faked a mugging by coshing himself on the head but he didn't convince the authorities. The advent of safes in milk floats, in the late seventies and early eighties, lowered the risk of milkmen pulling off such stunts.

Other fiddles were played out in the round's book. One milkman listed fictitious addresses on his arrears sheets, suggesting there were payments outstanding, and then he pocketed that money. Another looked for empty houses and listed them as substantial bad debts, even though the milkman had never delivered any milk there. But some of the fiddles directed at the dairy were erased by the intro-duction of franchising.

The job's independence was an asset for milkmen but it made life difficult for supervisors. 'I was up to here with people,' said one foreman, holding his hand to his forehead and explaining why he'd handed in his notice. 'I had to go to court just because I happened to catch a bloke fiddling. In the end I didn't want to know, I just did not want to know.'

A milkman often knew when a customer was away on holiday, and that sort of information was a burglar's dream. Burglars spent a lot of time in pubs listening for such inside knowledge. Milkmen were generally aware that such infor-mation was sensitive, but sometimes it came out.

In 1961 a milkman from Bedford became a money-lender because some of his customers were on the skids. Unfortunately he charged 600 per cent per annum inter-est on loans and that brought him to the notice of the authorities. He was fined £25 for running a moneylending business without an excise licence.

Another milkman gained £650,000 through fraud. The milkman had registered with a Welfare Scheme to supply milk for pregnant women and mothers with young children, but many of his so-called customers didn't exist and some who did exist had never heard of the scheme.

Winning the Competition

There were competitions to see which milkman could increase his sales the most during a six-week period. Some milkmen prepared for the competition by reducing their sales in the build-up to the starting date.

On one occasion six milkmen colluded to make sure one of them would win the prize of a new car. One kept upping his order, day by day, before meeting the other five at a discreet spot where he could hand over a few crates to each of his mates. That way he was able to increase his sales from 700 pints a day to 1,500 pints a day, and it looked great on paper.

During the competition period, one of the gang was late to the dairy, so the man with 1,500 pints on board had to leave 200 pints for his mate on a street corner. Unfortunately his mate went floating past without noticing the milk. The dairy got a call and had to collect them. The dairy probably knew what was happening, but the star milkman (on paper) won the car anyway.

Out on the Round

'I've been looking for a plank that size,' one milkman told his mate, suddenly stopping the milk float next to a building site. He hopped off the van and moved the crates around to create a thin gap down the middle of the van. Then he looked around sheepishly, picked up the plank of wood, and slid it out of sight between the crates.

This was the sort of thing a milkman could do at five o'clock in the morning. One milkman told me that 5 a.m. was the time of day when he put his own personalised racing stripe down the side of any car whose owner had offended him. Another milkman used the dark mornings to his advantage if he needed new batteries for his torch. He looked around for a similar cycle lamp, checked that the batteries were working, and then switched the batteries with his own dud ones. Sometimes the dark had its advantages.

Some milkmen were looking to fiddle milk tokens and some customers were fiddling Social Security payments.

There was one block of flats in particular where we had a lot of DSS people living and when you went into those you got paid by picking up their Social Security slips. I never ever delivered any milk there. I only ever delivered pop and crisps and they paid with these milk things, which annoyed me. I said to the manager of the dairy, 'This is wrong, they can't do this.' 'Look,' he said. 'Don't say anything, we want the wheels to stay on the float.'

16

Returning to the Dairy

Please leave an extra pint of paralysed milk.

MILKMEN generally enjoyed independence on their rounds. Then came the point in the day when they returned to the dairy. This was a love–hate time. Milkmen loved the feeling of euphoria about finishing the round, driving back to base with a song on the brain at a time when other people were setting off for work, but they disliked the possibility of being overseen and regulated. On collecting days, they had the added task of counting their money and paying in at the office.

Milkmen were independent souls and the dairy was the only place where they gathered in small groups. There is no obvious collective noun for milkmen but suggestions have included a crate of milkmen, a delivery of milkmen, a depot of milkmen, a chorus of milkmen, a clatter of milkmen and a fleet of float drivers.

The Dairy

The final part of the day usually began with a milkman driving into the dairy (unless the float had to be towed in). The dairy had a sour smell. Some milkmen liked the smell of milk but many were offended by it. When dairy workers opened up metal gratings you could be sick at the smell, especially in summer. Also noticeable was the wetness underfoot. But, hey, it was no use crying over spilt milk. The dairy workers wore wellington boots and got on with the job.

Some of the dairy staff worked in a large fridge. When anyone opened the door to come in, a person inside might shout, 'Shut the door, it's getting warm in here.' Inside the dairy a cadre of workers prepared the milk.

Milkmen drove their floats into a designated area and spent a few minutes offloading crates of empty bottles (in the days before plastic bottles). Then they drove to another loading bay where a foreman checked in unsold milk. The foreman counted the returns and breakages and made a note against the round number. If you had only a few left he might give you a respectful comment ('Good, boy') and if you had a couple of crates of full pints the retort would be fierce ('Cut back on your milk tomorrow'). On collecting days milkmen parked the van and then visited the office to pay in the money. There were usually a few other milkmen around and inevitably a few stories to tell. Here are two examples:

A customer annoyed me one day. I walked across his grass and he bawled me out: 'That grass isn't for walking on.' I said I was sorry but he kept rabbiting on about it. He was the type who cut their grass without walking on it. You know the type – really superior. I said I was sorry but he didn't let up. Now I had a friend at Fison's at the time, so I said to my friend, 'Have you got anything good that kills grass?' and he gave me something. The next time I went back I sprinkled it on the customer's lawn.

One day a spare milkman was using an electric float to ferry some goods around the dairy. One of the inside workers, a dairy hand, came out from the pub and saw the float.

'How do you drive one of these?' the dairy hand asked.

'You just put your foot on this,' the milkman said. He got out of the float and when he looked back the float was moving and the dairy hand was behind the wheel, shouting, 'Which is the brake?'

The van smacked straight into the big Dodge wagon and caused a tremendous amount of damage. The roof of the milk float caved in. The dairy hand would have lost his job but the milkman signed the accident form.

Paying in at the Office

Returning to the dairy was a mixed blessing. It meant welcome relief at the end of the day and a chance to chat to colleagues, but it was also a time when a milkman learnt about a customer's complaint, a shortage in the books or a management decision which affected the round.

Collecting days were extended by the need to pay in takings at the office. Some customers posted cheques to the dairy and others called in to pay cash. In those cases the accounts office liaised with milkmen so that payments could be crossed off in the round's book.

Sometimes customers disappeared without paying their milk bill and the debt had to be written off. There might be a relevant sign in the office: 'All disputed or bad debts should be entered on this form immediately it occurs and handed into the office for action.' At the end of the financial year other signs would go up asking the milkmen to collect as much money as they could.

One old-timer used to welcome newcomers with a piece of advice: 'Stay on top of the job and don't let the job get on top of you. When it comes to shortages, there's only three places it can be – in the ledger, in the book, or in your pocket.'

Problems at the Dairy

Some milkmen disliked returning to the dairy because they might have to face a customer's complaint or some problem with the round's accounts. One customer complained about a milkman knocking on her caravan door at 8 a.m. on a collecting day and the complaint pulled in everybody up to the chief executive.

On another occasion a milkman's float nearly hit a man on a tricycle. When the tricycle rider sought a confrontation, the milkman stuck up two fingers and gave his name as 'Joe Bloggs'. Two weeks later, the milkman returned to the dairy after his round and the foreman shouted across to him: 'Hey, Joe Bloggs, the manager wants to see you.'

Other difficulties were caused by management making changes without consultation. One milkman lost two streets and he was annoyed at the loss of money from his round's expected income. He told the customers and they gave him lots of tips as he wouldn't see them again. Then the dairy management reconsidered and gave him back the two streets and he had to face the customers again. Should he return the tips?

One day a customer complained to the dairy about a milkman who'd got mad at her. That made the milkman even madder. The next day he went back to her house, picked up four yoghurts from his van and, one by one, slung them at the garage doors. Splat! Splat! Splat! Splat! All down the doors.

Other problems came when paying in. The office administration was always a good target for criticism.

'They'd let any new calls go through, bad debts and all,' moaned one milkman.

'They gave me a house of squatters once,' said another. 'I wasn't serving them.'

Sometimes the office staff took money from a customer and they weren't sure which round the house was on. Other times there was a dispute about the precise amount of cash the milkman was paying in. The dairy had two separate worlds – an outdoor life and an indoor life – and both sides had to accept the different functions. Money was the key factor in the dairy's survival. Money was what the milkman tried to earn.

Occasionally a milkman's wife would visit the dairy to pick up her sick spouse's wages. The wife could find the dairy an intimidating place. It was a male enclave with a lot of swearing and the wife would have to walk through a messy environment while being ogled by men dressed in overalls and wellington boots. When she reached the office, the milkmen counting their money might turn and stare.

A Dead-end Job?

Some milkmen hung around the dairy. It was a chance to catch up with gossip and, if there was a recreation room, an opportunity to play some darts, pool or table tennis. In their heyday dairies organised dances, competitions and outings, and there were dairy sports clubs.

> One Sunday afternoon our dairy played cricket against a pub side. The dairy team fielded first. The pub team's scorer shouted, 'Bowler's name?' and a fielder shouted back, 'Milkman.'

Returning to the dairy also provided an opportunity to have a word with the shop steward or sound off about a festering complaint. But milkmen's trade unions were difficult to galvanise because the members were a collection of individuals who were working all over the region.

The main union body was The Transport & General Workers' Union. Alex Kitson started his working career as a milkman in Edinburgh and progressed to number three in the Transport & General's leadership. In his milkman days of the 1930s Kitson recognised that it was a very hard battle just to get raincoats for the workers in Edinburgh, even though milkmen were frequently soaked and freezing cold on the rounds.

There was no shop floor, no easy way for milkmen to assemble and a big turnover of staff:

> I remember attending a union meeting in a pub during a really bad winter. About half the dairy's roundsmen had turned out, which was quite unusual. The milkmen wanted

'snow money', winter holidays and free footwear, but the debate went all over the place. I don't think we had much group cohesion. Each roundsman had his own issues with the management. Those battles took place in the foremen's office or in the manager's room, and they were usually one to one.

The money was good during the sixties and seventies because it was hard for dairies to retain staff. John Williams left his job as a teacher and enjoyed a 60 per cent wage rise by signing up as a milkman. He stayed on the milk for thirty months.

Milkmen were not located in a career structure. It was possible to gain promotion to foreman, senior foreman and management, but openings were scarce and most milkmen turned down the chance of progression because they didn't see 'foreman' as a high-status position (despite the more regular hours). 'Look at him,' said one roundsman, pointing to a foreman. 'They only gave him a foreman's job because he couldn't handle a round.'

A lifetime as a milkman was unusual. Relatively few retired from the job. Many milkmen were temporary workers who preferred to describe themselves by another trade.

Putting up the Milk Float

Back in the dairy, after a day out, there was usually a good feeling of having done a satisfactory job. Having offloaded empties and paid in money (if it was a collecting day) milkmen checked in unsold goods and put in an order for the next day's milk and goods. Frank Bingley found the advent of computers helpful for planning the order:

> Before [computers], it was a bit of a guessing game really with the old books. You could look back to the week before and see what you roughly sold on that day the previous week, but that didn't take into account the extra couple of pints that Mrs Townsend wants or the extra bag of potatoes, or the ones that were away, and things like that. And of course this computer has everything like that stored in it. When you want to know what to order for the next day, you just press a button on the computer and you get a print-out of exactly what you need to do the round, right down to the last detail, which is a phenomenal help really.

About once a week milk floats were washed down with a brush and hosepipe. The final act of the milkman's day was to drive the van into its appropriate fleet-number slot in the garage. The milkman switched off the ignition, changed the controls to 'charge' and plugged the lead into the electric socket. Then the milkman checked that the goods box was locked before collecting belongings for the journey home. To use the dairy lingo, the milkman had 'put the van up'.

Most milkmen then got into their cars and adjusted to a much-faster pace. They went home, but sometimes milk was sold through the night. I have heard of one dairy which had a coin-operated milk machine in an outside wall until the late forties. The machine dispensed loose milk into customers' jugs when the dairy was closed. In the fifties and early sixties milk could be obtained from automated vending machines at dairies.

Finally, the milkman's working day was over . . . or nearly over. 'Sometimes I lie awake wondering whether I've remembered to plug the float into the battery charger,' said one milkman.

17

Milk Containers

Please shut the gate because the birds keep pecking the tops off.

Over the last 150 years milk vessels have changed from jugs and pails (loose milk) to glass bottles (from the 1920s), cartons (in the eighties) and plastic bottles (from the late nineties). The biggest milk container is a juggernaut. There is a technology story associated with the development of milk containers but I shall bypass most of that here as it might take us too far away from milkmen.

Loose Milk

Early milk delivery saw milk poured into jugs on the doorstep. This was followed by churns with draw-off taps, but they were liable to rust and leak. Then came cylindrical mushroom-lidded churns in the late twenties. At that time London still had cow-keepers who delivered milk in pails or sold it straight from the hatch. Some cow-keepers went on to bottle their milk and start proper dairies, but most sold loose milk. In the twenties and thirties, dairies moved from loose milk to glass bottles, albeit at different paces.

In the nineties, Mike Hull, co-editor or editor of *Milk Bottle News* from 1984 to 2000, wrote about loose milk:

> Personally, I remember, in 1940, a milk float with a churn and a row of dripping measures coming through the streets of a small Norfolk town, but most people in the town had their milk delivered in bottles. A newspaper cutting from Dave Hallett shows that there was loose milk delivery even in London during the Blitz. Two East London friends swear that they can remember carts with loose milk after World War Two; while Tony Pickford assures me that in Derbyshire villages milk was still sold from pails in 1950. Mrs Crew, whose husband ran the dairy at Pontings Farm, Chalford, near Stroud, says that two pails of milk on a yoke were carried by women during the war through the village to their customers' houses, until her husband managed to get a Land Rover after the War. Jeff Small can remember unbottled milk being delivered after the War. David Pimm has written that his mother's dairy used serving buckets, and a few bottles, into the early fifties. He also said that Pallance Dairy was selling unbottled milk in Cowes as late as 1956; many customers did not trust the bottled stuff.

Some traditionalists continued to serve loose milk. A 'soor milk cairt' operated in the Muirkirk, Ayrshire, until 1972 or 1973, and as late as 1985 there were stories about elderly farmers selling milk straight from the churn.

Glass Bottles

The first glass bottles appeared around 1880, and aqua and coloured glass bottles came in about 1910. The Coventry Co-operative Society bottled milk in 1913, but it wasn't until the twenties, when heat-treatment legislation came in, that glass bottles became more common in milk delivery. Milk prams were converted to carry crates of bottles and new prams were designed.

The early history of milk bottles includes a long quest to find a suitable seal to keep the milk safe from dust, dirt and foreign objects. Sterilised milk came in bottles with thin necks. 'Society is like a bottle of sterilised milk,' wrote one graffiti artist, many decades later. 'There's plenty of room at the bottom, but not much of an opening at the top.'

In the inter-war period some suppliers used fibre caps and paper caps, and others used crimped metal crown tops. From the twenties to the early fifties most bottles were sealed by cardboard discs inset into the rim. Cardboard caps carried messages:

> LONG LIVE THE KING
> *Milk is the path to health*
> DON'T PLAY ON THE ROAD
> *A Merry Christmas*

The main problem with cardboard discs was that the pouring rim was exposed to dust and dirt. This hygiene problem was solved by the gradual introduction of foil caps. For years people were able to identify the type of milk by the colour of its cap: silver top was pasteurised milk with cream on top; gold top was milk from Channel

Island cows; green top was unpasteurised milk; and red top had cream mixed with the milk.

During the 1926 General Strike provincial farmers brought milk into London and set up a base in Hyde Park for distributing milk to needy residents. By the end of the operation Hyde Park was awash with churns, so a new organisation, Milk Vessel Recovery (MVR), was set up. MVR established regional depots, used lorries to collect 'foreign' vessels from dairies, cleaned the bottles and redistributed the 'foreigners' to rightful owners. A dairy could be fined for using another dairy's bottles.

According to the trivia book published in installments from 1937–38 *Everybody's Enquire Within*, about 250 million milk bottles were in use in 1936 and over thirteen million were lost each year. Some were stolen, others broken, and many discarded in places such as beaches, camp sites, fairgrounds, sports grounds and the countryside. In 1936 about 1.5 million bottles were reclaimed by local authorities via dustbinmen. Over fifty years later, when cartons were established, the MVR system was redundant and it became the vogue for dairies to put any remaining 'foreigners' in a cullet skip.

Cardboard caps were phased out by the 1949 Milk Regulations and 1950 Hygiene Act. Thereafter containers had to be tightly closed and securely fastened with a cap (or cover) overlapping the lip of the container. This paved the way for the almost total dominance of glass bottles and their aluminium-foil caps. Half-pints were the most common bottle types in the thirties, when there were two deliveries a day, but they had disappeared by the eighties, and quart bottles went the same way. In the early forties quarts formed 10 per cent of the sales, pints 50 per cent, half-pints 30 per cent, and third-of-a-pint school bottles the rest.

An empty milk bottle on a doorstep is one of the greatest symbols of recycling ever constructed. The number of journeys made by a glass bottle – known in the trade as 'trippage' – was a very important issue. Figures varied from forty to eighty journeys during the thirties and forties, and in 1943 Arthur Guy Enock reported an average of sixty-three journeys. But those were the days of heavier, less destructible bottles.

In the post-war period some neighbourhoods had much lower trippage figures than others. After the 1981 riots, when milk bottles were used for Molotov cocktails or as fighting weapons, dairies were asked to notify the Metropolitan Police if lots of milk bottles disappeared as that might signify more riots to come. Other customers kept bottles – you might say 'stole bottles' – and used them as flower vases, rolling pins or, in the case of sterilised bottles, for home-brewed beer.

The weight of glass milk bottles was much reduced over the years and trippage figures more than halved between 1971 and 2001. A bottle of milk weighed about nineteen ounces in 1938. In the sixties the Co-op (CWS) continued with seventeen-ounce bottles made by United Glass, but other dairies changed to fourteen-ounce bottles. The first mention of the 'pintie', a short, squat milk bottle carrying a pint, came in 1968. Pinties could weigh as little as six or eight ounces. They used less space when stacked in crates and were cheaper to buy. Murchie of Edinburgh started using the pintie in 1974, and Unigate followed shortly afterwards. One milkman remembered their introduction:

When the pinties first came out people started calling them 'the dumpy' and the dairy industry put out this blurb – 'do not call it the dumpy, people will think that they've got to throw it away' – so they called it 'the pintie'. The difference in the weight was incredible – the old taller bottles were twice as heavy. And the other big change that made a difference to the weight that you carried was the crates, because when I started it was all wire crates and then it went on to plastic crates. Wire crates used to be lethal, bits of wire sticking out the side of them. The plastic crates were a lot better, a lot lighter, much easier to handle, and it was less weight on the van as well, not so noisy.

Design guru Sir Terence Conran named the classic glass milk bottle among his ten favourite items:

Everything is absolutely right about milk bottles. I like the noise they make when they are placed outside on the door-step. They are a superb piece of recyclable packaging and I like the feel of them. On top of that they are aesthetically pleasing enough to be able to place on the table, which you certainly couldn't do with a milk carton.

The aesthetic quality of milk bottles has attracted a number of artists. Charlotte Hughes Martin bought bottles from the milkman, engraved farmyard designs on them and left them randomly on doorsteps. Glass designer Sam Sweet produced cut-glass milk bottles in lead crystal with individual designs. And Michael Craig-Martin created a piece of art with fifteen bottles on a sloping shelf, all partly filled with water in such a way that it created a level horizontal water line.

Messages on a Bottle

Glass bottles were on loan to the customer. The right of ownership was reinforced by messages stating the dairy's name. The tone of this message could be polite ('Please rinse and return'), officious ('This bottle to be washed and returned') or regulatory ('2d charged for bottle if not returned'). Here are other examples of messages about the ownership of bottles:

DON'T THROW ME AWAY, I'LL BRING YOUR MILK ANOTHER DAY.
This bottle costs three-pence, It's as precious as 'owt, If tha' breaks it or lose it, We're working for nowt.

USE OF PLASTIC IS RATHER DRASTIC, USING GLASS IS FIRST CLASS
It would be a sin to put me in a bin – please rinse and return.

IF BY CHANCE I SHOULD ROAM, RINSE ME OUT AND SEND ME HOME.
The milk is thine, the bottle mine.

ON EACH NEW DAY YOUR MILKMAN COLLECTS, BOTTLES BY THE SCORE, BUT WHAT WILL PLEASE HIM MOST OF ALL? YOUR EMPTIES BY THE DOOR.
Please rinse and return it! Thank you.

Through the rationing days of the forties and early fifties, it was very important for customers to return bottles. The message to the customer was reinforced: PLEASE RINSE AND RETURN, ROUNDSMAN IS CHARGED FOR THE BOTTLE.

Milk Containers

Early bottles often had pictures of landscapes and buildings, such as Grantham parish church or Gloucester Cathedral. Later, dairy poets constructed pithy ditties about the quality of their milk. In the forties and fifties Clyde Higgs in Leamington Spa was a contender for Lactose Poet Laureate:

CLEOPATRA SHOULD HAVE HAD, HER BATH IN BEST
CLYDE HIGGS, FOUR HUNDRED PINTAS EVERY DAY,
AND EXTRA FOR THE WIGS.
Tots and teens, Grow like beans, When their mums, Fill their tums, With Clyde Higgs milk.

CLYDE HIGGS MILK IN A CUPPA, LIVENS UP THE
BREAD AND BUTTER.
Oh Jubilee, Oh Jubilation, we drink a toast across the nation, for twenty-five years of grace and charm, purest milk from Clyde Higgs farm.

HIGGS MILK, HIGGS HEGGS, KEEP THE WORKERS ON
THEIR LEGS.
Clyde Higgs milk in a bottle really ought to be in your throttle.

Other slogan writers tried hard during the post-war period:

NO MILK FOR SEVEN DAYS MAKES ONE WEAK.
Drink it neat for the tastiest treat.

A BOTTLE A DAY KEEPS THE DOCTOR AWAY.
The cows that graze round Snitterfield, give a most delicious yield.

No Milk Today

YOU CAN WHIP OUR CREAM BUT YOU
CAN'T BEAT OUR MILK.
Best by test.

ONE EXTRA BOTTLE A DAY KEEPS YOU
HEALTHY AND GAY.
Drink it neat for the tastiest treat.

YOUR CAT MIAOWS AT MILK FROM OUR COWS.

Milk Bottle Collectors

As a boy Steve Wheeler didn't particularly like the taste of milk, but as an adult he became a big collector of British milk bottles. His private museum, at the back of his house in Malvern, Worcestershire, holds nearly 20,000 bottles in buildings he has constructed himself. His collection began one day in the early eighties while walking in the Brecon Beacons:

I found this milk bottle just lying there and I put it in my rucksack. It was Goodwin's Dairy of Whitchurch in Shropshire. The thing that fascinated me was the telephone design on the side with the old 'hold up to your ear and wind' phone which was obviously in fashion well before this bottle was made, and the dairy had kept that design. I made a few enquiries and found out that the dairy was closing down. When I did more research I found that a lot of dairies were closing down and their bottles were vanishing, so I started getting modern bottles from any dairies I could find. I remember getting my hundredth bottle and thinking, Yes, I've arrived, a hundred bottles. And it's literally gone from there.

Milk Containers

Milkmen were doing their job when they collected empty bottles from doorsteps, but milk-bottle collectors were hobbyists who picked up milk bottles from anywhere except the doorstep. Milk bottles could travel hundreds of miles. Naomi and Mike Hull found a good spot at Stockton Wood, Wiltshire, with lots of discarded bottles within throwing distance of the A303 road. They reckoned the reservoir of milk bottles formed because the site was about halfway between London and the seaside resorts of Devon. The Hulls' collection reached 13,000 bottles by 1986 and they arranged them by traditional county names. Eventually they passed on their large collection and kept a small number of treasures.

Steve Wheeler, a retired exporter of Hereford cattle, learnt to search for old milk bottles when dairies closed down. He found them in allotment sheds, basements and under floorboards.

I've been in some places and the bottles were still in the cellar from the forties or fifties, underneath the solicitor's office. The solicitor put a filing cabinet against the door to the cellar and never went down there. I had the nod and they said I could have a look, and the bottles were down there, caked in dust. I got some super bottles out of there.

Wheeler's museum includes special Electrolux milk bottles used in showroom fridges, very rare litre and litre-and-a-half bottles, and bottles advertising funeral directors. The lettering on the bottles could be acid-etched, embossed, sandblasted or, later, silkscreen printed. Overall, he found collecting milk bottles a very satisfying hobby:

The bottles have all got stories. The great thing from my point of view – and it's incidental to collecting bottles – is all the people that I meet. That is great, especially when people tell me about milk bottles and the production of them. I like the social history, I like the designs, and the advertising they put on the bottles. I find it fascinating about the number of times it went back and forth from the milkman to the customer. The secret is that if you want to collect something then make sure it is fun and doesn't cost anything.

The Milk Bottle Collectors' Society magazine, *Milk Bottle News*, began in 1984. It featured bottles from various sources and, as we have seen, a variety of slogans. The collectors are much in demand by theatre groups looking for milk-bottle props for plays set in a certain period, such as Ronald Harwood's *The Dresser*, which takes place during World War Two.

Milk Campaigns

British people had confidence in milk in the fifties, when evidence showed that it improved physiques, health and academic performance. Poster advertisements featured a milkman ('You have to be made of the right stuff to deliver the white stuff'), a nurse ('Pick up a midday pinta') and the comedian Norman Wisdom ('You'll feel a lot better if you drink milk').

In the fifties the Milk Marketing Board's poster girl was Zoey Newton, who was only 5ft tall and weighed little more than seven stones. The diminutive Newton's wholesome image and bubbly personality enthused people and she was associated with slogan-backed marketing campaigns such as DRINKA PINTA MILKA DAY. In the late 1960s the Milk Marketing Board targeted children (GO TO SCHOOL ON A PINTA).

The big campaign of the eighties was based on GOTTA LOTTA BOTTLE. When Oxford United Football Club manager Maurice Evans saw the slogan at Wembley Stadium, halfway through the 1986 Milk Cup Final, he motivated his players by asking them if they had the bottle to win the match (which they did).

The slogan of the new century was THE WHITE STUFF. Many other catch phrases were developed at national or local level:

> *Drive safely on milk.*
> DRINK YOUR HEALTH IN MILK EVERY DAY.
> *Are you getting enough?*
> MILKMEN DO IT ON YOUR DOORSTEP.
> *If you need a little extra ask your milkman.*
> WATCH OUT, A HUMPHREY'S ABOUT.
> *Have you got the bottle?*
> MILK AND DRIVING – ALL SURVIVING

Steve Wheeler recognised the value of local advertising for local dairies:

When the bigger dairies started to take over from smaller dairies in the sixties, seventies and eighties, the smaller dairies were on the edge of going out of business. Then someone had a bright idea: Why don't we advertise local products? Whether it's the local garage, the person doing estate agency or a florist, the milk bottle could be printed at the cost of the advertiser. So they got a bottle for free. And this kept smaller dairies going for a long time.

The Milk Marketing Board and major dairies did their best to arrest the sector's decline. Bottle slogans moved from promoting the milk itself to milk-related products such as drinking chocolate, breakfast cereals, yoghurts and bread sauces. Customers were sometimes given gifts, such as recipe books or cereal bowls, to encourage them to buy more milk-related goods.

In the sixties various winning FA Cup Final football teams celebrated their success with milk, and the Dairy Council sponsored football's Milk Cup between 1982 and 1986. Cycling's Milk Race was sponsored by the Milk Marketing Board between 1958 and 1993, when the board was disbanded, but the race was resurrected in 2013 with sponsorship from the Dairy Council and the Milk Marketing Forum.

Cartons

The competition between cartons and bottles began in the post-war period. Express Dairies had introduced paper cartons in 1926, but the idea proved unpopular with housewives. In the fifties, however, British entrepreneurs looked towards New York City, where 85 per cent of milk was sold in cartons. Designers were set to work on cartons but customers still had mixed feelings about them. Those in favour stressed a number of advantages: cartons could be used in Automatic Vending Machines (AVMs); they took up half the space of bottles on a milk float; broken cartons were less dangerous than broken bottles; cleaning and replacing bottles was a costly process; and bottles could litter the countryside. But the anti-carton brigade argued in favour of bottles. Cartons created a bigger countryside litter problem because people knew they were designed for one trip, and, besides, everyone had trouble opening a carton. In 1968, Sunderland's cleansing superintendent told the annual conference of the Institute of Public Cleansing that replacing glass bottles with disposable containers would create a serious refuse-disposal problem.

In 1960, Lord Rayleigh's Dairies changed from glass bottles to cartons (Tetrapaks) but the milkmen's customers didn't like them. The 1963 Weights and Measures Bill allowed sixpenny cartons to be on sale in automatic vending machines (AVMs) but they had to carry clear 'AVM-only' labels. Stroud Creamery introduced milk in cartons in 1964, but this wasn't financially viable. In the sixties, therefore, the initial winner was the milk bottle. Bottles were heavier than cartons but the customers seemed happy to continue with them, and the doorstep delivery service was much loved.

In 1968, Pricerite became the first supermarket to stock UHT milk in cartons. The percentage of carton sales of milk increased from 5 per cent in the early seventies to 16 per cent in the early eighties. But the Milk Marketing Board's control kept carton prices higher than bottle prices.

Even in the nineties, though, people had trouble opening cartons, especially people with hand disabilities. When they opened a carton it might mean milk on their clothes. Scissors could help but they could also cause accidents, especially when frustrated people tried to stick the scissors through the packaging. The Rausing brothers made a fortune out of Tetrapak carton manufacturing and at one time they were the richest people in Britain, but, as *The Times* columnist Giles Coren once pointed out, just imagine how rich they'd have become if the cartons had worked.

In the early nineties Adrian Lawton wrote an under-graduate thesis about reusable containers such as glass bottles. Lawton found that supermarkets acknowledged environmental issues – 'We have been at the forefront of commerce in the development of environmental initia-tives over the past decade,' said Tesco – but they showed little interest in recycling bottles. Environmental groups supported various schemes, including litter taxes, bans on one-trip containers and recycling, but retailers and drinks companies were unwilling to stock glass bottles. And there was little chance of governments agreeing to such schemes. Instead politicians in office generally supported profitable one-trip packaging.

In 1995, Michael J Holmes wrote to the *Independent on Sunday* to point out that the milkman's customers were subsidising supermarkets. His argument was that there was a significant burden associated with disposing of plastic supermarket milk cartons and that this burden was being met by taxpayers through refuse collection and the cost of landfill sites. Meanwhile some milkmen were still collecting empty glass bottles for recycling in the dairies.

Milk cartons successfully caught people's eye in one way. In 1997 the National Missing Persons Helpline liaised with the supermarket chain Iceland to put photographs of missing children on milk cartons in an attempt to reunite more families. In 2002 cartons of milk were used for messages to reduce Christmas crime. They were also used to promote an unmarried Welsh farmer's chances of meeting the woman of his dreams.

Plastic Milk Bottles

In 1983, Joe Ashton, the MP for Bassetlaw, South Yorkshire, was concerned about a possible shift from milk bottles to cartons or other vessels. Speaking in the House of Commons, he pointed out that his constituency had the largest milk-bottle manufacturers in the country, perhaps even in Europe, and 460 people were employed in the making of 100 million bottles a year, a third of the country's milk-bottle production.

Ashton was right to be concerned. By the mid-nineties supermarkets were phasing out milk bottles and cartons, and they were replacing them with plastic bottles with screw tops. These plastic replicas of milk bottles proved more acceptable to members of the public, and the growth of recycling schemes for cardboard and plastic helped to alleviate some of the environmental issues caused by cartons. About 35 per cent of plastic bottles were recycled, but comparing plastic bottles with glass milk bottles for recycling benefits is a complex matter.

The milkmen increasingly delivered cheaper, lighter, one-trip, plastic pint containers rather than traditional bottles. Plastic bottles meant that the milk had to be homogenised, so customers lost the cream-on-top presentation of silver-top milk, and some people thought the milk tasted different. In 1974, 94 per cent of milk was put into glass bottles. By August 2008, about 80 per cent of milk went into plastic containers, 11 per cent into glass bottles and 9 per cent in cartons. The glass bottle share fell to 4 per cent by 2014.

Many customers preferred four- or two-pint plastic bottles to one-pint glass bottles.

Plastic bottles could be squarer or more rectangular than pint bottles, and that meant they stacked better. They also fitted better in lorries and household fridges. In September 2014, Dairy Crest announced it would close its Hanworth bottling plant in two years' time and convert to plastic bottles. By 2015 there were only three companies making milk bottles in the United Kingdom – Rockware, United Glass and Redfearn.

18

Family Life

No milk today: Is it a boy or a girl?

A MILKMAN'S family sometimes found it difficult to predict when the milkman would be home. The normal working week was supposed to be forty to forty-eight hours, but many milkmen were out for longer than that. When they arrived home they were often suffering from fatigue.

Physical Health

'Tell me a milkman who isn't tired when he's finished for the day,' a milkman told a group of his colleagues. Well, nobody could tell him one.

The cumulative tiredness came to rest in the family home. Most milkmen kept going until their days off. The early starts seemed disruptive to some people's body rhythm. Others stopped playing sport because that was more of the same physicality.

No Milk Today

The family home had a particular milkman smell. The odour of stale milk seeped into jeans, gloves, coats and nostrils. Girlfriends and wives didn't always kiss the milkman goodbye in the morning.

'My normally awake and active husband was asleep in the chair by 8.30 p.m. in readiness for a 3.30 a.m. start,' one wife told me about her husband's short spell as a milkman. 'His energy for domestic jobs was nil.'

Here are other stories of tiredness:

The first six months were fine, and then I got gradually worn down. I realised I was going downhill physically. I became so used to feeling rough. Headaches. Eyes hurting. You'd get into bed and your body would be still going, tingling all over. I'd take Anadins. Sometimes I hardly spent any wages. I was in bed when I wasn't working.

My mate was a big shit-stirrer. He was another milkman. He had his afternoon sleep and then he came round to my house and said to the wife, 'He's not sleeping, is he? He's always sleeping.'

Back home I'd doze off and wake up in the middle of a dream where the dairy manager was telling me I was £100 short in balancing the book. My home routine varied with the weather. I'd stay up through a sunny day, and I'd go to bed if it was a dull afternoon. Friends told me that I was carrying a hazy, lazy, sleepy look. Sometimes I'd dream of ones and twos, and other milk orders.

Getting home there were so many things to deal with. It was a matter of deciding on the order of things – a soak in the bath, food, drink, sleep or washing clothes? When I looked at myself in the bath I noticed chubby fingers with scars on them. I saw the bruises on my thighs from the crates and the van. My back and shoulders ached. And I felt other aches and strains from all the twisting and turning. My resistance got really low.

One time I woke up at midnight and felt awful. I was shivery and my whole body felt strained. I got up at 4.20 and phoned the dairy. I told the foreman I was unwell. 'Leave your book on the doorstep,' he said.

Some milkmen suffered from knobbly fingers, known as *granuloma annulare* (GA). Workers in other jobs suffered from GA but usually only in one hand; milkmen could get it in *both* hands because that was how they carried bottles.

New milkmen sometimes got cramp in their legs or their muscles tightened. Jean Cogar was one of many who struggled at first. In the first few weeks she ached all over and had to bandage her ankles. But she soon gained expertise lifting crates. She did the job for years.

Strange Hours
Milkmen worked unsociable hours in the sense that they got up in the night and did parts of the round in the dark. But their hours could be very sociable because they could see spouses, children, relations and friends during the day-time and evenings. They could also watch their children on sports days and help them with their homework.

I'd been a farm-worker and then spent five years as a cab-driver. While I was working long hours on the taxi, I came home one day and heard one of my children say, 'Daddy, when are you going to take me out – I never see you.' The next day I decided I would watch my kids grow up, so I became a milkman.

I was home by one, early for a Friday, and I got some kip before my evening out. Sometimes the hours could be overly social. People were around in the mornings, the afternoons, and the evenings. My sleep was often and shallow, and it always seemed like morning. I ate four breakfasts every day.

One time I worked thirteen successive weeks. I was considering working my next holiday too. Then the wife told me, 'If you do, it'll be no sex, no food.'

My major sleep is four or five hours in the afternoon. It's a bit of a nightmare in the summer when all the kids are on holiday and they're screaming out the front and you're trying to get off to sleep. But normally you are so tired you just nod off straight away.

A new way of working, in the eighties and nineties, meant many milkmen started the job at midnight or 1 a.m. Mike Yeo was a good example. In his early thirties, he was off to bed about 5 p.m. and that was earlier than the bedtimes of his four young children. But Yeo was back home by 10.30 a.m. and that gave him more time with his kids. He could do things with his children during school holidays. Many other milkmen saw this as an attractive side of the job. They enjoyed seeing their kids grow up.

Husband and Wife

When milkman Richard Smith married Carly Taylor, in 2013, the wedding took place after a heavy snowfall. Carly's father had planned to drive his daughter to the registrar's office but his vehicle was snowed in. The bride-to-be appealed to the local media for help and a volunteer collected Carly in a 4 x 4 vehicle. Meanwhile, the groom borrowed his work transport and arrived for the ceremony. The couple drove away from the register office in Richard Smith's milk float (JUST MARRIED).

Here is another tale of a milk float substituting for a wedding car. This event took place in the mid-fifties:

> In Gerard Street we had a Co-op milkman called Albert. In Grey Street there was a woman who lived over the brush [out of wedlock] with a man. They had a son called Johnny who had a permanent nasal discharge and was known to the rest of us kids as 'Candle fat'. Anyway, she contracted cancer and decided to get married to give Johnny an official father. They were very poor so on the appointed day Albert the milkman gave the woman a lift to the register office in his milk float. I can see her now, in the cab, a frail little woman carrying a small posy of flowers. Milkmen performed many social functions.

Some milkmen's wives helped with the round. John Prout found that the unusual hours made it possible for him to contribute to the care of his four children, and his wife Veronica reciprocated by helping to deliver the milk. Jimmy Jones and his wife were well known in the City of London. They delivered milk and ran a cafe for lunchtime meals.

Other husband-and-wife teams shared the work. In one case the man got up at 3 a.m. and started the milk round. Then his wife rose at 5 a.m. to do a cleaning job. They each returned to the house about 7 a.m. and had a proper breakfast. Then they went out together and finished the milk round. This arrangement was made easier by the franchise system and self-employment.

The Family Budget

In the sixties and seventies, a milkman's wage was good enough to sustain a family. The bonuses included commission, a bit of fiddling and tips. But it became harder for milkmen in the eighties and nineties. The terms of employment changed, customers shifted their loyalties from doorstep delivery to supermarkets, and milkmen had to adjust to the franchise ethic.

Finishing the round by nine or ten o'clock allowed milkmen time to supplement their income with some moonlighting – decorating, landscape gardening, building, window-cleaning, taxi-driving, plumbing, etc. One milkman told me that he used his float as a removals van.

The big financial bonus came with Christmas tips. Many milkmen stayed until the Christmas gratuity season and then left at the start of the New Year. A big exodus – maybe 10 or 20 per cent of staff – took place early in the New Year.

Leaving the Job

Milkmen who left within months of starting the job blamed the strange hours as a major cause of discontent. It was supposed to be a forty-eight-hour week, although a high proportion of milkmen worked longer than that.

The dairy could have done more to help. Yes, they explained about the early mornings and the hours but I am not sure they recruited people who were physically fit and capable. People dropped out because they weren't really prepared for it.

Essentially there was too little preparation for what you were expected to do. The senior staff were so familiar with the job that they no longer pointed out the basic issues. Half the people who packed it in would have made satisfactory roundsmen in time.

I was affected, physically and mentally, by both the physical work and the bad sleep pattern. I felt all right on the round, all rosy-cheeked, and I certainly got fit. Then, after nine months, I couldn't cope. It was too long a day. I never slept in though. I was used to getting up and getting out and about.

Maybe the job was more sustainable when there was a family tradition. David Hargreaves of Bolton took over the family business at seventeen. His father and grandfather had also been milkmen. For some it was all they'd ever known.

In the sixties, a young bespectacled Mancunian called Freddie Garrity was working as a milkman while playing in a pop group called Freddie and the Dreamers. When Garrity heard of a possible BBC Manchester audition, he rounded up the Dreamers and drove his milk float as fast as he could to Television Centre, Manchester. The group went on to hit the big time. Another milkman-singer was Matt Munro (real name Terry Parsons), whose record 'Born Free' was a major hit.

Milkmanship was good training for a career in boxing . . . or was it the other way round? Wally Smith, Dick Richardson, Freddie Mills and Andy Till all combined boxing with delivering milk. Till, known as 'the Northolt milkman', became the British light-heavyweight champion in the nineties. In 1993 he described how he'd integrated his two worlds:

> I've been a milkman for seven years, getting up at 4.30 in the morning. It's a form of training, I suppose. I'm out in all weather, sun, rain, frost – the lot. I dream of the day when I've earned enough money from boxing to be able to give it up and have a lay-in.

Eddie Hapgood, a milkman during the mid-1920s, later captained the Arsenal and England football teams. Ron Staniforth, a horse-and-cart milkman, signed as a professional footballer, at twenty-two, and later played for England. Doing a milk round also sparked the comic genius of Ronald Shiner, Benny Hill, Jimmy Tarbuck, Harry Enfield and Brendon O'Carroll.

19

Retirement

On holiday next week.

MANY milkmen came and went within months, but some spent much of their working life in the trade. Veterans faced a period of adjustment when it came to retirement. Their new life usually started with a farewell party, a suitable tribute and a present from customers. Local newspapers honoured these retirements with headlines such as 'I'VE HAD A CRATE TIME' or 'MILKMAN'S GOT THE BOTTLE'.

The decision to retire was a big one. The reasons could be injury, a general world-weariness, a desire to spend more time with the family or some other significant incident.

When Charlie Edmonds retired in 1982, it was because new ministry regulations meant he would have to change all the labels on his products. Edmonds had started delivering milk aged thirteen, in 1923, after his father had

had a heart attack. His dairy didn't bottle their milk until the early sixties. His round grew smaller and smaller, and by the time he retired he was delivering thirty-two pints to twenty-one houses. The regulatory change was the final straw.

Here is another veteran milkman speaking about his retirement:

> I did the job for forty-five years. I started in June 1966 and England won the World Cup the month after I'd started. I used to say I'll keep doing the job until we win the World Cup again, but I gave up the job in 2011, when I thought they were never going to win it . . . Deciding to retire was a combination of things. I was nearly sixty-five, the family had been nagging me for ages to give it up, and it was getting less and less viable. I thought, That's it, I've had enough. It's not an old man's game. It is physically hard work. After I retired I kept waking up at 3 a.m. for the first year.

Retirement Parties

Brian Tilley was sixty-five when he retired from Kirby & West Dairies in 2004. He had done the same round for thirty years. At a party to thank him for his contribution to the community, he was given several presents, including an aerial photograph of his milk round.

One of his customers, Malcolm Dilks, paid Tilley a great tribute: 'We thank Brian for being a kindly uncle to our children and grandchildren, for spoiling our dogs with biscuits – that may be a clever ploy – for keeping a concerned eye on our frail residents, and for exciting our womenfolk when he wears his shorts.'

When Roy Burton left his Thames Ditton round, in 1998, his twenty-seven years of service was celebrated by a surprise party at the Angel pub. Burton's customers clubbed together and gave him a whisky decanter, a set of glasses and a bottle of whisky. Sometimes customers collected money for the milkman to buy what he wished. Other times it was a carefully considered gift. Malcolm McDougal was presented with an engraved silver salver by villagers after thirty-three years on 'a mobile neighbourhood watch scheme'. Another milkman was honoured with a street named after him – Godfrey Close in Radford Semele, Warwickshire.

Very occasionally the natural order was reversed and someone became a milkman after retirement from another job. Schoolteacher Pat Gater's retirement present from her colleagues and pupils was the opportunity to drive a milk float. The present was kept a secret until her final day. Then she was given a white jacket and a milkman's hat. As she drove the milk float around the playground, the school loudspeakers blared out 'Ernie (The Fastest Milkman in the West)'.

Some retired milkmen hung on to their working clothes. They came in handy for fancy-dress parties.

Readjustment

'When I was working, people would talk about all these TV programmes they liked, and I wouldn't know what the heck they were talking about,' said Sid Hogg, who retired in 2009. 'I can catch up with all that now.'

Hogg delivered over ten million pints of milk in his career. Halfway through he took a week's holiday, his only holiday in forty-three years as a milkman. His North Yorkshire route covered Burton-in-Lonsdale and the Benthams.

Some retiring milkmen looked forward to lie-ins, but others didn't expect their routine to change. When John Prout retired aged sixty-eight in 2000, after thirty years delivering to Coaley, Gloucestershire, he told his local newspaper that he wouldn't be staying in bed as he'd been getting up early for too long to lie in. Julian Kearvell of Tunbridge Wells joked that his wife would have to get used to waking up next to him again now that he had retired. Kearvell reckoned he had delivered 4.5 million pints in a thirty-year career.

Here are four more milkmen talking about the transition to retirement:

I will miss the contact with people. I have seen families grow up. You see the dawn break every morning and at the weekend you see the youngsters, who have been out nightclubbing, on their way home, still out in the mornings.

I have made some great friends and have been able to watch families grow up. I will probably still get up at 1 a.m. and nip downstairs to watch a film or two on TV. I am so used to getting up now. I don't think I would know what a lie-in is!

I will always treasure my years as a milkman, but now I'm looking forward to being able to spend more time with my family. I want to start fishing again and have been targeted with a lot of decorating and gardening jobs. I will probably be busier now than I was when I was at work. At first I wasn't looking forward to it and didn't want to retire, but my knees have gone and I have to pack up.

I have been really lucky because my customers are so nice. I can't praise them enough. I have grown up with them and watched their children and grandchildren grow. I'll miss them all like mad. It has been a real wrench to leave. I hope I served them well and never let them down.

Second Careers

Rotherham milkman Edwin Wraith had a ready-made second career for when he retired. One day in 1980, when he was fifty-two, he slipped on his milk round and broke his ankle. It was six months before he was fit for work and during that time he started painting and drawing. He went on to exhibit and sell his art work. The ankle fracture turned out to be a lucky break.

Reg Gauge's retirement from United Dairies lasted nearly forty years, until he passed away in his sleep when he was 104 years old. At the start of his career Gauge delivered milk from a cart pulled by a horse called Joey. Gauge lived in Lewisham and worked the Lee Green round for thirty-nine years before retiring in 1974. Then he played bowls until he was into his late nineties. At one point he put up a challenge that he could beat any person over ninety at the game.

Other retired milkmen became passionate about a hobby. In a series of letters in a national newspaper, correspondents suggested all sorts of possible pursuits for a retiring milkman, including bell-ringing, bird-watching, whist, bridge, golf and collecting milk bottles. Tony Geake of Exeter started collecting milk bottles because he enjoyed the adverts on bottles (e.g. 'Eggs are smashing for breakfast'). Other retired milkmen thought that collecting milk bottles was too much like doing the job – they'd already been collecting empty milk bottles for years.

Retired Milk Floats

Electric milk floats could retire too. A lot of them became available in the eighties and nineties when customers deserted the milkman, the number of rounds was reduced and diesel vans were needed to cover larger territories. When Lester McDermott retired, he continued to drive a milk float around Sherborne, Dorset as it was his preferred method of transport. In the seventies Keith Moon, drummer for The Who, bought a milk float for his home in Chertsey, Surrey.

Purpose-designed electric vehicles can be seen at hospitals, airports and rail stations. In the past they have also been designed for fuel delivery and street-cleaning. Second-hand milk floats have been put to all sorts of uses, including ferrying goods around industrial estates, as mobile community shops, delivering local vegetable boxes and transporting builders' supplies. They have been used for produce delivery by organisations such as Rachel's Organic and Arthur Street Trading Company.

Milk floats have also featured in charity rides. In *Three Men in a Float*, Dan Kieran and Ian Vince wrote about three weeks in 2007 when they used their 1958 electric milk float to travel from England's east coast (Lowestoft) to west coast (Land's End). The float had delivered milk in

Oxford for over forty years before working at Birmingham Airport. In the early twenty-first century the vehicle was still reliable but needed daily thirty-two amp charges from the equivalent of a cooker socket. Finding a suitable electric charge was a daily quest, but Kieran, Vince and their electrician Prasanth Visweswaran succeeded in completing their trip.

Kieran and Vince had bought their milk float, nicknamed 'The Mighty One', from Stuart Billingshurst, who had used it for commuting to work. Billingshurst had discovered that his journey took about the same amount of time in a milk float as by car because all vehicles were similarly held up, but, unlike cars and lorries, milk floats used no extra energy when stationary at traffic lights. A few years later, Billingshurst and his partner bought a sixties milk float and converted it into a bed-and-breakfast hotel room with a double bed, shower, toilet and lounge area.

Milk Dynasties
The Bryant family served the public around Warmley and Kingswood, on the outskirts of Bristol, for about seventy-five years. There were three generations of independent milkmen – Alan Bryant, Denis Bryant (Alan's father) and Fred Bryant (Alan's grandfather) – and the dynasty lasted from 1935, when Fred Bryant arrived in the area, to 2010, when Alan Bryant retired. Typically, however, the round fell from 600 customers in 1980 to 300 in 2010, when it was taken over by Dairy Crest. The drop in the number of customers was caused solely by natural wastage – death or migration – rather than through any dissatisfaction.

Alan Bryant described his milk heritage to the *Bristol Evening Post*:

> My grandfather, Fred Bryant, owned the dairy farm that stood on this very spot – Crown Farm. They moved here from Goose Green in Siston [a mile away] and during the first two or three days several people asked if there would be milk deliveries to neighbouring farms. My grandfather, who farmed the fifty-five-acre piece of land, agreed that my dad, who was fifteen at the time, could deliver milk in between his other duties. That's how the round was born, with Dad walking around the district with a large milk can. Soon after, he bought a bicycle with a milk-can on each handlebar. [During World War Two] he used to carry his Home Guard helmet and rifle with him on his rounds, just in case.

Alan Bryant was four when he started helping his dad and his siblings with the milk round. He was paid sixpence a day. He worked with his dad for twenty years and then his dad retired in 1986. 'These people are much more than customers to me,' Alan said, when he retired, 'and they have been incredibly loyal over the years.' One elderly woman had lived in the same house for fifty-six years. She had seen Alan Bryant develop from a very young boy to a retired milkman.

Dave Sutton was another example of 'like father, like son'. When Sutton was nine, he got up early and earned some money working on his dad's milk round. After working as an artist for a wrought-iron company and as a welder, he followed his father into the milk-delivery business. Here he recalls his father's death:

The last time I saw him he was sitting up in bed in hospital and as I was leaving I shook his hand and looked him in the eyes. I think we both knew that was the last we would see of each other in this world . . . He died soon afterwards. I lost a very dear friend and a fantastic dad but like to think that if there is a next world he is back delivering milk with his horse and cart and that the weather is forever sunny.

Funerals

When Brian Townsend embarked on his milkman career, at the age of fourteen, he delivered from a horse and cart. He worked in the Blackburn area – Brookhouse, Audley and Johnston Street – and retired in 1990. After his death, in 1997, a horse-drawn Victorian hearse took him on his final journey. The floral tributes included a milk crate full of flowers from his eight siblings and a milk-bottle arrangement from his twelve grandchildren.

A horse-drawn funeral was organised for James Shawcross of Gwernaffield, Flintshire. The delivery vehicle carrying the coffin was similar to the one Shawcross had used around Mold at the start of his career (before he converted to a van). He retired, aged seventy-seven, after serving the community for sixty-four years. Horses were his passion and he raced them at Prestatyn Raceway. At the funeral the horse travelled from the family home, Cae Rhug Farm, and along the lane to the church. After the ceremony the horse and carriage took James Shawcross to his resting place in the cemetery.

There have been other considered tributes to milkmen who have passed away while employed as milkmen. When John Whittington died suddenly, at the age of forty-two, his customers dedicated a room at Hangleton community centre to his memory. Whittington had done a round in Hangleton (Brighton and Hove) for twenty-three years.

In 2007, Allan Knight died aged fifty-three while working on his round, and his funeral took place in the Hampshire village of Ropley. At the funeral the rector of Ropley, Reverend Royston Such, spoke movingly to over three hundred people about Allan Knight's life:

So many have spoken of him in many different ways but they have always spoken of a good man. I will remember Mr Knight for his smile. It was not a public smile. It was a special smile linked to a sort of sensitivity that not many human beings possess. I shall remember it because I know it was genuine. He had a habit of leaving a bottle of milk and a loaf of bread by a tree in Brighton for a local tramp. The tramp would pay Mr Knight when he could but often Allan would make up the difference himself. My guess is in reality this was just one of many occasions like this, but that it had happened to come to the attention of someone. This goes some way to explaining what kind of man he was and why so many have turned out to pay their respects today.

20

The Vanishing Milkman

Cancel one pint the day after the day after today.

OVER the last forty years the most significant thing about milkmen is that they have been disappearing from British society. In the sixties and seventies the main problem for dairies was a shortage of milkmen. Recruitment drives were common, regular men did overtime and consideration was given to a six-day delivery system with no Sunday deliveries. Two decades later it was all about reducing staff numbers, restructuring the dairy (e.g. five rounds rather than six) and reviewing business practices (e.g. the introduction of franchising).

Whichever figures you look at – number of milkmen, percentage of households served, number of milk rounds, value of business sectors – there is no escaping the harsh truth that doorstep milk delivery has been on the way out.

Meanwhile, milk sold in supermarkets and convenience stores has been on the way in.

In the fifties and sixties, milkmen took their products to about 99 per cent of houses. Those were the golden years for British milk. The product was clean, fresh, good for you and cost the same on your doorstep as at the corner shop. Young people congregated in milk bars, where milk shakes were much in demand, and Italian immigrants served excellent milky coffee in cafes.

Thereafter the percentage of households visited by milkmen was much reduced – from 99 per cent (in 1970) to 94 (1974), 86 (1982) and 62 (1990). Then came a sudden collapse in the mid-nineties – from 58 per cent of households (in 1994) to 45 (1995) and 39 (1996). The figures continued to fall – to 26 per cent (in 2000) and 11 per cent (2014). The number of milk rounds dropped from over 40,000 (in the late sixties) to just under 20,000 (1994) and just over 11,000 (2000).

This chapter looks at the decline.

The Price of Milk

The Milk Marketing Board, formed in 1933, set a national price for dairy farmers and a standard price for door-step-delivered milk. The system safeguarded the vagaries of milk production and distribution. During World War II, milkmen swapped customers so that they had tight rounds which saved resources. After the war it took a few years before customers had the freedom to choose a milkman. In the fifties dairymen's profits were rigidly controlled by the Ministry of Food.

The government milk subsidy for farmers was removed

on 2 September 1962, but the costs of milk distribution and dairyman's profits were still strictly controlled by the ministry. The Milk Marketing Board and the government continued to set the price for selling and delivering to customers. In the seventies, a time of inflation, increases in price were commonplace. The doorstep selling price climbed in small increments from 5p a pint (in 1970) to 12½p (1977), 20p (1982) and 30p (1989).

In the early eighties the combination of government reforms and European regulations paved the way for radical changes in the milk market. In 1984 there was a big increase in supermarkets' share of the retail milk business. In the late eighties there was a tipping point whereby it was cheaper for customers to buy milk in supermarkets than from milkmen. By then it was clear that supermarkets would win in the end.

In the early nineties, the doorstep-delivery business faced two more challenges – escalating EC interventionism and the impending dissolution of the Milk Marketing Board at home. The board had safeguarded milk delivery for sixty years, but the government of the early nineties saw it as outdated socialism. By 1994, the market for milk sales had been totally deregulated and a court case failed to overturn the decision. In August 1994, the Milk Marketing Board was replaced by Milk Marque, an independent cooperative which relied on voluntary membership. Milkmen realised that this was another step towards the job's demise, as one recalled:

The price regulation was great. It worked. It worked for the farmers, it worked for the milkmen and it worked for the customers. But once they scrapped that it was all downhill really, wasn't it?

In the summer of 1995 a pint of supermarket milk sold for 28p and a four-pint plastic bottle cost only 22p a pint. In comparison, a pint of milk on the doorstep sold for between 36p and 41p. By 1999, the doorstep pint sold at 60p (about 17p more than a supermarket pint). By 2001, supermarkets were selling milk at cheaper prices than the milkman could buy it for. Ten years later, there were considerable variations in pricing. In one region milk cost customers 68p a pint on the doorstep while nearby supermarkets sold it for under 50p. A West Yorkshire resident spotted that four pints of milk cost £1 at Lidl, £2 at Tesco and £2.34 by doorstep delivery. By 2014, supermarkets had 65 per cent of the market and convenience stores 20 per cent. Doorstep delivery was left with only 7 per cent, because those customers remaining in the delivery system (e.g. pensioners) generally had smaller orders.

Supermarket Milk

In 1981, Sir John Sainsbury described doorstep delivery as 'too easy for the inefficient and too profitable for the efficient'. Sainsbury, a marketing adviser to the Minister of Agriculture, Fisheries and Food, pointed out that grocers were prevented from offering milk bargains.

In November 1983, Baroness Fisher of Rednal put the case for the milkman to the House of Lords:

> If the doorstep delivery of milk is stopped, it will mean treks to supermarkets three, four, five miles away, in order to fill

up a pram with milk . . . As your lordships will remember, last year we had a lot of snow and bad weather. Pictures on television showed the milkman constantly getting on to the doorstep in all parts of the country. In some isolated areas the milkman found that the people were completely cut off and he signalled for the helicopter to come in with food for those places. We must not let the doorstep delivery go by default.

Baroness Fisher was powerless because more and more customers chose to do most of their shopping in one place and business people were monitoring more supermarket opportunities.

In the eighties Robert Wiseman, head of Robert Wiseman Dairies, saw the future as dairies supplying large shops rather than customers' houses. Articulated lorries could carry more milk than milk floats. Wiseman's new Bellshill dairy opened in 1989 and the business continued to expand, creating a direct link between big dairies and supermarkets.

Many customers began to buy milk in supermarkets, where milk was sometimes a loss-leader sold at prices favourable to customers. Experienced milkmen kept some calls because of their long-standing relationships with customers, but, when they retired, a change in personnel and a new delivery schedule meant customers often converted to supermarket purchases. Driving to a supermarket just to buy a pint of milk was clearly an expensive way to buy milk (when petrol costs were included) but people could also buy a trolley-load of other goods. And, if you did visit a supermarket for milk alone, the place was often designed so that you had to walk past other tempting goods to find the milk near the back of the store.

Supermarket milk is a story of economies of scale, improved refrigeration (milk can be kept for a week), changing packaging (cartons and plastic bottles rather than glass bottles) and larger containers (two pints, four pints and even six pints). It is also the tale of roll containers, i.e. three- or four-shelf milk trolleys which could be rolled on to lorries, rolled into supermarkets (where there was more space for storage) and rolled into supermarket aisles.

In the nineties, the shelf life and quality of milk improved dramatically. Milk could be pre-cooled and kept below five degrees centigrade until it was sold in supermarkets. In 1997, a cut in supermarket milk prices came as a shock to the market, and milkmen were even more disadvantaged. The competition between supermarkets and doorstep delivery became even more one-sided. Ultimately, milkmen and dairy farmers were the losers. Here is milkman Frank Bingley speaking in 2007:

> Over the years I've noticed that the amount of calls per round has been dropping slowly. When I first started, many rounds had over 500 calls, but nowadays, well, the round I do has 360 calls and that is quite a good size . . . With this shrinking customer base we've had to adapt. Rounds have been taken out and their calls distributed amongst the remaining rounds and things like that. And, also, when we first started, the main thing we delivered was milk but now we sell other things as well, like water and potatoes and all that sort of thing. There is a good profit at the end of the

year, so I can see us going for a bit yet, but unfortunately it will come to an end.

Doorstep delivery was also affected by changing diets. The amount of milk consumed fell from 4.89 pints a week (in 1965) to 4.33 pints a week (in 1985). By the late eighties a glass of milk had to compete with alcoholic drinks, sports drinks, fruit juices, other soft drinks and a wide selection of teas (including herbal teas). The custom retained by milkmen was biased towards the single-person households of elderly people, thus restricting the milkmen's aggregate sale. In the past a significant amount of milk was drunk by cats, but researchers discovered that lactose-intolerant adult cats could develop tummy upsets, vomiting and diarrhoea by drinking milk. The nutritional value of milk was debated more and more, especially when an increasing number of people were diagnosed as lactose intolerant.

Between January 1993 and January 1996, liquid milk consumption fell by 14 per cent. Women were no longer at home during the day, so traditional fares such as milky drinks, rice pudding and custard were threatened by convenience foods purchased at supermarkets. The modern era was one of sports drinks, the worldwide marketing of Pepsi and Coca-Cola, and packaged food purchased from supermarkets. Milkmen had no influence on supermarkets.

Dairy Farming
In 1950 the UK had about 196,000 dairy farms, but the numbers dropped to around 35,000 (in 1995) and 13,000 (2014). The underlying trend was towards a few large-scale dairy producers at the expense of many smaller ones.

In the fifties and sixties, the dairy farming financial system was so complex that some ministers at the Ministry of Agriculture failed to understand it. An outbreak of foot-and-mouth disease caused problems in 1967, but, overall, rigid government price controls allowed local dairies to sustain their businesses through the seventies.

Dairy farmers sold milk to processors, who packaged the milk into churns, bottles and cartons. Then the processors sold milk to dairies (depots), bottled-milk buyers and, increasingly, supermarkets. The dairies and bottled-milk buyers then sold their milk to either household customers (via doorstep delivery) or to 'middle ground' customers (i.e. small retail shops, garages, cafes and restaurants). The catering trade turned milk into products known as 'bakes, cakes and shakes'. Overall, about half of dairy production has gone into the liquid market (milk) and half into manufactured products (cheese, butter, yoghurts, milk powder, cream, etc.).

During the period from 1980 to 2010, the milkman's doorstep visits fell from 90 per cent of households to 26 per cent. This was also an uncertain period for dairy farmers. The driving forces behind the vulnerability of dairy farmers and milkmen were the withdrawal of traditional price controls, an increase in food imports and the power of supermarkets, who sometimes gave farmers a good deal for the first year and then offered tougher deals thereafter.

In 2007, when author Richard Askwith was researching his book *The Lost Village*, a dairy farmer told him, 'The last few years have been absolutely soul-destroying.' It had been downhill ever since the outbreaks of BSE (from 1997) and foot-and-mouth (from 2001), and some farmers also had to deal with outbreaks of cows aborting their calves after eating dog faeces and digesting *neospora caninum*. A 2003 survey found that farmers were twice as likely to contemplate suicide as other people in Britain.

In the new century, dairy farmers' production costs went up and milk prices went down. It was hard work with little reward, and most farmers found it hard to balance their books. In 2007, a quarter of the remaining dairy farms ran at a loss. Two years later, Jim Leaver, owner of Swanage Dairy, spoke about the farmers' plight:

> You are seeing the death of the milk round. The traditional milkman is facing competition from the large multiples who can sell milk cheaper. Now the supermarkets dictate what they will pay for it because they know someone will supply it at that price. The only way they can sustain these low prices is by paying the farmer less.

In 2011, the Office of Fair Trading fined a number of supermarkets a total of £49.5 million for fixing cheese and milk prices (offences from 2003). More and more farmland was being turned into housing, and the number of people employed in agriculture fell by about a third in twenty years. In 2012, a group of dairymen, Farmers for Action, blockaded roads and processing plants to protest about having to sell their milk at a loss; they won a few concessions from the processors and supermarkets.

A few small dairies have been revived with the help of special products such as organic milk and traditional local cheese. Micro-dairies and organic-milk producers were successful by selling something that supermarkets didn't sell, e.g. unhomogenised, twenty-four-hour-old, fresh local milk. The cows were milked at 9 a.m. one day and the milk could be on your doorstep by 9 a.m. the next morning. But the cows needed milking 365 days a year. Dairy farming was a relentless life.

Another change for dairies was the legal requirement for a piece of equipment called a sidewall scanner. Such scanners could spot dirt in the milk, but their introduction caused a loss of revenue because dairies could no longer print advertisements on bottles as the scanner would reject them. Up to this point there had only been a bottom-wall scanner which looked through the bottom to see if anything had settled out.

According to Steve Wheeler, the sidewall scanner caused some dairies to be turned into a block of flats, a supermarket, a vet's headquarters, a holiday home or a housing estate:

> There are so few small dairies left, with the exception of maybe places like Lancashire and Yorkshire, and the North East, where the small dairies keep going for two reasons. One is that they don't use sidewall scanners up there, and the other reason is because there are loads of little hamlets and villages in amongst hills with no supermarkets. If you don't have a supermarket you don't have anyone buying the milk and selling it as a loss-leader to get you in there. To this day those dairies have survived and are still doing adverts on bottles. Whether it will last, I don't know.

Technology moved on. Modern dairy farming could involve automatic laser-guiding milking machines so that cows can use milking facilities whenever they wish. In large processing plants, robots take milk on trolleys to the loading stations.

Responses

In March 2004, Gwyneth Dunwoody, MP for Crewe and Nantwich, spoke on behalf of the troubled milkman: 'Delivering to customers in inner-city areas has become so difficult that many milkmen do not know how to proceed. One unfortunate milkman incurred £450 worth of [parking] fines in one week, which was more than he earned.'

Competition from supermarkets and convenience stores meant that the remaining dairies and surviving milkmen had to become more efficient. After 6 a.m. the traffic in cities jammed up, so more milkmen started their rounds at midnight or soon afterwards. By the new century many remaining milkmen were expanding the range of goods on sale, and milk floats became general stores on wheels. In the seventies the basic range of goods had included a range of milks, cream, yoghurts, juice and eggs. When bread roundsmen began to disappear, milkmen took over some bread and cake deliveries. By the twenty-first century, however, Parker Dairies of Walthamstow were also delivering cereals, bakery products, groceries, pet food, household goods and gardening materials (and their milkmen were engaging with customers through Twitter and Facebook). Dairy Crest, a nationalised dairy company set up by the Milk Marketing Board, introduced an online ordering service called Milk & More for about 1.6 million customers and that helped to create some recovery. M-box, linked to Express Dairies, also extended the milkman's product list to include all sorts of goods available via internet ordering. The term 'milkman' was no longer apt because his range of goods included nappies, newspapers, fireworks, rubbish bags, wine boxes and television sets. 'We'll be delivering three-piece suites to customers before too long,' moaned a milkman from the Midlands.

Franchising of rounds began around 1970. It became a more widespread business model in the mid-eighties, when milkmen at Northern Dairies were made redundant and then offered their old rounds on a franchise basis. 'When I was franchised the only thing the dairy was interested in was whether I paid my cheque every week,' said one franchisee.

Milk was promoted through advertisements, marketing and websites. The electric milk float still held advantages – it issued no fumes, needed no petrol and made little noise when compared with juggernauts – and glass bottles lasted far longer than other containers. But, when milk rounds spread over greater areas with fewer customers, costlier diesels replaced electric vehicles, and even the best milkmen lost out. Tony Fowler, an award-winning milkman from Leicestershire, lost eighteen customers in nine months in 2014, and a further seventy-two customers had reduced their orders.

Attempts to save the milkman included The Freedom Campaign (Friends Electing for Delivery of Milk), National Milkman Week and support from members of the Maternity Alliance and the Health Visitors Association. But milkmen were losing the battle. The differential between milk float sales and supermarket sales grew larger. The percentage of people moving accommodation each year had increased (to 20 per cent in London) and therefore tracking bills and customers became more difficult. Milkmen also noticed that the average age of customers was increasing:

> It was the old people that still wanted it delivered. The trouble is that they don't buy the quantity. They are buying two or three pints a week. The ones you need are the families buying three or four pints a day to make the job viable and that was the ones you were losing. The trouble was that as soon as somebody moved out you didn't get the people coming in. That was the way the job was going and I was getting too old anyway.

The Vanishing Milkman

Over a forty-year period – 1974 to 2014 – the population of milkmen fell from about 40,000 to around 4,000. Many other community roles were much reduced during that same period. British society lost coalmen, park-keepers, bus conductors, railway porters, station-masters, bread roundsmen, petrol station attendants and lavatory attendants. Supermarkets had also helped to put many high street butchers, fishmongers and greengrocers out of existence, and the number of independent grocers dropped from 116,000 (in 1961) to 31,000 (in 1995). One wag suggested that postmen would disappear next and we'd have to pick up our mail from supermarkets.

Once upon a time Brian Belcher worked as a baker and a milkman in the Leicester area. In the forties, when he was growing up, his street had three dairies, at least two bakers, a greengrocer and a tea seller. They have all disappeared now.

In 2000, *Bolton Evening News* reporter Frank Wood rued the change:

> Like sub-post offices, newspapers boys, corner shops and beat bobbies, the milkman is a vital part of the wider community. You may be able to buy milk a lot cheaper at a superstore, but there are many thousands of people, such as the elderly, who haven't got a car to load up from a trolley. And the reassuring clink of bottles in the morning is a godsend. Milkmen deliver friendship as well as the right stuff.

Lost community gatekeepers have sometimes been replaced by technology (e.g. CCTV) and volunteerism (e.g. Neighbourhood Watch), but many gatekeepers have disappeared. The milkman has been superseded by supermarkets and something has been lost. A supermarket first-aider might treat an elderly customer who collapses in a supermarket aisle but won't spot someone who has collapsed in their own home (as vigilant milkmen did in the past).

In 1984, The Earl of Kinnoull spoke in the House of Lords about the milkmen's role:

> Milkmen are one of the few unsung heroes who give a service to our communities. They offer a vital service. They are inevitably cheerful, helpful people, who work very unsocial hours, and they are often very kind to the elderly. Along with postmen, they have a very special place in our society. Any threat to the future of milkmen, whether from importing long-life milk or from some repercussion from these awful regulations, will, I hope, be strongly resisted.

The Earl of Kinnoull failed to get his wish. The remaining milkmen became more distanced from their customers than their predecessors. Earlier starts meant they could do their round before many customers were awake, and direct debit payments reduced the number of face-to-face meetings. Milkmen embraced new technology – electronic round's books, internet ordering, computerised billing, etc. – but this distanced them from their clientele. Customers talked about how they hadn't seen their milkman for ten years and, for all they knew, a robot was bringing the milk.

In the fifties, some customers said, 'I never see my milkman', but more and more said it in the eighties and nineties. Gone was the highly visible milkman who provided a local bush telegraph news service. Phil Wark, writing in 2008, suggested it would need Ghostbusters or a private detective to find a milkman in the modern era.

In November 2013, Margaret Hancock of Yateley, Hampshire, wrote to the *Daily Telegraph* to say that she had remained loyal to doorstep milk delivery because it created jobs, encouraged entrepreneurship and provided regular social interaction for the lonely. But now she had no contact with her milkman and she paid her milk bill by bank transfer. The price difference – 75p on the doorstep, under 50p in supermarkets – meant she was supporting a pricey anachronism when she needed to economise.

Milkmen might have been the eyes and ears of the community, but their managers were increasingly concerned with balance sheets. Journalist Brian Viner lost his doorstep delivery in rural Herefordshire in 2014. His milkman had made a significant contribution to the Herefordshire community, but the business folk in Cheltenham decided to cut the round. Viner wrote:

> Our milkman told his bosses that on a round as rural as ours, sometimes with miles between one house and the next, him arriving with the milk and newspapers is the only human interaction some people enjoy all day. They told him they were operating a business, not a social service, which is unarguably true. Yet the end of his milk round – proper old-fashioned bottle of milk, too – represents another tiny rip in the fabric of rural England. I now have to drive five miles to a service station to buy milk.

More and more customers wrote notes to their milkmen to say that they didn't want to see him again, and neglected housewives had to go elsewhere for their jollies. Milkmen and customers had shared many fulfilling relationships, but the job was now spiralling towards its end. Did you hear about the woman who recently had an affair with her milkman? No, I guess you didn't. These days it is really difficult for a customer to have face-to-face contact with a milkman, let alone body-to-body. And men working behind the scenes in supermarket chains don't seem to have the same pizzazz and allure as traditional milkmen.

Postscript

The Milkman in the Arts

Please leave one pint of skimmed or semi-skimmed milk only.
I have just watched a horrific film on FAT.

THE milkman has made memorable appearances in songs, novels, plays, films and TV programmes. He has also been commemorated in the names of musicians (e.g. *The Milkman's Sons*), pubs (e.g. The Jolly Milkman at Mortlake), greyhounds (e.g. Mick the Milkman), racehorses (e.g. The Milkman) and comedy troupes (e.g. All the Milkman's Children). It is very difficult to be comprehensive about the milkman and the arts, but here are a few thoughts.

Literature

Toni Morrison's *The Song of Solomon* (1977) is reportedly Barack Obama's favourite book. Morrison's novel is part of education courses around the world and has spawned much love, analysis and literary criticism. The book's central character, Macon Dead Junior, is nicknamed 'Milkman' because his mother breast-fed him until he was four years old. Milkman's left leg was shorter than his right, but he managed to turn his limp into a strut and he found a way of dancing that attracted the girls.

William Sansom wrote a collection of stories called *The Ulcerated Milkman* (1966). The title story is about a milkman who hates milk. When the milkman delivers the bottles he slams them down and he doesn't care if he breaks them, so the cats follow him around and lap up the milk. The denouement comes when the milkman is taken to hospital with a perforated ulcer and is prescribed a milk-only diet.

Stephen King created sinister milkmen for *Skeleton Crew* (1985), a bumper collection of King's shorter works. In 'Morning Deliveries (Milkman no. 1)' the villain, Spike, conceals venomous spiders, acid gel, cyanide gas and a bloodstained meat hook in threatening places. In 'Big Wheels: A Tale of the Laundry Game (Milkman no. 2)', laundry-worker Rocky attempts to take revenge on Spike, who has got Rocky's wife pregnant.

In *David Copperfield* (1850) by Charles Dickens, the eponymous hero visits Tommy Traddles, an old school friend who lives in an undesirable street. Just before David arrives at the front door, the milkman turns up to see Traddles. When a servant answers the door, the milkman tries to collect an outstanding bill, adopting a truculent manner: 'That there little bill has been running so long, that I believe it's run away altogether and never won't be heerd of.' The milkman threatens to stop the house's milk but reluctantly opens his can and deposits today's milk in the family jug.

David Storey won the 1976 Booker Prize for his novel *Saville*. The book contains an evocative scene featuring a milkman in a black bowler hat and brown smock. Storey describes the days of the milkman's horse and cart when there were jugs on doorsteps, metal scoops and milk ladled from shiny, oval cans. Saville, his wife and their young child are off on holiday. They are walking to the railway station with heavy bags when the milkman kindly gives them a lift.

Confessions of a Milkman (1976) by Timothy Lea (real name Christopher Wood) is a low-brow view of the milkman with plenty of sex scenes. The main character works for Meadow Fresh Dairy and is as fresh as his milk. He is usually on the job when he should be on the job, and he asks housewives whether they'd like it delivered to the front or the back.

The milkman is a more lovable character in children's stories. In Flack and Templeton's *Angus Lost* (1932) the hero, a Scottie dog, is given a lift into town by the milkman. In the *Big Alfie and Annie Rose Storybook* (1990), created by Shirley Hughes, Alfie is good friends with the milkman. And Enid Blyton's Toytown milkman always cheered up when he rang Noddy's bell.

A novel by Max Bygraves, *The Milkman's on his Way* (1971), is more about the music business than the milk trade. Young Harry Selfridge gets a job at Dutton's Dairies. He is trained by milkman Jimmy Lloyd, who has swapped his previous career in the Royal Navy, where superiors were hanging over him twenty-four hours a day, for a more independent lifestyle. Harry and Jimmy sing together in the evenings, and Harry goes on to make a number-one record. Later, Harry throws off the gangsters of the music business and returns to Dutton's Dairies, where the boss is surprised to see him. 'I ran out of milk in Las Vegas,' says Harry.

Perhaps the most controversial contribution to milkman literature is *The Milkman's on His Way* (1982) by David Rees. This is young-adult fiction with explicit scenes of homosexuality. The book was mentioned in Parliament on several occasions, particularly during debates about whether or not homosexual issues should be taught in schools. Baroness Knight bemoaned the glorification of the book because it 'explicitly described homosexual intercourse' and encouraged 'youngsters to believe that it was better than any other sexual way of life'. Colin Moynihan described it as 'depraved and corrupt literature'. Baroness Cox wondered whether the book should be classified as pornography and whether it was appropriate in the age of AIDS. The Earl of Caithness described the book as 'odious' and Michael Howard criticised Haringey Library for making it available in the children's section.

In Dylan Thomas's *Under Milk Wood* (1954), Ocky Milkman's milk is 'as fresh as the dew' but only because the milk is half dew because it is watered-down. Elsewhere, customers have been inspired to write verse for their milkman. Some poems explicitly declared amorous intentions; others offered thanks for travelling through bad weather and providing a great service. Adrienne Rich's poem 'Living in Sin' is about an affair with the milkman.

In John Buchan's *The Thirty-nine Steps* (1915), the

milkman provides an escape route for an innocent murder suspect called Richard Hannay. Hannay hands over a sovereign to borrow the milkman's cap and overall, allegedly for a bet, and the two men exchange places. 'I haven't got time to explain, but to win it [the bet] I've got to be a milkman for the next ten minutes,' Hannay tells the milkman. 'All you've got to do is stay here till I come back. You'll be a bit late, but nobody will complain, and you'll have that quid for yourself.'

Hannay sticks on the milkman's flat blue hat and white overall, picks up the cans, bangs the door and goes whistling downstairs. The porter tells Hannay to shut his jaw, and Hannay takes that as a sign that he looks convincing. This milkman scene is legendary. It appears in several film versions of the book . . .

Cinema

At least three film versions of *The 39 Steps* have included the milkman scene. The first was directed by Alfred Hitchcock in 1935 and starred Frederick Piper as the milkman, although I suppose Robert Donat (Richard Hannay) and Madeleine Carroll (Pamela) deserve a modicum of praise. The second version of *The 39 Steps*, directed by Ralph Thomas in 1959, saw Leslie Dwyer as the milkman while Kenneth More (Hannay) and Taina Elg (Fisher) did their best to steal the limelight. In another remake, in 1978, Robert Powell (Hannay) and Karen Dotrice (Alex) were totally upstaged by the brief appearance of Leo Dolan as the milkman . . . or maybe I'm biased.

A couple of short American films are praiseworthy. *Your Milkman* (Daniel Skubel, 2012), set in 1953 when the USA still had milkmen, shows a meeting between a milkman and a housewife in a diner. The housewife knows that the milkman is sexually involved with other women on her round so she attempts to seduce the milkman, but the story takes a twist.

The second short film, *The Milkman* (Mark Nicholson, 2008), has a violent plot based on a 1952 true story. A milkman mixes with the wrong crowd and has to protect his family from villains.

The premise of *The Calcium Kid* (Alex De Raikoff, 2004) is that boxer Jimmy Connelly has strong bones because he drinks lots of milk and therefore has a high calcium intake. Connelly demonstrates the power of his fist by injuring a championship contender. He deputises in a major fight and his career is launched.

In *Melvin and Howard* (Jonathan Demme, 1980), milkman Melvin Dummar (Paul Le Mat) gives a tramp (Jason Roberts) a lift to Las Vegas. The passenger says he is Howard Hughes, the wealthy recluse, but Dunbar doesn't believe him. Years later, Dunmar receives a $136 million inheritance from the Hughes estate. Based on a true story, the film has scenes set within the milkman culture. In one, Dummar is seduced by an older female customer. In another, he sings a milkman's song in order to woo his wife. Other scenes show his relationship with the dairy manager. David Robinson, film reviewer for *The Times*, chose *Melvin and Howard* as his desert-island film.

The Trials of a Milkman (1916), an early silent movie, offers a guide to what milkmen had to put up with in those days. Nearly half a century later, there was plenty to test a milkman's resolve in a slapstick comedy called

The Early Bird (Robert Asher, 1965). A milkman called Pitkin (Norman Wisdom) delivers milk for a traditional dairy with the help of a horse called Nellie. Meanwhile, Austin (Bryan Pringle), who drives an electric milk float, looks for every chance to outdo his rival (e.g. smashing Pitkin's empty bottles). Pitkin's horse is poisoned by Austin, so Pitkin has to push a handcart up a steep slope. His churn falls off and rolls downhill. *The Early Bird* is a little like Mr Pastry meeting Mr Bean with lots of milk and cream.

The Amorous Milkman (Derren Nesbitt, 1975) is set around bored housewives and a virile milkman called Davy (Brendon Price). The fashions and vehicles have some historical interest, but the tone of the film can be judged by milk-float slogans such as ARE YOU GETTING PLENTY? ASK YOUR MILKMAN.

Sixteen minutes into *The Girl Can't Help It* (Frank Tashlin, 1956), the ultra-curvy Jerri Jordan (Jayne Mansfield) pays a visit to a press agent called Tom Miller (Tom Ewell). While walking towards Miller's apartment, Jordan passes a laundry man who lets off steam and a milkman, whose bottle of milk bubbles over. The milkman is standing transfixed, holding his milk bottle at waist level as the contents erupt like a geyser. The film could have won an Academy Award for 'sneaking a scene past a censor'.

Other actors depicting milkmen in major films include Clark Gable in *The Easiest Way* (1931), Harold Lloyd in *The Milky Way* (1936), James Gleason in *The Clock* (1945), Danny Kaye in *The Kid from Brooklyn* (1946), Michael Crawford in *The Games* (1970), Adam Bareham in *Victims* (1979) and Max Beesley in *The Match* (1999).

Music

Here is my choice for a sing-along in the milk float:

Benny Hill: 'Ernie (The Fastest Milkman in the West)' (written by Benny Hill, 1971). This was a number-one record for ex-milkman Hill, who was famous as a comedian with his own shows. The song has a well-constructed storyline involving the widow Sue, bread-roundsman Ted and milkman Ernie. In 2006, David Cameron chose *Ernie* as one of his records on Radio 4's *Desert Island Discs*.

Fats Waller: 'My Very Good Friend the Milkman Says' (Jimmy Burke and Harold Spiner, 1935). This record was a surprise hit for Fats Waller. The singer's confidant is a milkman who gives advice. Eric Clapton, George Melly and Paul McCartney made later versions.

Billy Bragg: 'The Milkman of Human Kindness' (Billy Bragg, 1983). A Shakespearian line of verse – 'the milk of human kindness' – came to mean compassion, even though Lady Macbeth's use of the expression, in *Macbeth*, was more sinister. Billy Bragg's website has offered a 'Milkman of Human Kindness' T-shirt with a picture of an electric milk float and a distinctive number plate: BR4GG.

Ian Hardie: 'The Poetic Milkman' (Ian Hardie, 1986). This tune is written in honour of Bobby Service, a milkman in Kirk Yetholm in the Scottish Borders, a great character and the first Kelso laddie. It first appeared on the album *A Breath of Fresh Airs* (1986) and was re-released in 2012. Ian Hardie's song has also been recorded by Scottish band Breabach.

Topol: 'If I Were a Rich Man' (Sheldon Harnick and Jerry Bock, 1964). The milkman Tevye sings this song in the stage play and film of *Fiddler on the Roof.* Tevye is delivering milk with a lame horse when he dreams of what life could be. Topol and his understudy Paul Lipson have both performed the song thousands of times on stage.

George Formby: 'Delivering the Morning Milk' (Fred Cliffe, Harry Gifford, George Formby, 1941). Taking the voice of a milkman, Formby observes various sexual shenanigans on his round. This is possibly the only song to have ever rhymed 'rope', 'soap' and 'elope'. The sexual innuendo of the lyrics was toned down for the film version *Much Too Shy* (1942).

Level 42: 'Kansas City Milkman' (Mark King, Mick Lindup, Phil Gould, Wally Badarou, 1984). The son of a dairyman, Mark King delivered milk on the Isle of Wight and in London. The Level 42 song can be linked to a fictional newspaper office motto ('write it so a Kansas City milkman can understand it') and Reynolds Packard's 1950 novel *The Kansas City Milkman.*

Ugly Kid Joe: 'Milkman's Son' (Whitfield Crane and Dave Fortman, 1995). Featuring on the album *Menace to Society*, the song is about a young man who has broken up with his girlfriend and is feeling like the milkman's son.

Herman's Hermits: 'No Milk Today' (Graham Gouldman, 1966). In his distinctive voice Peter Noone explains that his lover has left him and the milkman doesn't need to call any more.

Ella Mae Morse: 'Milkman, Keep Those Bottles Quiet' (Don Raye and Gene de Paul, 1943). The song was popularised by Nancy Walker in the film *Broadway* (1944). It was later covered by many artists, including The Pied Pipers and the Raeburn Band.

Tony Bennett and Barbra Streisand: 'Lullaby of Broadway' (Harry Warren and Al Dubin, 1935). The numerous versions of this song include those by The Andrews Sisters, Connie Francis and Bette Midler. Bennett and Streisand's appears on the 2006 album *Duets*. The singer says goodnight to his girl in the early hours of the morning, when the milkman is delivering.

Kentucky Headhunters: 'My Daddy was a Milkman' (Kentucky Headhunters, 1989). The song tells the story of a white-coated milkman who delivers to an American house. While the father is serving abroad in the forces, the mother of the house takes up with the milkman.

Captain Beefheart and his Magic Band: 'Safe as Milk' (Don Van Vliet, 1967). The title song was a bonus track on an album called *Safe as Milk*. A young Ry Cooder was part of the band.

Martha Tilston: 'Milkmaid' (Martha Tilston, 2006). Here the singer-songwriter honours her great grandmother, also called Martha Tilston, who worked as a milkmaid in North Wales. The song appears on her second album, *Of Milkmaids and Architects*.

Anne McCue: 'Milkman's Daughter' (Anne McCue, 2004). McCue is an Australian singer with a big following in North America. This song appears on her album *Roll*.

Peter Mulvey: 'Remember the Milkman' (Matt Lorenz and Peter Mulvey, 2014). This track, from Mulvey's *Silver Ladder* album, captures the loss of North American milkmen.

Max Miller: 'Mary from the Dairy' (Sam Kern, Max Miller and James Walsh, 1936). The original title was 'Mary at the Milk Bar', but the final choice clearly benefited from rhyming Mary with dairy. The song became Miller's signature tune and he sang it in the 1940 film *Hoots Mon!*

Paul Hone and Stephen Hone: 'On the Milk Round' (Paul Hone and Stephen Hone, 2007). The Hone brothers pay tribute to 1963, when, as children, they helped to deliver milk on their father's round in Uxbridge.

Katie Lawrence: 'Mary met the Milkman at the Corner' (Harry Allen and J P Harrington, 1903). Lawrence was a dancer and singer who achieved music-hall fame in her teens and then became a superstar in her twenties. Her other songs included 'A Bicycle made for Two'.

Traditional: 'Martha, the Milkman's Daughter' (G W Hunt, 1866): The young male narrator is in love with the milkman's daughter but the milkman refuses to let him near the girl. In the end the milkman's daughter throws herself in the Hudson River.

Television and Radio

The milkman in *EastEnders*, played by Michael Leader, did not speak during his first ten years in the role. Yet Leader researched his role thoroughly. He had a family background in milk – his grandparents owned a dairy in London's East End – and he continued to visit milkmen at Express Dairies to keep up with trends. The milkman's voice finally broke through when he returned Kat Slater to her father's door. As Charlie Slater answered the door, the milkman pointed to Charlie's daughter on the back of the milk float and said, 'This yours, squire?'

Milkmen have appeared in many other TV series. Geoffrey Brightman played one in *Coronation Street* and in one episode he helped to rescue the injured Albert Tatlock. Barbara Flynn was the milkwoman in *Open All Hours*, and she enticed the shopkeeper's nephew, Granville (David Jason), into a brief fling. In one long-running radio series, *The Archers*, Mike Tucker and Jazzer McCready delivered milk around Ambridge.

A twenty-minute episode of the American series *Tales from the Darkside* features a milkman who offers to satisfy customers' requests if they leave notes about their fantasies. The milkman is never seen, but his customers get what they asked for. The tale heads towards a dark ending when an impotent man leaves a note asking for a child.

ITV screened *Bottle Boys* in the mid-eighties. Set in the fictional Dawson Dairy, starring Robin Askwith, the show ran to two series with thirteen thirty-minute episodes in total. According to the author and historian Mark Lewisohn, *Bottle Boys* was 'blokish and berkish'. The show didn't do much to promote political correctness and Lewisohn saw it as one of the worst-ever sitcoms. It also showed little about the milkman's job. '*Bottle Boys* did not achieve the success I had hoped for,' said Vince Powell, who wrote the series. 'Some you win, some you lose: this was one I lost.'

The second series of *Whatever Happened to the Likely Lads?* has a show called 'Someday we'll laugh about this'. It contains a cheeky milkman called Les, played by Tony Haygarth.

Acknowledgements

I STARTED this book when I worked as a relief milkman in the late 1970s and it took me nearly thirty-eight years to complete the project. Oh well, better late with the book than late with the milk.

I sensed there was a book to be written from the moment my father forwarded my master's degree apparel after I'd been unable to attend the convocation at my Canadian university. My dad enclosed a short note: 'This blue-and-white hood will go well with your blue Co-op uniform.'

I realised then that I should combine my research background with my milkman's job, so I wrote notes about my experiences, kept a milkman's diary and saved newspaper cuttings. Over the years I interviewed twenty-two milkmen and four milkwomen, and I am very grateful to them: Barry, Bert, Brian, Chris, Dave, Derek, Derrick,

Acknowledgements

Eric, Gerry, Gill, Graham, Henry, Jan, Jeff, John, Kevin, Liz, Paul D, Paul J, Paul W, Pete, Ray, Roger G, Roger M, Steve and Sue. Where quotations are unattributed, they are from my interviews or my diary.

The notes for milkmen, displayed at the beginning of each chapter, came from a number of sources, including Steve Wheeler, Ken Forester, Ann Baker, Phil Reilly, Peter Hall, my own scrapbook, the *Newcastle Journal* (26 August 1993), and *Milk Bottle News* 55 (winter 1998).

Milk Bottle News was a wonderful source for milk-related tales. Set up in 1984, the newsletter's first editors were Mike Hull and Margaret Barber. Then Mike Hull was sole editor from autumn 1987 until Paul Lake took over in 2001. Naomi and Mike Hull allowed me access to material, provided support and helped with the manuscript.

Dave Sutton very kindly allowed me to reproduce nine short extracts from his blog, *Confessions of a Unigate Milkman*, and I found his work inspirational. Steve Wheeler's milk bottle museum was suitably quirky and informative, and his willingness to share knowledge was much appreciated. Teresa Reynolds provided her customary insight while the manuscript was at an early stage, and Steve Troup supplied me with literature on paternal discrepancy.

Milkmen and milkwomen were my local heroes. As their numbers dwindled, I've missed them more and more, but memories of them remain and I hope this book plays a small part in consolidating their place in history.

Sources

Introduction

'Quigley': *Belfast Newsletter*, 18 Sep 2003

1. Off to Work

'Duncan': *Kilmarnock Standard*, 2 Aug 2012

'Kearvell': *Kent & Sussex Courier*, 4 Sep 2015

'Teesside milkman': *The Times*, 11 Dec 1993

'Roy Dyer': BBC News website, 29 Jun 2005; *Guardian*, 18 Feb 2007; BBC, 22 Nov 2013; *ENP Newswire*, 25 Nov 2013

'Hadley': *Newark Advertiser*, 9 Oct 2009

'first started': Frank Bingley, 'The Last Milkman', YouTube, 30 Jun 2007

'Gaunt': Anne Stewart, *The Milkman*, Hamish Hamilton, London, 1983

2. 'Good morning, Milkman'

'Cogar': *Oxford Journal* magazine, 1984

'Travelling grocery': *Choosing a Job: Milkman*, Wayland, London, 1973, p. 18

'Williams': *Daily Post*, 6 Aug 2015

Sources

'Cannabis': BBC News, 6 Feb 2009

'Midlands dairy': Voices of Kingstanding internet forum

'Rolls': *The Times*, 1 May 2001

'Contented cow': *The Milky Way: How to Become a Star Milkman*, Joint Committee of the Milk Marketing Board and The Dairy Trade Federation, and the Food, Drink and Tobacco Industry Training Board, 1977, p. 8.

3. Different Types of Milkmen

'when I worked': firbeck, Nottingham forums, 2 Oct 2014

'Qualter': *Exeter Express & Echo*, 28 Jul 2010; *Clevedon Mercury*, 30 Sep 2010; Gary Qualter's walking blog

'Redrup': *The Times*, 11 Apr 1958

'Kane': *Hansard*, 2 Feb 1989; *Wikipedia*, retrieved 24 Sep 2015

'Billson': *The Times*, 8 Jun 1987

'Arch': BBC News, 9 Feb 2009; *Daily Express*; 12 Feb 2009; *Daily Mail*, 6 Mar 2014

'Moon': *Sun*, 7 Mar 2003; *The Times*, 25 Feb 2004; *Express*, 25 Feb 2004

'Robins': *The Times*, 30 Dec 2000; *Wiltshire County Publications*, 2 Sep 2003

'Tisdale': *Shropshire Star*, 11 Jul 2014

'Maclean': *Caithness Courier*, 8 Sep 2010

'Survey of customers': *The Milky Way*, op. cit. p. 31

'Unigate training': *Tim Wood, My Job – Milkman*, Franklin Watts, London, 1989

'Sheldons Dairies': www.sheldonsdairy.co.uk

'Gifford': *Daily Mail*, 12 Jul 2013; *Sun*, 13 Jul 2013; *Leicester Mercury*, 19 Jul 2013

'Moore': *Coventry Telegraph*, 13 Oct 2000

'McCartney': *The Spectator*, 29 Mar 2014

Quentin Falk, *The Musical Milkman Murder*, John Blake, London, 2012

'Service': email correspondence with Viv Hardie, Nov 2015

4. Doorstep Delivery

'1986 survey': *The Times*, 29 Jul 1986

'number of fridges': *Daily Telegraph*, 3 Jul 2011

'jockeys': Voices of Kingstanding forum (Co-op dairy), 2012

Sting, *Broken Music*, Simon & Schuster, London, 2003, pp. 28–29, 86–87

'rheumatology research': C A Speed, J N Fordham, J L Cunningham, 'Bilateral tibial stress fractures in a fifteen-year-old milkman', *Rheumatology*, 1996

'Frankland': *South Wales Echo*, 4 Sep 2007; *South Wales Echo*, 24 Apr 2014; *Sun*, 27 Apr 2014

'On the milk': Kevin Murphy, textubation.com, 28 Jan 2009

'It was grim': 'Jean Donaldson Remembers: Delivering the Milk', YouTube

Willie Robertson, *On the Milk*, Hachette, Scotland, 2010, pp. 28–32

'Carl Giles': *The Times*, 1 Dec 1998, 4 Dec 1998; *Coventry Telegraph*, 16 Jun 1999

'Park Hill': *The Times* 28 Aug 1998, 11 Aug 1999; *The Stuart Hall Project*, directed by John Akomfrah, 2013

'local football ground': John Huins, *Choosing a Job: Milkman*, Wayland, London, 1973, p. 41

'The Olympic Milkman': *Spitalfields Life*, 16 Oct 2009

Sir Timothy Kitson MP, House of Commons, 22 May 1978

'house in Adelaide': *The Times*, 18 Jun 1963

'Isle of Wight': *Milk Bottle News* 31

'R A Claydon': *Milk Bottle News: Collectors' Handbook* I-24

'zoning': John Strachey MP, House of Commons, 22 Jan 1947; fourteen letters to *The Times*, from 3 Aug 1955 to 12 Aug 1955; *Milk Bottle News* 33, summer 1992

'soothed the animals': *Express Journey, 1864–1964*, Newman Neame, London, 1964, pp. 97–98; Kingstanding internet forum

5. The Milkman's Year

'Acorn Dairy milkmen': Acorn Dairy, *Winter News*, 2013

Sources

'differences in climate': Met Office historic station data

'Harry James': *The Sentinel*, 15 Mar 2011

Alan Jenkins, *Drinka Pinta*, Heinemann, London, 1970, p. 140

'first school': *Gloucestershire Within Living Memory*, Countryside Books, Newbury, Berks, 1996 p. 108

'no lights': Frederick Cowley, MP, House of Commons, 11 May 1897

John LaRizzio, *Hey, Milkman!*, Dog Ear Publishing, Indianapolis, 2011, pp. 17–18

'Arch': BBC News, 9 Feb 2009

'Gary Cowley': interview by Naomi Hull, *Milk Bottle News* 17, summer 1988

'Windsor Floods': *Windlesora Magazine*, 1981

'fur collar': letter to *The Times* by Barbara Davis, Chelmsford, 17 Dec 1979

'great storm': BBC memories of 16 Oct 1987, Paul Slade, Cliftonville, and Mike Bentley, Ambulance technician, accessed 2013

Leonard Hill, *Saucy Boy: The Life Story of Benny Hill*, Grafton Books, 1990, p. 100, p. 270; 'Benny by Lenny', *The Times*, 31 Jul 2004; *Benny*, Dennis Kirkland with Hilary Bonner, Smith Gryphon, London 1992

6. 'Merry Christmas, Milkman'

'Ashworth': *The Times*, 30 Dec 1967

'Briggs': *Father Christmas*, Hamish Hamilton, London, 1973

'Greenham': *Western Gazette*, 29 Apr 2010

'Wilson': *Black County Bugle*, 11 Mar 2004

'Christmas always seemed special': Dave Sutton, *Confessions of a Unigate Milkman: A Milkman's Blog*, 25 May 2011. Reproduced by permission of the author

'Poltimore Arms': *Mid-Devon Gazette*, 12 Apr 2014

7. The Amorous Milkman

Otis E Bigus, 'The Milkman and His Customer: A Cultivated Relationship', *Journal of Contemporary Ethnography*, 1972

Ann Oakley, *Housewives*, Allen Lane: London, 1974 p. 101

Jokes from various forums, including jokebudda.com, and adapted from G Legman, *The Rationale of the Dirty Joke: Part II*, Granada, London, 1972, p. 345

'Sunday mornings': Sutton, op. cit. 11 Mar 2011. Reproduced by permission of the author

'Affair': Birmingham Co-op dairy forum.

'female customers could fantasise': G Legman, op. cit. p. 326, discusses 'the sexual folk beliefs of people who, themselves, make love only in a very routine fashion in bed, after the cat and milk bottles have been dutifully put out'

'two rounds at Sherwood': Bilbraborn, Nottingham Forums, 10 Oct 2013

The Milkman Cometh, Kate Richards, Decadent Publishing, USA

Sting, op. cit. p. 49

Grayson Perry (with Wendy Jones), *Portrait of the Artist as a Young Girl*, 2007, pp. 7–13

'Angie Smith': *Daily Mirror*, 8 Jun 2015

'two suspicious characters': Naomi Hull, op. cit.

'getting old': *Worcestershire County Publications*, 6 Apr 2007

'milkman's fault': Letter from M Brookes, Wrexham, to *Daily Mirror*, 19 Oct 2011

'take your knickers off': old joke

'paternal discrepancy': Mark A Bellis, Karen Hughes, Sara Hughes and John R Ashton, 'Measuring Paternal Discrepancy and its Public Health Consequences', *Journal of Epidemiology and Community Health*, 59, 2005: 749–754

8. Never Work with Animals

Huins, op. cit. p. 54

'dog at the wheel': *Birmingham Post*, 24 Jan 2004; *Glasgow Evening Times*, 24 Jan 2004

'Roberts': *Lancashire County Publications*, 29 Jun 1998

'Cooper': *Macclesfield Express*, 28 May 2008

Sources

'Burton': *Greater London, Kent and Surrey Publications*, 14 Feb 1998

'On one delivery': Sutton, op. cit. 25 Apr 2015. Reproduced by
  permission of the author

'Siamese cats': Sutton, op. cit. 25 Apr 2015. Reproduced by
  permission of the author

'a snail had eaten': *The Times*, letter from Michael Nicholas,
  19 Jun 2000

'a new scarecrow': *The Times*, 13 May 2006

'monkey called Mickey': *The Times*, 1 Jun 1965

'heavy cough': Naomi Hull, op. cit.

'Weaver': 'The Milkman,' *Guardian*, 3 Oct 2009

9. Injuries, Crashes and Emergencies

'Greenham': *Western Gazette Series*, Yeovil, 15 Apr 2010

'Pettitt': *Greater London, Kent and Surrey Counties Publications*,
  7 Nov 2002

'Bell': *Daily Express*, 30 Dec 2006

Lionel Jones, 'A Dursley Milkman's Day', *The Dursley Lantern* (2010),
  pp. 4–5. Reproduced by permission of Lionel Jones and the editor
  of the *Dursley Lantern*

'Had trouble parking, did you?' *Oxford Journal*, 9 Aug 1984

'two cars written off': *Bristol Evening Post*, 30 Oct 1999; *The Times*,
  1 Nov 1999; *Western Daily Press*, 1 Nov 1999

'Frank Kidwell': *The Times*, 19 Feb 1973, 31 Mar 1973

'Leonard Munson': *The Times*, 11 Nov 1974

'Ronnie Kettridge': *The Times*, 24 Apr 2003

'Thomas Cahill': *The Times*, 20 Jul 1973

'Trevor Close': *The Times*, 27 May 1983

'Paddy Brady': *The Times*, 17 Nov 1984

'Geoff Reynolds': *Wiltshire County Publications*, 25 Oct 2006

'Allan Knight': *Hampshire County Publications*, 13 Jul 2007, 18 Jul 2007

'Christopher John Losper': *Mail* online, 14 Mar 2007

'Nicholas Sutton': *Oxford Times*, 14 Jun 1991

'milkman on a bicycle': Frederick Kellaway, MP, House of Commons, 30 Jul 1912

'Greenford milkman': *The Times* 29 Aug 1957

'Owen Whymark': *The Times*, 5 Sep 1973

'Brian Hockley, MBE': 'Delivering criminals to police is all part of the life of Brian', Emma Hardwick, *Dunmow Broadcast*, 16 Oct 2013

'Police escorts': Simon Hughes, MP, House of Commons, 11 Dec 1985; *The Times*, 6 Jun 1987

'Superglue': *The Times*, 30 Dec 1992, 30 Jan 1993

'Dyer': op. cit.

'Boyce': *The Times*, 6 Mar 1991

'eighteen-year-old burglar': *The Times*, 13 Aug 1998

'Munley': *East Sussex County Publications*, 15 Nov 2000, 7 Dec 2000

Bates: *Hertfordshire County Publications*, 16 May 2001

'Aryan Strike Force': *Northern Echo*, 16 Apr 2010, 30 Apr 2010; *The Jewish Chronicle*, 14 May 2010

'Finchley milkman': *Daily Mail*, 30 Oct 2009

'Milkman arrested': *South Wales Echo*, 7 Jun 2011; BBC News 20 Jun 2011; *Western Mail* 21 Jun 2011

'Float watch': *Liverpool Echo*, 26 Dec 2002

'Normanton milkman': *Express on Sunday*, 4 Feb 2007

'Arnold milkman': *Nottingham Post*, 10 May 2013

'float hijack': *Nottingham Post*, 10 May 2013

'Rhondda Dairy milkmen': *South Wales Echo*, 27 Aug 2005

'Cardiff milkman': *South Wales Echo*, 20 Jun 2011, 21 Jun 2011

'teenage gang': *Daily Mail*, 20 May 2008

'Brown': *Liverpool Echo*, 9 Apr 2009

'Cambridge milkman': *The Times*, 25 Apr 1972

'Taylor': *Daily Post*, 1 May 2014, *Caernarfon & Denbigh Herald*, 1 May 2014

'rescued child', *The Times*, 15 Nov 1923

'milkman from Ely': Alf Morris, MP, House of Commons, 16 Nov 1983

Sources

'Frame': *Wilshaw Post*, 15 Jan 2014

'Knipe': *Westmorland Gazette*, 26 Jun 2003

10. Community Workers

'Clark': *Daily Mirror*, 23 Aug 1994

Paul Radford fitted the false leg, *Birmingham Mail*, 25 Jan 1999

Lord Taylor, House of Lords, 9 Mar 1961

'Crocker': *The Times*, 31 Dec 2003

'Trotter': *Harrogate Advertiser*, 9 Mar 2007

'Clark' and 'Hollinrake': *Yorkshire Post*, 22 Jun 2015

'Trevor Jones MBE': *South Wales Argus*, 16 Sep 2015

'Stoneman': *Essex County Publications*, 25 Feb 2008

'Edmondson': *Swindon Advertiser*, 15 Feb 2013

'Pierce': *EDF* 24, 16 Aug 2006

'Haynes': BBC website, 30 Dec 2010

'Milington': *Oxford Mail*, 17 May 2014

'O'Malley': *Guardian*, 24 Mar 1995

'Weaver': op. cit.

'Locke': *The Times*, 13 Jul 1988

'Simpson': *Lancashire County Publications*, 10 Oct 1996

Eroline O'Keeffe, *Fatal Journey: The Murder of Trevor O'Keeffe*, O'Brien Press, Dublin, 2006

'Watson': *Sheffield Star*, 7 Oct 2011

'Fry': getwest London.co.uk, 27 Jun 2014

'Care Code': Tom Phelps, *The British Milkman*, Shire Publications, Oxford, 2010, p. 51; *The Milky Way*, op. cit. p. 19

'Smith': *Nottingham Evening Post*, 24 Dec 2009

'I used to help': mega monty, Sheffieldforum.co.uk

'one time': Lee Cordrey, *Guardian*, 3 Feb 2010

'Greenhalgh', *Radcliffe Times*, Nov 1962

'Williams': *Solihull News*, 27 Sep 2013

'Truro': *The Times*, 6 Apr 2000

'Sargeant': *Brentwood Gazette*, 4 Mar 2009

'Wood': *Bolton Evening News*, 6 Jul 2000

'Nock': *Birmingham Mail*, 10 Nov 2008

'Spurr': *Drinka Pinta*, op. cit. pp. 204–5

'Tony Fowler': *Leicester Mercury*, 28 Mar 2000, 12 Feb 2005, 7 Jul 2007, 2 Mar 2010; *Daily Express*, 4 Mar 2009; *Nottingham Evening Post*, 1 May 2010, *Sun*, 10 Jun 2010; *Weekender*, 10 Mar 2013.

11. Collecting the Money

'giro': *The Times*, 24 Sep 1971

'Quentin Thompson': *Daily Mail*, 16 Jan 2014

'Arch': op. cit.

'I'm Josie': letter from Edna Ledsam, Cardiff, *The People*, 2 May 2004

'Reed': *Sunday Times*, 11 Nov 2012

'Stevens': Dr Bicknell and Fred Stevens, Pathé News 1947

'Sutton': op. cit. 19 Feb 2011. Reproduced by permission of the author

Robertson, op. cit. pp. 41–44

'Tokens': BBC programme 'History of the World'; Mark Hudson, *Milk Bottle News* 40, spring 1994

'Sterilised lady': *Thanet Gazette*, 1961

13. Milkwomen and Milkmen

'Hicks': *Western Morning News*, 9 Apr 2001

14. The Milkman's Vehicles

'tractors': *Dursley Gazette*, 24 Mar 2000.

'last horse and float': *The Times*, 24 Feb 1953

'Wilkins': *Gloucestershire Within Living Memory*, op. cit. p. 65

'a very young boy': Lionel Jones, op. cit.

'Leslie May': 'Delivering the Milk' chapter in Henry Buckton, *Yesterday's Country Village*, David & Charles, Devon, 2005

'Pedometer': *Drinka Pinta*, op. cit. p. 65

Sources

'Kimmins', *Milk Bottle News* 19, winter 1989, interviewed by Michael Harmer

Lord Rayleigh Dairies: *Milk Bottle News* 39, winter 1993

'Welsh cobs': *The Times*, 24 Feb 1953

'Well, the first': Emily Filmer, interviewed by Cyril Weeden in 1974, *Milk Bottle News* 7, winter 1985–6

'1920s': *Gloucestershire Within Living Memory*, op. cit. p. 65

'Horses understand': Jack Jones, MP, House of Commons, 29 Jan 1954

'Our horse': Frank, 'The Old Milkmen of Brum', Birmingham Forum, 20 Mar 2010

'Queenie': *Lancashire County Publications*, 10 Dec 1999, 14 Jan 2000, 4 Feb 2000

'Jenkins': *The Times*, 25 Mar 1995

Sean Connery: *Being A Scot*, Weidenfeld & Nicolson, London, 2008, pp. 6, 16–20, 23, 79, 84; Christopher Bray: *Sean Connery: The Measure of a Man*, Faber & Faber, London, 2010, p. 14; Andrew Yule: *Sean Connery: Neither Shaken nor Stirred*, Sphere, London, 1993, p. 19

'Redford': *The Times*, 3 Aug 1998

'Moore': *Express,* 30 Sep 2012; Moore's website

'Hill plaque': *Hampshire County Publications*, 19 Jul 1999

'William Bailey': *Milk Bottle News* 27, winter 1991

'Bolting horse': *The Times*, 23 May 1961

'last in 25 races': www.ukjockey.com/jokes

'Greenhalgh': op. cit.

'Express Dairies', *Drinka Pinta*, op. cit. p. 55

'Hygienic Dairies': www.milkbottlenews, 1984–2014

'Wimbledon Common Ranger': *Express Journey*, op. cit. p. 119

'Edgar's Dairies': *Milk Bottle News* 27 p. 288; *Milk Bottle News* 43

'motorised transport': Lionel Jones, op. cit.

'Old Farm Dairy': *Drinka Pinta*, op. cit. pp. 53–55

'Trevor Jones': *South Wales Argus*, op. cit.

James Hay, MP, House of Commons, 17 Jul 1962

'Electrics': *Express Journey,* op. cit., Keith Roberts, *Electric Avenue: The Story of Morrison-Electricar,* Bryngold Books, Neath, South Wales, 2010

'Banks': *Nottingham Post,* 21 Feb 2012

'Lewis of Camden Town': *Drinka Pinta,* op. cit. p. 55

'Nesting dove': *Scunthorpe Evening Telegraph,* 1 May 2008

'Milkman on M1': *Milk Bottle News* 55, winter 1998

'Wheel-clamped': *The Times,* 29 Apr 1991

Dave Sutton, op. cit. 9 May 2011. Reproduced by permission of the author

'Linford Christie': YouTube, 11 Jun 2012

'55,000 battery-operated': LJK Setright: *Drive On! A Social History of the Motor Car,* Granta, London, 2004 p. 124

'Dean': *Lancashire County Publications,* 28 Feb 1998

'lent some props': Stan Wilson, *Black Country Bugle,* 11 Mar 2004

'Test valley': gransnet forum

15. Petty Crime

'short measures': William Eaton, *The Times,* 31 Oct 1918; William Smith, *The Times*; 17 Dec 1918; Henry Hornsby, *The Times,* 25 Aug 1921

'a major concern': Lionel Jones, op. cit.

'white thumb': Letter to *Daily Mail* from Ted Lacey, Southampton, reproduced in *Milk Bottle News* 55, winter 1998

'Rowner Infant School': *Portsmouth Evening News,* 17 Nov 2008

Cynon Valley: *Cynon Valley Leader,* 27 Nov 2013

'fifty-five pints': *Crewe Chronicle,* 12 Feb 2014

'Rayne': *Essex County Publications,* 9 Aug 1999

Dave Sutton, op. cit. 9 Feb 2011, 12 Feb 2011. Reproduced by permission of the author

Gerald Mars, *Cheats at Work,* George Allen & Unwin, London 1982 pp. 192–193; see also Jason Ditton, *Part-time Crime,* Macmillan, London & Basingstoke, 1977

'nearly 600 pints': *Cambridge Evening News,* 30 Mar 1982

'Milkman in Wales': *The Times*, 15 Feb 1993

'money-lender': *The Times*, 13 Dec 1961

'£650,000 through fraud': *The Times*, 20 Jan 2001

16. Returning to the Dairy

'Alex Kitson': Ian MacDougall, *Voices from Work and Home*, Mercat Press, Edinburgh, 2000, pp. 1–66

'Williams': *The Times*, 13 Sep 1972

Frank Bingley, op. cit.

17. Milk Containers

'Cowkeepers': conversation with Steve Wheeler

'Plastic bottles': *The Times*, 25 Apr 1995

Mike Hull, *Milk Bottle News: Collectors' Handbook* (1994); 'Milk Bottles' by Mike Hull, in Susanna Johnston and Tim Beddow, *Collecting: The Passionate Pastime*, Viking, Harmondsworth, Middlesex, 1986

Hull: op. cit. p. II

'Muirkirk': Hull, op. cit.

'Slogans': *Milk Bottle News* 30, autumn 1991

Charles Ray (editor), *Everybody's Enquire Within*, Amalgamated Press, London, 1938

Arthur Guy Enock, *This Milk Business: A Study from 1895 to 1943*, Lewis & Co, London, 1943

'Molotov cocktails': *The Times*, 6 Jul 1981

'Warning of riots': *Guardian*, 19 Oct 1985

'Pintie': Mike Hull, op. cit. pp. 1–7

'Bottle Weights': *Milk from Earliest Times to the Machine Age: Teachers' Notes*, Dairy Council, c1984

'Conran': *Milk Bottle News* 52, spring 1997

'Charlotte Hughes Martin': *Daily Mail*, 23 Aug 2008, *The Times*, 24 Sep 2008

'Sam Sweet': 'Contemporary Applied Arts Sam Sweet', accessed Oct 2015

'Craig-Martin': A Retrospective, *Milk Bottle News* 23, winter 1990

'Messages on a Bottle': *Milk Bottle News* 1, summer 1984, *Milk Bottle News* 2, autumn 1984, *Milk Bottle News* 8, spring 1986, *Milk Bottle News* 13, summer 1987, *Milk Bottle News* 34, autumn 1992, *Milk Bottle News* 41, summer 1994

'Wheeler': *Mail Online*, 28 Aug 2013

'Milk campaigns': Jenkins, op cit., p. 205

'Maurice Evans': Geron Swann and Andrew Ward, *The Boys from up the Hill*, Crowberry 1996 pp. 165–6

'paper cartons in 1926': *Milk from Earliest Times to the Machine Age: Teachers' Notes*, National Dairy Council, 1984 p. 5

'New York City figures': *The Times*, 26 Aug 1957

'cleansing department': *The Times*, 12 Jan 1968

'Lord Rayleigh's Dairy': op. cit.

'Pricerite': *The Times*, 24 Apr 1968

'Coren': *The Times*, 19 Mar 2002

Adrian Lawton, *An Investigation into Reusable Glass Beverage Container systems and the Barriers Preventing their Wider Establishment*, BSc (Hons) undergraduate dissertation, University of Huddersfield, 1993

'Holmes letter': *Independent on Sunday*, 18 Jun 2010

'Photos on Cartons': *The Times*, 16 Apr 1997

Joe Ashton, MP, House of Commons, 16 Nov 1983

'Ninety-four per cent': Ray Georgeson, 'The Demise of the Milkman', *Resource Magazine*, 6 Feb 2013; Tom Hayden, 'Nostalgia for an old-fashioned milk bottle', *BBC News Magazine*,

'Hanworth bottling plant': *Sunday Express*, 28 Sep 2014

18. Family Life

Cogar, op. cit.

'My major sleep': Lee Cordrey, op. cit.

'Yeo': *The People*, 19 Aug 2012

'Smith and Taylor': *Swindon Advertiser*, 18 Jan 2013

'Albert': email from Anton Rippon, author of *A Derby Boy*, Sutton, Stroud, 2007.

Sources

'Prout': *Dursley Gazette*, 24 Mar 2000

'Morton': *Western Gazette Series*, 10 Feb 2010

'Jones': David Mitchell, MP, House of Commons, 15 Jan 1975

'shared the work': BBC Radio Leicester interview with Arthur
    Beyless, 1999, the British Library

'Hargreaves': *Lancashire County Publications*, 16 Aug 2001

'Garrity': *The Times*, 4 May 1992

'Munro': *The Times*, 8 Feb 1985

'Mills': *The Times*, 2 Sep 2000

'Till': *The Times*, 15 Apr 1993

19. Retirement

'Edmonds': *Milk Bottle News* 54, autumn 1997

'Tilley': *Leicester Mercury*, 18 Oct 2004

'Burton': *Greater London, Kent and Surrey County Publications*,
    14 Feb 1998

'McDougal': *Western Daily Press*, 24 Nov 2000

'Gater': *Greater Manchester & Merseyside Publications*,
    26 Jul 2007

'Godfrey Close': *The Times*, 26 Feb 1969

'Hogg': *Westmorland Gazette*, 26 Oct 2009

'Prout': op. cit.

'Kearvell': op. cit.

'will miss the contact', *Western Gazette, Dorset*, 4 Feb 2010

'some great friends', *Birmingham Evening Mail*, 16 Oct 2001

'treasure my years', Peter Fry, op. cit.

'really lucky': *Greater London, Kent & Surrey Counties newspapers*,
    10 Sep 2002

'Wraith': *Sheffield Star*, 30 Apr 2013

'Gauge': *News Shopper*, 1 Oct 2013

'Geake': *Telegraph*, 6 Jun 2014, 10 Jun 2014

'McDermott': *The People*, 6 Apr 2014

Dan Kieran and Ian Vince, *Three Men in a Float*, John Murray, London, 2008

'Billingshurst': *Daily Mail*, 19 Nov 2013

'Bryant': *Bristol Evening Post*, 24 Jun 2010; *Sun*, 26 Jun 2010

Dave Sutton, op. cit. 25 Mar 2011. Reproduced by permission of the author

'Townsend': *Lancashire County Publications*, 30 May 1997

'Shawcross': *Liverpool Daily Post*, 8 Feb 2002

'Whittington': *East Sussex County Publications*, 1 Sep 1999

'Knight': *Hampshire County Publications*, 13 Jul 2007, 18 Jul 2007

20. The Vanishing Milkman

'In the fifties and sixties': *Milk Bottle News* 65, summer 2000

'Young people congregated': Philip Wilkinson, *The High Street*, Quercus, London, 2010, p. 203; *The Times*, 4 Sep 1936, 4 May 1970, 8 May 1999

'percentage of households': Dairy UK figures, *The Times*, 24 March 1995

'Milk Marketing Board': Stanley Baker, *Milk to Market*, Heinemann, London, 1973

Shortage of milkmen: *The Times*, 28 Mar 1962

'West Yorkshire resident': *Huddersfield Daily Examiner*, 7 May 2011

'Sainsbury': *The Times*, 3 Feb 1981

Baroness Fisher, House of Lords, 24 Nov 1983

'Wiseman': *The Times*, 7 Jun 2003

'Bingley': op. cit.

'milk consumed': *Observer*, 30 Jun 1985

'cats': yourcat.co.uk

'dairy farm numbers': Barry Wilson, editor *Dairy Industry Newsletter*, letter to the *Guardian*, 7 Oct 2014

'financial system': *The Times*, 20 May 1967

'soul destroying': Richard Askwith, *The Lost Village*, Ebury Press, 2008

Sources

'2003 survey': Askwith, op. cit. p. 74

'Leaver': *Bournemouth Daily Echo*, 19 Feb 2009

Gwyneth Dunwoody, MP, House of Commons, 16 Mar 2004

'Parker Dairies': www.parkerdairies,co.uk

'Fowler': op. cit.

'Freedom campaign': *The Times*, 16 Apr 1992; *People,* 20 Sep 1992; *Milk Bottle News* 34, autumn 1992.

'National Milkman Week': described as 'hardly noticed' in *Milk Bottle News* 34, autumn 1992

'Belcher': *Leicester Mercury*, 26 Sep 2014

'one wag': *The Times*, 28 May 2002

'Wood': *Bolton Evening News*, 6 Jul 2000

The Earl of Kinnoull, House of Lords, 20 Jul 1984

'Wark': *The Times*, 2 Jan 2008

'Hancock': letter, *Daily Telegraph*, 23 Nov 2013

'Viner': *Mail Online*, 28 Feb 2014

Postscript: The Milkman in the Arts

'Rees book': Baroness Cox, House of Lords, 4 Feb 1987; Colin Moynihan, MP, House of Commons, 11 May 1987; Earl of Caithness, House of Lords, 1 Feb 1988; Michael Howard, MP, House of Commons, 9 Mar 1988; Baroness Knight, House of Lords, 6 Dec 1999

'desert-island film': *The Times*, 15 May 1981

'David Cameron's choice': *Daily Mail*, 25 May 2006

'Leader': *The Times*, 13 Nov 2001; *Guardian*, 16 Nov 2001

Index

Index

Index

Hadley, Jim 7
Haines, Les 176
hand injuries 101-3
handcarts 168, 169
    electric 177-8
Hapgood, Eddie 228
Hardie, Ian 33, 262-3
Hargreaves, David 227
Hay, James 177
Haygarth, Tony 267
Haynes, Mark 124
health problems 2, 3, 8,
    24, 36-7, 58, 101, 223
    see also injuries;
    tiredness
hedgehogs 96, 97
Herman's Hermits 264
heroism 51, 55, 63-4, 116,
    117, 127
Hicks, Annette 153
Higgs, Clyde 211
high-rise buildings 40-1,
    149
Hill, Benny 26, 64-5,
    173-4, 228, 262
Hockley, Brian 112
Hogg, Sid 231-2
Hollinrake, Kevin 122
Holmes, Michael J 218
homogenised milk 62, 219
Hone, Paul and Stephen
    265
horse and cart 49, 166,
    167, 169-75, 177
    bolting horses 174
    Welsh cobs 169
house fires, and rescues
    116, 117
house keys 119-20
Huins, John 91
Hull, Naomi and Mike
    205, 213

injuries 19, 99-103
    see also fatalities

inner-city riots 112, 208

Jackson, Malcolm 175
James, Harry 52
Jan (milkwoman) 154-7
Jeff (milkman) 147-52
Jenkins, Alan 55
Jenkins, Simon 172
Jersey milk 62, 206-7
'jockeys' 36
Jones, Jimmy 225
Jones, Lionel 103-4, 175-6,
    186
Jones, Trevor 122, 171-2,
    176
journey to work 9-10

Kane, Jock 23
Kaye, Danny 261
Kearvell, Julian 2, 232
Kentucky Headhunters
    264
Kettridge, Ronnie 109
Kidwell, Frank 109
Kieran, Dan 234
Kimmins, Mr (milkman)
    168-9
King, Mark 263
Kinnoull, Earl of 252
Kitson, Alex 200
Kitson, Sir Timothy 44
Knight, Allan 110, 238
Knight, Dennis and Jean
    125-6
Knipe, David 117
kosher milk 52

lactose intolerance 245
LaRizzio, John C 58-9
lateness, fear of 2, 6
Lawrence, Katie 265
Lawton, Adrian 218
Leader, Michael 266
Leaver, Jim 247
leaving the job 226-8

see also retirement
Level 42 263
Linda (milkwoman)
    159-63
listening ear 126-7, 130
literature, milkmen in
    255-9
'Living in Sin' (Adrienne
    Rich) 258
Lloyd, Harold 261
Locke, Bobby 125
loose milk 204-5
Losper, Christopher John
    110

M-box 249-50
McCartney, Paul 33, 262
McCready, Jazzer 266
McCue, Anne 265
McDermott, Lester 234
McDougal, Malcolm 231
mackintoshes 7, 8, 200
Maclean, Alistair 26
Mansfield, Jayne 261
Mars, Gerry 189-90
Martin, Charlotte Hughes
    209
May, Leslie 167
meals 3, 138, 139, 156, 158,
    159, 161
Melly, George 262
Melvin and Howard (film)
    260
milk
    consumption, falling
        245
    price of 145, 240-2, 244
    shelf life 244
    smell of 61, 156, 163,
        196, 222
Milk & Moore 249
Milk Bottle News
    (magazine) 205, 214,
    269
Milk Cup 215, 216

Index